Wealth and Poverty in Close Personal Relationships

At a time of global and domestic economic crisis, the financial aspects of domestic and familial relationships are more important and more strained than ever before. The focus of this book is on the distribution of wealth and poverty in traditional and non-traditional familial relationships. The volume takes an interdisciplinary approach to explore the way in which money matters are structured and governed within close personal relationships and the extent to which they have an impact on the nature and economic dynamics of relationships. As such, the key areas of investigation are the extent to which participation in the labour market, unpaid caregiving, inheritance, pensions and welfare reform have an impact on familial relationships. The authors explore governmental and legal responses by investigating the privileging of certain types of domestic relationships, through fiscal and non-fiscal measures, and the differential provision on relationship breakdown. The impact of budget and welfare cuts is also examined for their effect on equality in domestic relationships.

Susan Millns is Professor of Law and Head of the Law School at the University of Sussex. Her research lies in the area of European Human Rights Law and European Constitutional Law. She has a particular interest in feminist legal studies and gender equality and has written extensively on gender and public law issues.

Simone Wong is a Reader in Law at the University of Kent. In addition to being a member of Lincoln's Inn in the UK, she has been called to the Bar in Malaysia, Singapore and Australian Capital Territory. Prior to her joining Kent in 1998, Simone had practised in Malaysia (1986–1989) and Singapore (1990–1994). She teaches Banking Law as well as Equity and Trusts. Her research interests are primarily in Equity, Trusts, Cohabitation and other Domestic Relationships, and Banking.

Wealth and Poverty in Close Personal Relationships

Money Matters

Edited by
Susan Millns and
Simone Wong

LONDON AND NEW YORK

First published 2017
by Routledge
2 Park Square, Milton Park, Abingdon, Oxon OX14 4RN

and by Routledge
711 Third Avenue, New York, NY 10017

Routledge is an imprint of the Taylor & Francis Group, an informa business

© 2017 selection and editorial matter, Susan Millns and Simone Wong; individual chapters, the contributors

The right of Susan Millns and Simone Wong to be identified as the authors of the editorial material, and of the authors for their individual chapters, has been asserted in accordance with sections 77 and 78 of the Copyright, Designs and Patents Act 1988.

All rights reserved. No part of this book may be reprinted or reproduced or utilised in any form or by any electronic, mechanical, or other means, now known or hereafter invented, including photocopying and recording, or in any information storage or retrieval system, without permission in writing from the publishers.

Trademark notice: Product or corporate names may be trademarks or registered trademarks, and are used only for identification and explanation without intent to infringe.

British Library Cataloguing-in-Publication Data
A catalogue record for this book is available from the British Library

Library of Congress Cataloging-in-Publication Data
A catalog record for this book has been requested

ISBN: 978-1-4724-6986-1 (hbk)
ISBN: 978-1-315-54758-9 (ebk)

Typeset in Galliard
by Florence Production Ltd, Stoodleigh, Devon, UK

Contents

Table of cases	vii
Table of legislation	ix
List of contributors	xiii

	Introduction	1
	SUSAN MILLNS AND SIMONE WONG	
1	**Credit and debt in close personal relationships**	7
	JACKIE GOODE	
2	**Intra-household inequality, poverty and well-being**	21
	SARA CANTILLON AND MARIE MORAN	
3	**The ownership and distribution of money in Spanish dual-income couples: gender differences and the effects of some public policies**	39
	SANDRA DEMA MORENO AND CAPITOLINA DIAZ MARTINEZ	
4	**Money practices among older couples: patterns of continuity, change, conflict and resistance**	58
	DEBORA PRICE, DINAH BISDEE AND TOM DALY	
5	**Austerity, solidarity and equality: a European Union perspective on gender and wealth**	74
	SUSAN MILLNS	
6	**Contractual thinking in couple relationships**	89
	TONE SVERDRUP	
7	**Marriage and the data on same-sex couples**	101
	ROBERT LECKEY	

8	Value in personal relationships and the reallocation of property on divorce CRAIG LIND	118
9	Intestate succession and the property of unmarried cohabitants in England and Wales SIMONE WONG	134
10	The role of child support in tackling child poverty HEATHER KEATING	148
11	The Universal Credit: a 'great rationaliser' for the 21st century ANN MUMFORD	166
	Index	183

Table of cases

Bailey, Re [1977] 1 WLR 278 18
Baker, Re [2008] 2 FLR 767 137
Baumbast and R v Secretary of State for the Home Department [2002]
  ECR I-7091 82
Best v Samuel Fox Co. Ltd. [1952] 2 All ER 394 125
Browne (formerly Pritchard) v Pritchard [1975] 1 WLR 1366 121
Burden v UK [2007] 44 EHRR 51; [2008] 47 EHRR 38 144–5

Charman v Charman [2006] EWHC (Fam) 1879 125
Conran v Conran [1997] 2 FLR 617 .... 121, 128
Coventry, Re [1980] Ch 480 137
Cowan v Cowan [2001] EWCA (Civ) 679 125
Crozier v Crozier [1994] Fam 114 (Fam Div) 152

Dano v Jobcenter Leipzig, Case C-333/13, 11 November 2014.
  EU:C:2014:2358 84
Dart v Dart [1996] 2 FLR 286, CA 121, 128
Defrenne v SABENA (No. 2), Case 43/75 [1976] ECR 455 79
Delaney v Delaney [1990] 2 FLR 457 (Fam Div) 149
Dennis, Re [1981] 2 All ER 140 137
Dereci, Case C-256/11 [2011] ECR I-11315 84

Egan v Canada [1995] 2 SCR 513 107

Ghaidan v Mendoza [2004] 3 All ER 411 140
Graham v Murphy [1997] 1 FLR 860 137
Granatino v Radmacher [2010] UKSC 42 [2011] 1 AC 534 .... 103, 125
Grzelczyk v Centre Public d'Aide Sociale d'Ottignes-Louvain-la-Neuve (CPAS),
  Case C-184/99 [2001] ECR I-6193 82

Halpern v Canada (Attorney General) [2003] 65 OR (3d) 161 .... 105, 108
Hartshorne v Hartshorne 2004 SCC 22 [2004] 1 SCR 550 103
Hendricks v Québec (Procureur général) [2002] RJQ 2506 105
Holland v IRC [2003] STC (SCD) 43 144

Johnston v Ireland (App No 9697/82) (18 December 1986) 145

viii Table of cases

Kehoe v UK [2008] 2 FLR 1014 (ECHR) 151
Kerr v Baranow [2011] SCC 10 [2011] 1 SCR 269 .... 95, 99

Lawrence v Gallagher [2012] EWCA Civ 394 .... 112, 115
Ligue catholique pour les droits de l'homme c Hendricks [2004] RJQ 851 (CA) 105
Lindsay v UK [1987] 9 EHRR CD555 145

M v H [1999] 2 SCR 3 107
McCarthy, Case C-434/09 [2011] ECR I-3375 84
McFarlane v Macfarlane [2006] UKHL 24 [2006] 2 AC 618 .... 111, 121
Martinez Sala v Freistaat Bayern, Case C-85/96 [1998] ECR I-2691 .... 81–2, 84
Miller v Miller, McFarlane v McFarlane [2006] UKHL 24 .... 90, 111, 121–2, 132
Minton v Minton [1979] AC 593 120
Moge v Moge [1992] 3 SCR 813 112

Negus v Bahouse [2008] EWCA Civ 1002 137

O'D v O'D [1976] Fam 83 121

Page v Page (1981) 2 FLR 198 121
Phillips v Pearce [1996] 2 FLR 230 (Fam Div) 154
Piglowska v Piglowska [1999] 1 WLR 1360 137
Preston v Preston [1982] Fam 17 121

R (Fawcett Society) v Chancellor of the Exchequer [2010] EWHC 3522 86
R (JG and MB) v Lancashire County Council [2011] EWHC 2295 85
R (Rahman) v Birmingham City Council [2011] EWHC 944 85
R (WM and Others) v Birmingham City Council [2011] EWHC 1147 85
R v Sec of State for Work and Pensions ex parte Kehoe [2006] 1 AC 42 (HL) 151
Ruiz Zambrano v ONEM, Case C-34/09 [2010] ECR I-1177 83–4

Serife Yigit v Turkey [2011] 53 EHRR 25 145
Shackell v UK (App No 45851/99) (27 April 2000, unreported) 145
Sorrell v Sorrell [2005] EWHC (Fam) 1717 125
South Africa, Kritzinger v Kritzinger [1989] 1 All SA 325 125
Stack v Dowden [2007] UKHL 17 99

Wachtel v Wachtel [1973] Fam 72 121
Watson, Re [1999] 1 FLR 878 137
White v White [2001] 1 AC 596 .... 90, 111, 120–2, 132

Zhu and Chen v Secretary of State for the Home Department, Case C-200/02,
    [2004] ECR I-9925 83

Table of legislation

Austria
Constitution, Art 7 80

Canada
Divorce Act 106

Council of Europe
European Convention on Human Rights (ECHR) 144
    Art 8 .... 82, 144–5
    Art 14 144–5
    Protocol 1, Art 1 144–5

European Union
Charter of Fundamental Rights 80, 87
    Art 20 80
    Art 21 80
    Art 23 80
Directive 75/117/EEC Equal Pay 78
Directive 76/207/EEC Equal Treatment 78
Directive 2002/73/EC, Equal Treatment Amendment Directive 79
Directive 2004/113/EC Access to and Supply of Goods and Services 79
Treaty of Lisbon 75, 80
Treaty on European Union (TEU) 75, 81
    Art 2 76
    Art 7 75
    Art 9 81
Treaty on the Functioning of the European Union (TFEU) 75, 81
    Art 18 81–2
    Art 20 81
    Arts 20-24 81
    Art 157 78

Finland
Constitution
    Art 1 76
    Art 6 80

x   Table of legislation

France
Civil Code 76
Constitution, Art 1 .... 76, 80

Ireland
Constitution, preamble 76

Italy
Constitution
    Art 1 76
    Art 3 80

Netherlands
Constitution, Art 1 80

Portugal
Constitution, Art 1 76

Spain
Constitution
    Art 1 76
    Art 2 80

Sweden
Constitution
    Art 2 80

United Kingdom
Administration of Estates Act 1925 135
    s 46(2A) 134
Adoption and Children Act 2002 120
    s 144(4)(b) 140
Child Maintenance and Other Payments Act 2008 .... 5, 151, 155
    s 6 159
    s 15 151
    ss 27-30 154
Child Poverty Act 2010 .... 156, 162, 174
Child Support Act 1991 .... 5, 148–51
    s 3 150
    s 6 151
    s 6(2) 151
    s 46 151
Child Support Fees Regulations 2014 160
Children Act 1989 120
Civil Partnership Act 2004 104
Equality Act 2010 176
    s 149 85
    s 149(1) 85

Family Law Act 1996, s 62(1)(a)	140
Family Procedure Rules, Pt 9	127
Fatal Accidents Act 1976, s 1(3)	140
Human Rights Act 1998	144–5
s 3(1)	145
Inheritance (Provision for Family and Dependants) Act 1975	134–6, 139, 144
s 1(1)(ba)	134, 136
s 1(1)(d)	143
s 1(1)(e)	136
s 1(1A)	134, 136, 140
s 1(1B)	134, 136
s 1(2)(a)	136
s 1(2)(aa)	136
s 1(2)(b)	136
s 2	137
s 3(1)(a)-(g)	137
s 3(2A)	137
Inheritance and Trustees' Powers Act 2014	135
Inheritance Tax Act 1984	143
s 1	144
s 2(1)	144
s 3(1)	144
s 8A	144
s 18	144, 146
s 146	144
Jobseeker's Act 1995	173
Marriage (Same Sex Couples) Act 2013	2, 104
Matrimonial Causes Act 1973	111, 120, 124, 127
s 1(1)	120
s 1(2)	120
ss 23-24D	120
s 25(1)	120
s 25(2)(a)	121
s 25(2)(b)	121
s 25(2)(c)	121
s 25(2)(d)	121
s 25(2)(f)	106, 121
s 25A	120
Social Security Contributions and Benefits Act 1992	
s 124	173
s 130	173
s 131	173
Tax Credits Act 2002	168, 173
Welfare Reform Act 2007	173
Welfare Reform Act 2012	158, 167
s 33(1)(a)	173
s 33(1)(b)	173
s 33(1)(c)	173

xii *Table of legislation*

    s 33(1)(d) 173
    s 33(1)(e) 173
    s 33(1)(f) 173
    s 136 158
    ss 140-141 159
    Sch 14(1) 168
Welfare Reform and Pensions Act 1999 (Commencement Order 1999)
    Order 1999, 1999 No. 3309 174

Contributors

Dinah Bisdee, whose first degree was obtained at Oxford University, returned to studying in 2002 after a long career in marketing and market research. She completed her PhD in social psychology at the University of Surrey in 2008. Her thesis was on 'Ageism in the Workplace', and her research investigated the root causes of prejudice against older (50+) people in terms of employment, promotion and training opportunities. Since then she has been working with Debora Price at King's College London on the 'Behind Closed Doors' project on older couples' management of household finances. She has also taught Social Psychology and Research Methods at the University of Surrey. Dinah has three grown-up children and lives in Guildford.

Sara Cantillon is Professor of Gender and Economics at Glasgow Caledonian University and Director of the WiSE Research Centre. Previously, she was Head of the School of Social Justice and Director of the Equality Studies Centre at University College Dublin. Her main areas of research are equality, care, poverty, gender and intra-household distribution and she has published widely on these topics. Professor Cantillon was appointed by the Irish Minister for Education to the Expert Group on *Future Funding for Higher Education* 2014–2017.

Tom Daly retired from the National Audit Office in the early 1990s and joined the Sociology Department of the University of Surrey. Working within the Centre for Ageing and Gender, and the Department of Psychology, he undertook a number of studies on issues affecting older people. These included a study of the leisure activities of older men as part of the *Growing Older* programme, 'Older men: their social worlds and healthy lifestyles' and another on behalf of the Nuffield Foundation on End of Life Care, 'Older people and their families: autonomy and decision-making in later life'. He joined the Institute of Gerontology, Kings College London in 2008, and undertook further research on older people including the 'Behind Closed Doors' project on older couples' financial arrangements. In addition, within the University of Surrey, he continued to provide guidance to undergraduates and MSc students in social research mechanisms. This included the use of SPSS and other statistical techniques.

Sandra Dema Moreno is Associate Professor in the Department of Sociology, University of Oviedo (Spain). She has worked on numerous research projects analysing women's inequality, both in the field of public policies and within the family, focusing in the last years on the financial decision-making processes within couples. She has published several articles and books including two chapters in the book *Modern Couples Sharing Money, Sharing Life*, Palgrave Macmillan, New York, 2007 and the articles: 'Behind the negotiations: financial decision-making processes in Spanish dual-income couples', *Feminist Economics* 15(1), 2009 and 'Gender inequalities and the role of money in Spanish dual-income couples', *European Societies* 12(1), 2010. Her research also focuses on other questions related to the sociology of gender, such us feminist methodology and gender and development, two topics on which she also has several publications, for instance: 'Gender and organizations: The (re)production of gender inequalities within Development NGOs', *Women's Studies International Forum* 31, 2008. With Capitolina Diaz Martínez she has edited the book: *Sociología y Género, Tecnos*, Madrid, 2013, a handbook designed for graduate and postgraduate students enrolled in Gender Studies.

Capitolina Diaz Martínez is Associate Professor of Sociology (University of Valencia), President of the Spanish Association of Women Scientists and Technologists (AMIT). She has been General Director for Women and Employment (Ministry of Equality) (2008–2010), Counsellor of Science in the Spanish Representation in front of the EU (2008) and Director of the Women and Science Unit of the (Ministry of Education and Science) (2006–2008). Her main fields of research are Sociology of Gender, Gender Analysis Methodology and Sociology of Family. She has participated in more than 15 research projects and currently, she is the director of a European Research study on the Gender Salary Gap and Gender Care Gap. She is the author or co-author of approximately 100 publications, most of them in Spanish, but some of them in English, such as: 'Gender inequalities and the role of money in Spanish dual-income couples' (2010), *European Societies* 12(1); 'Mapping the maze. Getting more women to the top in research' (2008), European Commission; *Modern Couples Sharing Money, Sharing Life* (2007), Palgrave Macmillan. She teaches sociology of gender, and gender perspectives on scientific research.

Jackie Goode is a sociologist and Visiting Research Fellow in the Social Sciences Department at Loughborough University. She specialises in qualitative and ethnographic research methods and has published extensively on sociological and social policy issues relating to low-income families, including with Professor Ruth Lister on the intra-household distribution of income within families reliant on benefits; on feeding the family on a low income; on the use of credit and the acquisition of problematic debt by those on low incomes; and on men's household money management.

Heather Keating is Professor of Criminal Law and Criminal Responsibility at the University of Sussex. Her main areas of research are the criminal law and family (especially child) law and the role played in each by the concept(s) of responsibility. She is co-author of Keating, Cunningham, Walters and Elliot, *Criminal Law: Text and Materials* (eighth edn) (Sweet & Maxwell, 2014).

Robert Leckey is Dean and Samuel Gale Professor in the Faculty of Law, McGill University. He is the editor of *Marital Rights* (Routledge, 2016) and *After Legal Equality: Family, Sex, Kinship* (Routledge, 2015), co-editor of *Les apparences en droit civil* (Yvon Blais, 2015) and *Queer Theory: Law, Culture, Empire* (Routledge, 2010), and author of *Bills of Rights in the Common Law* (Cambridge University Press, 2015) and *Contextual Subjects: Family, State, and Relational Theory* (University of Toronto Press, 2008). He has received the International Academy of Comparative Law's Canada Prize (2010) and the (McGill) Principal's Prize for Excellence in Teaching (2010).

Craig Lind is Senior Lecturer in Law at the University of Sussex. His research lies in the area of domestic, international and comparative family law. He has written on unmarried cohabitation, the redistribution of assets and financial responsibility on divorce, parental status and parental responsibility and responsibility for decision-making relating to older people. He is also interested in issues of gender, sexuality and culture and has conducted research into the way in which sexual identity is understood in other cultures and the ways in which western regulatory regimes impact upon identity.

Susan Millns is Professor of Law and Head of the Law School at the University of Sussex. Her research lies in the area of European Human Rights Law and European Constitutional Law. She has a particular interest in feminist legal studies and gender equality and has written extensively on gender and public law issues.

Marie Moran is a Lecturer in Equality Studies at University College Dublin. She specialises in and has published in the fields of egalitarian theory, social justice, cultural political economy and cultural studies. Her first book, *Identity and Capitalism* was published by SAGE in 2015.

Ann Mumford is a Reader in The Dickson Poon School of Law, King's College London and specialises in tax law, fiscal institutions and equality. The scope of Ann's published work has ranged from feminist perspectives on taxation law to, as a contributor to the 'new' fiscal sociology movement, the integration of tax legal scholarship into the realm of economic sociology. Ann regularly supports non-governmental organisations working to further women's economic equality, and works with scholarly organisations to support socio-legal research in the law of taxation. In particular, as one of the convenors of the Law and Society Association's collaborative research networks, titled 'International socio-legal feminisms', Ann has served as an advocate for border-crossing research into the impact of global tax systems on equality and opportunity. As a researcher, more generally, Ann's work has focused on international, comparative, and socio-legal, feminist legal perspectives, particularly those that arise through taxation law. Ann is the author of two monographs, *Taxing Culture: Towards A Theory of Tax Collection Law* (2002, Ashgate: Socio-Legal Studies Series; General Editor: Philip A. Thomas), and *Tax Policy, Women and the Law: UK and Comparative Perspectives*, Cambridge University Press (2010, Cambridge Tax Law Series – General Editor, John Tiley).

Debora Price is Professor of Social Gerontology at the University of Manchester, where she is Director of MICRA, the Manchester Institute for Collaborative Research on Ageing. She is currently the President of the British Society of Gerontology (2016–2019). A sociologist and gerontologist, she was formerly a barrister and founding member of Coram Chambers, a set of barristers' chambers specialising in family law. Since completing her PhD on the impact of social change on pension scheme participation in the UK and entering academia, her research has focused on the study of poverty and inequality in later life. She specialises in the study of pensions, funding later life, and the sociology of money over the life course. She has been Principle or Co-Investigator on numerous research projects in these spheres including understanding the gendered impact of recent pension reforms in the UK, the impact of extending paid work in later life on health and well-being, grandparenting across Europe, older couples and the management of household money (the 'Behind Closed Doors' project), research into life-course influences on poverty and inequality in old age, and measuring the poverty of older people.

Tone Sverdrup holds a Chair in the Faculty of Law at the University of Oslo.

Simone Wong is a Reader in Law at the University of Kent. In addition to being a member of Lincoln's Inn in the UK, she has been called to the Bar in Malaysia, Singapore and Australian Capital Territory. Prior to her joining Kent in 1998, Simone had practised in Malaysia (1986–1989) and Singapore (1990–1994). She teaches Banking Law as well as Equity and Trusts. Her research interests are primarily in equity, trusts, cohabitation and other domestic relationships, and banking.

Introduction

Susan Millns and Simone Wong

At a time of global and domestic economic crisis, the financial aspects of domestic and familial relationships are more important and more strained than ever before. The focus of this collection is on the distribution of wealth and poverty in close personal relationships that are familial (traditional and non-traditional) and couple based. The collection is an interdisciplinary endeavour and brings together academics working in the fields of law, sociology, social policy and related disciplines (such as economics and political science), to explore the way in which money matters are structured and governed within close personal relationships and the extent to which they have an impact on the nature and economic dynamics of relationships. As such, one of the key areas of investigation is the extent to which matters such as participation in the labour market, unpaid caregiving, inheritance, pensions and welfare reform have an impact on familial relationships.

The collection explores relations of intimacy in close personal relationships and economic (inter)dependency, by interrogating how, when and why money matters in these relationships. In what way(s) does it affect or lead to individuals being, or being willing to become, economically vulnerable? Are some (women, for example) more prone to vulnerability than others? How do familial and domestic relationships affect the acquisition of wealth in households and, equally, how do they contribute to the poverty of individuals? The collection explores governmental and legal responses by investigating the privileging of certain types of close personal relationships (through fiscal and non-fiscal measures), and the differential provision on relationship breakdown. The impact of budget and welfare cuts is also examined for their effect on (in)equality in these relationships.

We hope that the chapters in the collection will encourage further dialogue and exchange between disciplines and across issues while also providing the conditions for these cross-disciplinary and cross jurisdictional encounters and offering new insights into the area. The chapters evaluate the ways in which law and policy, by regulating the financial aspects of close personal relationships, can be deployed as an effective instrument of governance, in 'stabilising' or 'mainstreaming' forms of domestic relations and in ending or perpetuating inequality in relationships.

The collection has been written as many countries in Europe are still pursuing policies of economic austerity resulting from the economic and financial crisis of 2007–2008 and its benefits lie in charting and explaining the current state of financial dependency and interdependency within close personal relationships. This has brought with it a need for public spending to be reduced with an immediate impact upon the provision of welfare and the tightening of fiscal policies. In such times of austerity, it is often the vulnerable in society, and particularly women, who bear the brunt of spending cuts.[1] A key aim of the collection is to demonstrate to policy makers, those in government, officials and experts, the extent to which those in relationships of dependency, through their familial and domestic relationships, are affected through changes in the labour market and in the regulation of areas such as inheritance, pensions and welfare. A further contemporary issue which chimes with the publication of the book is that in Europe many states have recently enacted forms of civil partnership and/or same-sex marriage which allow same-sex couples to formalise their relationships and thereby acquire effectively the same rights as married opposite-sex couples.[2] The passage of such legislation has served to highlight that, aside from marriage and civil partnerships, other forms of domestic relationships may warrant legal protection because of the economic vulnerability that parties to such relationships may suffer when the relationship breaks down.

The chapters in the collection have been grouped and divided into three thematic sections. The first section comprises chapters that consider, at a macro level, the sociological and legal aspects of the intra-household economy. A common theme linking the chapters in this section is the persistence of the gendered nature of economic inequalities within close personal relationships, where women are invariably placed in a psychologically and financially disadvantaged position. The section begins with a consideration of the impact of having to deal with over-indebtedness in low-income families (Goode (UK); Cantillon and Moran (Ireland)). Goode's chapter sets off the theme of the book by considering the intra-household economy and illustrating the tensions between public and private responsibilities for both human and social welfare. Her exploration of the experiences of low-income families in the United Kingdom (UK) in using credit and acquiring problematic personal debt (over-indebtedness) shows the complexities of interdependency and the importance of temporal factors on credit and debt outcomes. Goode highlights the failure of existing public policy, which promotes increasing private responsibility during this period of economic austerity, to take into account over-indebtedness. These measures have a negative impact on low-income families who are left struggling to manage over-indebtedness and keeping together their homes, work and family lives.

Cantillon and Moran's chapter, on the other hand, considers the relationship between intra-household inequality and psychological well-being of individual family members within the households of married couples in Ireland. Her chapter indicates the significant relationship between material deprivation, financial strain and psychological distress; intra-household inequality is not only gendered but also has an impact on the psychological well-being of individual family members. Wives who are burdened with managing scarce financial resources suffer higher levels of psychological distress.[3]

---

1 See M O'Hara, *Austerity Bites: A Journey to the Sharp End of Cuts in the UK* (Bristol, UK: Policy Press 2014); E Palmer *et al.* (eds), *Access to Justice: Beyond the Policies and Politics of Austerity* (Oxford: Hart 2016).
2 In the United Kingdom, the Marriage (Same Sex Couples) Act 2013 received Royal Assent on 17 July 2013 which enabled same-sex couples to marry when the Act came into force on 13 March 2014.
3 D Rottman, *Income Distribution within Irish Households* (Dublin: Combat Poverty Agency 1994) found a significant link between income sharing and levels of psychological distress. J Pahl, 'Household spending, personal spending and the control of money in marriage' (1990) 24(1) *J Br Sociological Assoc* 119, further found that women from lower income households normally undertook responsibility for managing scarce household resources. That, however, was perceived by them as a burden and a chore rather than a source of empowerment and control. See also C Vogler and J Pahl (1994), 'Money, power and inequality within marriage' (1994) 42(2) *The Sociological Review* 262.

These two chapters are followed by chapters examining the manner in which public policies, e.g. cuts to social welfare and changes to fiscal policies, affect the economic position of families as a whole as well as spouses and cohabitants individually (Dema Moreno and Diaz (Spain); Millns (EU)) and the money management patterns of older (ageing) couples (Price, Daly and Bisdee (UK)). Dema Moreno and Diaz, for instance, analyse the correlation between public policies and the perpetuation of gendered economic inequalities in close personal relationships. Focusing on three specific types of policy (pensions, conciliation and fiscal policies) implemented by the Spanish government, Dema Moreno and Diaz illustrate the ways that public policies serve to shape intra-household practices that reinforce the traditional 'male breadwinner/female homemaker' family model. The Spanish government's adherence to a traditional family model means that other inequalities can persist through certain practices such as gendered division of labour.[4] In doing so, gendered economic inequalities are perpetuated within Spanish families despite the increase in women's participation in paid labour and the rise of dual-income families, especially among the young aged between 16 and 34 years.

The perpetuation of abiding inequalities as a result of adherence to a traditional family model can equally be found in other jurisdictions as well as older couples. Looking further along the life course of individuals, Price, Daly and Bisdee's chapter considers the ways in which older couples in the UK manage their money and cope with major financial transitions such as retirement, bereavement and ill-health. Their chapter similarly reveals couples' money practices are difficult to change; gender imbalances persist and are generally resistant to change in older couples. The gendered economic inequalities that were sown earlier on in a relationship become embedded over time and resistant to change as the couple gets older.

Millns's chapter considers the austerity measures taken at the level of the European Union to tackle the financial crisis and, more particularly, their relationship with the values of solidarity and equality. The chapter explores the rhetoric of core European values and the way in which they have been harnessed to facilitate access to welfare by EU migrants invoking free movement and European citizenship rights while not fully recognising the care-work provided by women as contributing to the European single market. This chapter is further concerned with the potentially gendered impact of solidarity-driven, anti-EU and anti-migrant austerity measures at the domestic level in the UK. The increase in job losses and threats to social welfare benefits as a result of cuts in public spending, fuelled in part by fears of migration, are shown to have a greater impact on women than men, leaving them in financially more vulnerable and dependent positions within the family.

The second section of the book, comprising three chapters, focuses on the various theoretical approaches that might inform the legal regulation of close intimate relationships. Sverdrup's chapter questions the appropriateness of a private law contractarian approach to the regulation of couple relationships. Drawing on examples such as the approaches canvassed by the American Law Institute and the Law Commission of England and Wales, she argues that the private law approach that relies on contractual thinking in resolving financial and property matters upon relationship breakdown is problematic as couples do not deal with each at arm's length. Rather, their relationship is a form of partnership based on commitment which engenders emotional and financial interdependence, thereby making them act in more

---

4 C Carrasco and A Rodríguez 'Women, families, and work in Spain: structural changes and new demands' (2000) 6(1) *Feminist Economics* 45.

accommodating ways.[5] This resonates with the arguments made by others for a rethink of the way in which the law conceptualises close personal relationships and responds in terms of distribution of property and income when the relationship ends.[6]

Leckey, on the other hand, considers the way in which public law arguments were utilised in Canada to provide same-sex couples with the right to marry. These were based on constitutional arguments of equality, premised on the autonomy and dignity of individuals, regardless of their sexual orientation, to marry: that same-sex couples should be given equal treatment as opposite-sex couples by being allowed to marry. An oft-cited reason for justifying the right of same-sex couples to marry is the sameness of opposite- and same-sex relationships.[7] However, due to the limited empirical data available on same-sex relationships and how same-sex couples structure their household arrangements, Leckey questions whether access to a heterosexual marriage model, and particularly the obligations that arise for not only third parties but also as between spouses both during the marriage and on divorce, is apposite to same-sex couples.[8] In his chapter, Leckey argues that more empirical research is needed into same-sex relationships in order for the law to respond in a more nuanced way in terms of setting out these obligations.

Lind's chapter considers the legal rationale(s) for the distribution of property upon divorce and dissolution of civil partnerships under English law, which have mainly been framed along the lines of gender inequality (mostly women), and the public/private division. Lind, like Sverdrup in her chapter, observes that a consequence of focusing on either of these leads to a market-oriented legal rationality, where attempts are made at placing value on contributions made by the respective spouses in terms of the market. However, some contributions such as love, companionship, comfort, ease and contentment are intangible but equally invaluable to the relationship. Invaluable contributions further include the provision of unpaid domestic labour and caregiving, especially by women. All these intangible but invaluable contributions prove particularly difficult for the law to grapple with since they are not easily reduced to economic value and can also lead to economically irrational choices being made. The challenge for the law then is formulating a regime that will provide scope and ability to value the 'invaluable' and provide fairer compensation to the parties.

---

5 See, e.g. S Wong, 'Caring and sharing: interdependency as a basis for property redistribution?' in A Bottomley and S Wong (eds), *Changing Contours of Domestic Life, Family and Law: Caring and Sharing* (Oxford: Hart 2009); C Powell and M Van Vugt, 'Genuine giving or selfish sacrifice? The role of commitment and cost level upon willingness to sacrifice?' (2003) 33(3) *European Journal of Social Psychology* 403.

6 See, e.g. C Lind in this collection; A Bottomley and S Wong, 'Shared households: a new paradigm for thinking about the reform of domestic property relations' in A Diduck and K O'Donovan (eds), *Feminist Perspectives on Family Law* (Abingdon, UK: Routledge-Cavendish 2006).

7 Leckey observes that the call by same-sex couples for the right to marry is sometimes driven by the desire to make a political statement about equality of gays and lesbians with straight men and women and/or feminist arguments of equality between men and women. See also Badgett MVL, *When Gay People Get Married: What Happens When Societies Legalize Same-Sex Marriage* (New York: New York University 2009).

8 The limited socio-legal research on same-sex relationships is in part due to difficulties such as problems with sampling. What little research that has been conducted on same-sex relationships further provide a very mixed picture, indicating distinct differences between opposite- and same-sex relationships such as the latter being more egalitarian and for same-sex couples to adopt more individualised patterns of money management. See, e.g. M Burns, C Burgoyne and V Clarke, 'Financial affairs? Money management in same-sex relationships' (2008) 37(2) *Journal of Socio-Economics* 481; A Esmail, '"Negotiating fairness": A study on how lesbian family members evaluate, construct, and maintain "fairness" with the division of household labor' (2010) 57(5) *Journal of Homosexuality* 591.

Lind thus seeks to shift the analysis away from previous foci and argue instead for a more rigorous conceptual and normative critique of the notion of 'value' in these cases.

The final section of the book considers the public/private division at a micro level. The chapters deal in different ways with the impact of state intervention through public policy and/or law reform on couples and the household economy. The chapters indicate the increasing trend of privatisation of family responsibility. In these cases, this is done through public policies that promote conformity with a traditional form of family, e.g. by adhering to a marriage model, which in turn enable certain practices that allow abiding inequalities to persist are allowed to perpetuate. Wong's chapter focuses on recent proposals for the reform of the intestacy rules in the UK in relation to cohabitants. It examines whether the proposals are likely to benefit cohabitants and achieve their intended objective of alleviating their financial hardship in the event of the death of a partner. Likewise, Wong's chapter notes the conservative politics at play wherein the Law Commission of England and Wales reverted to a marriage-like definition in their reform proposals. The chapter considers the normative basis upon which intestacy rights are afforded to cohabitants and when and how they qualify for protection. It further considers the scope and extent of the rights provided and whether the distribution of the intestate partner's estate under the proposals will be done fairly. The extension of rights beyond spouses to other unmarried couples may seem progressive. However, the adherence to a marriage-like definition by the Law Commission has significant normative implications for cohabitants as it signals the state's pro-marriage stance in promoting and reinforcing only those relationships that follow a particular traditional form. Thus, the law serves to regulate and normalise seemingly deviant relationships.[9] The reform proposals may provide formal equality by extending protection to cohabitants but only to certain types of cohabitants, thereby rendering the scope of protection substantively more limited.

Keating's chapter is concerned with recent changes to child support provision in the UK. The Child Support Act 1991 was enacted in part to ensure that parents assume responsibility for the maintenance of their children where they are able to do so.[10] It was also hailed as legislation benefitting lower income families where there might be a higher incidence of 'absent fathers' failing to take financial responsibility for their children.[11] While there is a lack of consensus among academic commentators on the effectiveness of the Child Support Act 1991 in eradicating poverty, some see such legislation as having a role to play.[12] Legislative changes such as the Child Maintenance and Other Payments Act 2008, brought with it a shift in policy towards greater reprivatisation of child support. In her chapter, Keating examines this shift in policy to the promotion of individual responsibility and private agreement in relation to child support. She cautions that, in this austerity-driven era, the

---

9 A Diduck and K O'Donovan, 'Feminism and families: *plus ça change*?' in A Diduck and K O'Donovan (eds), *Feminist Perspectives on Family Law* (Abingdon, UK: Routledge-Cavendish 2006).
10 H Keating, 'Children come first?' (1995) 1 *Contemp. Issues L.* 29; J Carbone, 'Child support comes of age: an introduction to the laws of child support' in JT Oldham and MS Melli (eds), *Child Support: The Next Frontier* (Ann Arbor MI: University of Michigan Press 2000) 11.
11 R Collier, 'The campaign against the Child Support Act: "errant fathers" and family men' (July 1994) *Family L* 384.
12 See, e.g. P Parkinson, 'Re-engineering the Child Support Scheme: an Australian perspective on the British Government's proposals' (2007) 70 *MLR* 812; J Bradshaw, 'Child support and child Poverty' (2006) 14 *Benefits* 199; cf Carbone (n) who is doubtful that child support legislation alone can eradicate child poverty.

reprivatisation of responsibility is more likely to cause child poverty to rise substantially rather than be eradicated.

Last but not least, the final chapter is by Mumford, who seeks to adopt an isomorphic institutional analysis of the Universal Credit introduced in the UK by the previous Conservative-led Coalition government. The Universal Credit replaces a host of benefits including income-based jobseeker's allowance, child tax benefit, income support, council tax benefit and income-related employment and support allowance, and payment will be made to only one member of a couple. This in turn has raised concerns in some quarters about the financially detrimental effect that the Universal Credit will have on women.[13] Through an institutional analysis, Mumford seeks to examine the reasons for the introduction of the Universal Credit, which she suggests is more than a matter of bureaucracy. She further suggests that the area of tax, gender and, particularly, the Universal Credit is one that is ripe for further analysis through an institutionalist lens. It is still unclear the extent to which the Universal Credit will be able to address questions such as gender (in)equality, improvement of women's labour market participation and child poverty. Mumford's chapter, however, draws our attention to the potential for further work on this area to be undertaken through an isomorphic institutional analysis in order for us to acquire a better understanding of the way in which rights might be framed within a bureaucratic process as well as the impact of consequences, both intended and unintended, brought about by legislative changes.

This collection provides a timely analysis of the complexity of financial arrangements within close personal relationships. As we continue to experience the effects of the financial crisis in Europe and globally, the implications of legal and welfare reform, together with austerity measures, are beginning to be felt. We are mindful that this collection is limited to the impact of such reforms upon domestic relationships and gender relations and that there is much more to be said about their wider implications too in terms of the challenges to public and private life. What comes across especially, however, from the chapters in this collection is the resurgence of a rather traditional and conservative ideology within public policy, chiming with a move to the right in popular thinking,[14] yet allowing the continuation of norms that perpetuate, indeed exacerbate, existing economic inequalities, particularly for women.

---

13 See, e.g. Women's Budget Group, 'Universal credit and gender equality' (June 2011), at www.wbg.org.uk/RRB_Reports_13_4155103794.pdf.
14 As evidenced by the referendum vote in June 2016 in the United Kingdom to leave the European Union and the election of Donald Trump in November 2016 as the new President of the USA.

1 Credit and debt in close personal relationships

Jackie Goode

Introduction

At the beginning of 2012, when average incomes in the United Kingdom (UK) had fallen by nearly 3.5 per cent in real terms over the previous year, and consumers were still facing soaring bills, a survey[1] showed that UK households remained among the most indebted in the world, with British families averaging nearly £8,000 in debts from loans, overdrafts and credit cards. The research presented here explored experiences of using credit and acquiring problematic personal debt in low-income families in the UK, many of whom were reliant on welfare benefits. It draws on two projects, referred to as 'Credit and Debt' and 'Money Advice'. Those who are over-indebted and those reliant on benefits alike have traditionally attracted public disapprobation, in relation to the former in particular, through negative moral discourses of 'dependency'. This chapter examines the notion of '*inter*dependency', in two senses: in relation to intimate personal relationships between heterosexual partners, in which each is to some extent dependent on the other to varying degrees of complementarity; and in relation to the interdependent nature of contributory factors to over-indebtedness, as individuals try to manage the domains of home, work and family in which they are trying to maintain 'tenure'.

Security is a basic human need. And beyond a necessary level of ontological security, this includes social security – we live in relationships; in a series of social worlds. 'Close personal relationships' are defined in this chapter in terms of various forms of couple/family organisation. When it comes to money matters, however, there is a paradox. Despite the powerful discourse of 'sharing' in couple relationships, a growing body of research testifies to different degrees of 'separateness' and 'togetherness', influenced by factors such as: patterns of management and control;[2,3,4,5] sources of income;[6,7] identities and ideologies of

---

1 'Precious plastic' (Pricewaterhouse Coopers, 2012) www.pwc.co.uk/financial-services/publications/precious-plastic-2012-all-change-please.jhtml [accessed 19 September 2012].
2 V Wilson, *The Secret Life of Money* (St. Leonards, NSW: Allen and Unwin 1999).
3 J Pahl, 'Household spending, personal spending and the control of money in marriage' (1990) 24(1) *Sociology* 119.
4 K Rake and G Jayatilaka, *Home Truths: An Analysis of Financial Decision Making Within the Home* (London: Fawcett Society 2002).
5 C Vogler, 'Cohabiting couples: rethinking money in the household at the beginning of the twenty first century' (2005) 53(1) *Sociological Rev* 1.
6 J Goode *et al.*, *Purse or Wallet? Gender Inequalities and Income Distribution Within Families on Benefits* (London: Policy Studies Institute 1998).
7 D Molloy and D Snape, *Financial Arrangements of Couples on Benefit: A Review of the Literature* (UK: Department of Social Security 1999).

family and parenting;[8] and the status of the partnership (for example, whether heterosexual or same-sex partners;[9] whether married or cohabiting;[10,11,12] and whether it is a first or subsequent partnership).[13,14]

We also live 'in time'. Our lives change over time. As the above references to the stage of the relationship and to serial relationships suggest, the temporal aspects of close personal relationships are important for the distribution of income within the household. Is this true in relation to credit and debt too? How do credit and debt figure in the dynamics of partner interactions, in changes that occur across the life course, and in institutional changes at societal level? At the day-to-day interactional level, Kirchler and others highlight the temporal aspects of couples' decision-making around expenditure in which a kind of mental book-keeping takes place:

> When one partner resists the other's opinion and tries to win the argument . . . they may need not only to realise the personal goal represented by the decision, such as a desire to purchase, but to clarify the starting situation, that is, settle demands and commitments arising from the past, or to fulfil an overarching aim such as the maintenance or improvement of harmony in the relationship.[15]

In terms of the life course, Wilson[16] showed that money carries subjective meanings often acquired in childhood that partners then bring into couple relationships. Finney[17] also makes an important observation about the life course in relation to the established connections between financial difficulties and relationship breakdown. It is an over-simplification, she suggests, to view this connection in isolation from other factors. Rather, 'it should be seen in the wider context of relationship formation and duration, taking into account associated life events such as setting up home, becoming a parent and raising a family'.[18]

In terms of societal/institutional change, proponents of the individualisation thesis posit the idea that we now 'create our own biographies' as individuals rather than being 'relationally' or socially oriented:

> According to leading sociological theorists like Ulrich Beck[19] and Tony Giddens[20] we have now entered a 'late modern' epoch of 'de-traditionalisation' and 'individualisation'.

---

8   Goode *et al.* (n 6).
9   M Burns *et al.*, 'Financial affairs? Money management in same-sex relationships' (2008) 37(2) *J Socio-Economics* 481.
10 V Elizabeth, 'Managing money, managing coupledom' (2001) 49(3) *The Sociological Rev* 389.
11 Vogler (n 5).
12 C Burgoyne and S Sonnenberg, 'Financial practices in cohabiting heterosexual couples' in J Miles and R Probert (eds), *Sharing Lives, Dividing Assets* (Oxford: Hart 2009).
13 CB Burgoyne and V Morison, 'Money in remarriage: keeping things simple – and separate' (1997) 45(3) *Sociological Rev* 363.
14 Goode *et al.* (n 6).
15 E Kirchler *et al.*, *Conflict and Decision-Making in Close Relationships: Love, Money and Daily Routines* (Hove, UK: Psychology Press 2001) 169.
16 G Wilson, *Money in the Family: Financial Organisation and Women's Responsibility* (Aldershot, UK: Avebury 1987).
17 A Finney, 'The role of personal relationships in borrowing, saving and over-indebtedness' in Joanna Miles and Rebecca Probert (eds), *Sharing Lives, Dividing Assets* (Oxford: Hart 2009).
18 Ibid. 109.
19 U Beck, *Risk Society: Towards a New Modernity* (Thousand Oaks, CA: SAGE 1992).
20 A Giddens, *The Transformation of Intimacy: Sexuality, Love and Eroticism in Modern Societies* (Cambridge: Polity Press 1992).

Economic prosperity, education and the welfare state have freed us from externally imposed constraints, moral codes and traditional customs. The social structures of class, gender, religion and family are withering away, so that people no longer have pre-given life trajectories. Instead, individuals are compelled to reflexively make their own choices and hence create their own biographies. At the same time, the 'project of the self', with an emphasis on self-fulfilment and personal development, comes to replace relational, social aims.[21]

Meanwhile, politicians talk about, and valorise, 'hard-working families'. When they do this, they are conjuring up a picture of an ideal type of family comprising an (implicitly) heterosexual couple, one or both of whom is in paid employment and who live in their own or a rented house together, raising their children. And although this is also a model reproduced until very recently in the law,[22] it is very evidently no longer the only model of family to be found.

There have also been changes in relation to our financial institutions that impact on families. Pahl[23] showed, for example, how the advent of new forms of 'invisible' money such as credit cards and store cards, ushered in by the electronic economy, can act as an additional tool to facilitate individualised forms of spending within an ostensibly 'joint' model of household finances. Less than a decade later, the 'credit crunch' demonstrated only too well how decisions and actions taken at an earlier period in life, whether individually or jointly, can have long-lasting consequences for individuals, couples, families and whole economies, further down the line.

I would like to show therefore the ways in which the use of credit and the acquisition of problematic personal debt are embedded in the dynamics of the close personal relationships through which many of our lives are socially organised, how these relationships themselves are subject to development and change over time, and how they are being conducted in a changing 'structural' environment. What models of coupledom/family did the practices of these research participants constitute? Were they over-indebted individually or together? How did individualised forms of spending on credit at different stages in the life course figure in and impact upon couples' relationships now? Even for those who do match or aspire to the model of the family beloved of politicians in which children are brought up in a stable environment provided by married heterosexual parents in paid employment, it is not one that, for many, proves maintainable for any length of time. What was striking about the lives of those interviewed for this research was that they were characterised by fragility, insecurity, uncertainty and change, rather than by stability. In the aftermath of the credit crunch, they were frequently in transition in one way or another between one partnership, housing, or labour market status and another, and accompanied by a constant struggle to reduce rather than increase their debts.

---

21 S Duncan and D Smith, 'Individualisation versus the geography of "new" families' (2006) 1(2) *21st Century Society* 167.
22 A Diduck and F Kaganas, *Family Law, Gender and the State, Texts, Cases and Materials* (Oxford: Hart 1999).
23 J Pahl, 'Couples and their money: patterns of accounting and accountability in the domestic economy' (2000) 13(4) *Accounting, Auditing & Accountability J* 502.

Methods

Credit and debt

This study, funded by the Joseph Rowntree Foundation,[24] used a qualitative longitudinal approach, with repeated telephone and in-depth interviews, conducted between May 2008 and July 2009. Six groups were recruited – those with and those without children in each of three categories: the long-term low-waged; those in long-term receipt of benefits; and those who 'churn' between the two categories. These categories are not static, and the longitudinal nature of the methodology meant that movement between them during the course of the study could be mapped. Initial in-depth interviews were undertaken with 58 participants. On the basis of preliminary analysis of these, 12 were selected as in-depth case studies. Case study participants were re-interviewed every two months, over a period of a year, while the remaining 46 were interviewed by telephone every two months over the same period, to maintain briefer running updates of changing circumstances. This enabled mapping of the dynamics of change over time, but also allowed identification of critical moments/events. The time span of a year also allowed the capturing of seasonal and other time-specific demands on household income, such as birthdays, holidays, religious festivals and higher fuel consumption; emergencies such as washing machine or refrigerator breakdown; and the impact of price increases on food and consumer goods. At the end of the 12-month period of data collection, all participants were interviewed in depth once more, in order to clarify unresolved issues and expand on observations. Finally, participants were invited to a half-day workshop to solicit feedback on findings, and discuss and develop the policy implications of the study.

Money advice

A focus on targeting limited resources on women has been an important outcome, in policy terms, of research on the allocation of money within the household, due to revealed patterns of distribution in which men tend to have greater access to personal spending money and women tend to 'go without' in order to meet children's needs. Men, however, have traditionally been under-represented as participants 'in their own right' in such studies. They also tend to use advice services less frequently than women. In more recent research on *assets* (such as home ownership, pensions and savings) and debts,[25] men's voices *are* more prominent, but an overall imbalance remains. In 2010, this research, funded by the Money Advice Trust,[26] involved individual in-depth interviews with 20 men in low- to average-income households, about their experiences of household money management, debt and debt advice.

The methodology for this project meant that the kind of 'interactional' data between partners (where both are present and there is an element of dialogue between them), which were sometimes available in the Credit and Debt study, were forfeited here for men's speaking in their own right about how they had acquired problematic debts; how their domestic

---

24 www.jrf.org.uk.
25 K Rowlingson and R Joseph, *Assets and Debts within Couples: Ownership and Decision-Making* (York, UK: Friends Provident Foundation 2010).
26 www.moneyadvicetrust.org.

budgets, including their debts, were managed; and what their views and experiences were of debt advice. It also afforded the opportunity to interview some lone fathers.

Part of the brief for both projects was to identify 'triggers' into over-indebtedness. However, this signals a very specific conceptualisation of the acquisition of problematic debt – that is, that it results from a particular *event*. It is true that what has been referred to as 'adverse shocks' leading to a sudden and unanticipated loss of income or a sudden and unanticipated increase in expenditure proved significant for many in this research. However, in-depth interviews revealed a highly complex picture of credit use and over-indebtedness that did not necessarily accord with the notion that 'one-off events' were the key factor. *Problematic* debt was seen more as a characteristic of a gradual accumulation/unfolding of circumstances over time, sometimes in a fairly chaotic fashion that made it hard for people to maintain a clear picture of their overall circumstances, or to exercise financial control over it. In this sense, it was not so much a single 'trigger' that was responsible for their over-indebtedness but a matrix of interdependent factors. A number of case studies drawn from the two projects are now presented to explore and illustrate the complexities of 'interdependency' and the importance of temporal factors, as partners tried to maintain a foothold in the labour market, the housing market, and couple/family relationships in a context of problematic personal debt and economic crisis.

Family formation

The Chivers

A common refrain among interviewees was that of 'going mad with a credit card' when younger. Mr Chivers recounted how, when he first got his: 'I looked at it and thought "Shouldn't do anything silly with this". Managed for about two weeks and then walked into a record shop.'

When his wife then got her credit card, and they went to buy a PlayStation, he did ask her 'Are you sure you want to do that?' – but described this as 'putting up a very weak defence'. This kind of 'influencing' of one's partner in relation to decisions about expenditure is not uncommon, and not unique to couples with problematic debts. In low-income households, however, where there is little or no truly disposable income, and where it is usual for one person to have overall responsibility for budgeting, relationship dynamics that act effectively to 'sabotage' attempts to minimise all but essential expenditure can contribute to or exacerbate problematic debt. Dynamics can change however. Further along the life course, the Chivers now had two school-aged children and a baby on the way and were reliant solely on one wage. Mr Chivers felt that he and his wife were now much more responsible and organised and they actively managed their finances. They still had debts they felt were problematic, but they were also much more conscious of not leading each other into further debt.

The Nortons

Mr and Mrs Norton's problematic debt also arose from decisions that were located in the dynamics of their relationship at an earlier stage in their lives. Mr Norton lived with his wife, three-year-old twins and younger daughter. All the children had been conceived as a result of expensive IVF treatment. They had had a very stressful time after they had the twins, during which they first of all 'compensated' for failures to conceive a second time by 'treating themselves' to a bigger house, and then reversed their decision to accept having no more children, taking out another loan to 'have one more go' at IVF:

> we had two goes which cost £10,000. . . . I know it's probably off the subject a bit but it's financially draining and it's emotionally draining as well you see. And we moved house and 'treated' ourselves to a bigger house and everything – and then we decided to have one more last go. So I borrowed the money and that's where the loans come from.

Investing in family

The Hobsons

Mrs Hobson, a partnered woman with four resident and two adult non-resident children, became liable for debts accrued on her credit cards by her ex-husband when he became unemployed, thereby placing considerable strain on the income of her new re-constituted family. As she had still been employed when she and her current partner got together, she retained access to credit and store cards. He had a poor credit rating so she allowed him to use her cards. He also took over control of household finances.

Over a period of time, he 'maxed' all her cards, offering reassurances when she queried the levels of expenditure. When she started getting 'demanding' phone calls and the truth came out, they got a bank loan of £18,000 to consolidate their debts. However, her new partner then went on another substantial credit/store card spending spree, acquiring more debts. At the time of the first research interview, they owed around £30,000, including on rent arrears, 'pay as you view' purchases[27] (in this case, a hi-fi and car insurance), catalogues, and loans from doorstep lenders.

Mr and Mrs Hobson were both unskilled and had both become unemployed by the time the research started, remaining so throughout the year, apart from a couple of very short spells of 'agency' work. It had taken them a while to adjust to a substantial reduction in their benefit income when the two older children (one of whom had been in receipt of disability benefit) left home, but over the year, they began to reduce their debts – apart from what they felt to be the insurmountable loans and credit card debts, letters about which Mrs Hobson returned marked either 'deceased' or 'not known at this address'. They had very little in terms of consumer goods to show for their past level of credit spending, and it turned out that a considerable proportion of it had been incurred by Mr Hobson on clothes for the family and on taking them all out for meals on a regular basis. Mrs Hobson revealed, as the fieldwork progressed, that her partner tended even now to minimise their debts and arrears, and she explained this – and his incurring the debts in the way he had in the first place – in terms of his insecurities as both a partner and as a 'provider'. He separately revealed what he saw as *her* personal insecurities (around self/body image) in relation to their partnership, explaining that he continually had to try and convince her that he genuinely loved her. His 'treating' the family to clothes and meals out seems to have been viewed by both of them in the context of their personal relationship as a couple. The only way she could discharge 'her' debts, she recounted, would be to prosecute him.

---

27 Television viewing is accessed via paying into a meter attached to the TV, with variable tariffs set and adjusted by the loan company according to the rates at which householders are viewing/making repayments.

But who would do that, she asked? Such a course of action posed far too great a threat to their relationship, which was more important than being debt-free.

The Youngers

The cumulative process of a previous history of debt, unemployment and an insecure hold on housing were evident for the Youngers. At the beginning of the research, Louise Younger and her partner had just been re-housed after being made homeless, bringing with them credit card debts, undischarged loans and arrears on fuel from the former tenancy. Both were in receipt of benefits for the duration of the project. Louise's partner had participated in the 'New Deal' welfare programme in the past but he did not feel that this had helped him towards gaining a secure foothold in the labour market.

They bought new furniture on instalments and regularly incurred punitive bank charges by being overdrawn as they 'robbed Peter to pay Paul'. Their four children were all of primary school age and the birth of their fifth child during the period of research, while it brought them great happiness, also incurred additional expenditure on credit. Christmas presents for the children brought further debts. They were fairly accepting of this as they valued their children and their family life, with its hands-on 'dual-parenting' (as opposed to 'dual-earner') arrangement, very highly. They decided it was no good worrying about their finances as things were unlikely to change in the foreseeable future. Nevertheless, by the end of the project, they had stabilised their position with a debt consolidation loan.

In each of the above cases, the couple relationship had survived earlier periods of using credit and acquiring problematic debts intact. They all still had debts but these were either more manageable because they had been reduced or consolidated or they were being 'evaded' – for the time being at least. But family breakdown figured as a significant feature of problematic debt for others – in combination with loss of income associated with long-term unemployment, repeated redundancy or 'churning' in and out of work.

Family breakdown

Mr Compton

After his wife left, Mr Compton spent some time trying to care for his children while maintaining full-time work:

> I had the kids for the first few years, and then when she got another property, that is when she applied for the kids again . . . and then the children wanted to go back to their mum like, because I was rushing them to the childminders in the morning so I could work. And then come back home, get all the breakfasts ready for the next morning, put it on a tray like, cover it over, get the dinners ready soon as I got back, got them back home, then helping them with their school work and things like that at night.

When he started to get into arrears, he used a credit card to 'smooth' his income, but then 'suffered a breakdown' as a result of the pressure he was under and became unfit for work. He was unable to pay the mounting arrears from his Incapacity Benefit, and his inability to service his debts and manage on his income was further exacerbated during the period of the research by the loss of Child Benefit when the youngest child left school and also went to live with his mother.

Living alone now and with long-term mental health issues, Mr Compton reflected on an earlier period of his life when he had been employed, he and his wife had sat down regularly together to manage the household finances and they had had no unmanageable debts.

Mr Winters

Mr Winters was also a lone father. He had acquired substantial arrears in the period after he separated from his partner and moved into a council house of his own with their young son. He was employed for a short period of time but found it too difficult to keep work hours and care for his son at the same time. As for many lone mothers, and in contrast to some men who are relieved of any worry by virtue of their partners' bearing the responsibility for managing the household finances,[28] he found being responsible for his son while struggling with debts a source of enormous worry:

> It's got better since I've had him because I don't really want people knocking at the door. As it stands at the minute I ain't had no letters about no arrears for ages because the TV is sorted, the water rates is sorted, I get my gas and electric on a key meter. Housing benefit is covered and whatnot, so really, in that way, it's a lot better than it used to be. I used to get really worried and stressed out, sleepless nights and that, thinking the bailiffs were coming.

And again in common with many lone mothers, being unable to provide as well as he would like to for his son was a source of depression:

> I want a good life and I want nice things and I want to go on holidays . . . but it just ain't going to happen with the situation at the minute . . . that's only a dream . . . I must have applied for a hundred jobs in the last two months . . . I wake up in the morning with good intentions like looking for work, and then by the time I get back, it's just depression really. When I was a kid my mum and dad paid for me to go and watch (the local football team), go on these trips . . . I can't do none of that for my boy.

The Grahams

Partnership breakdown, unemployment and evictions were also part of the picture of the Grahams' problematic debts. Although Mr Graham had experienced a pattern of churning in and out of low-paid short-term jobs, delays in processing benefit claims only serving to exacerbate their debts, it was the breakdown of a former cohabitation and the commitments he had to the child of that partnership that meant that he not only came to his current marriage and new baby with problematic debt – but that he was now trying to support two families from an inconsistent income not adequate to the task. Mrs Graham had started a part-time degree with the intention of improving their prospects, but found it impossible to sustain and she now had an outstanding student loan to repay.

They had been evicted shortly before the research began and had eventually found another privately rented house, but they soon got into arrears again; this was followed by repeated

---

28 J Goode, 'Brothers are doing it for themselves? Men's experiences of getting into and getting out of debt' (2012) 41(3) *J of Socio-Economics* 327.

borrowing from the bank as and when Mr Graham was in employment, in order to pay off their earlier debts and try to contain the new arrears.

Further, although the Child Support Agency suspended payments to Mr Graham's 'non-resident' child from the benefit income he received when he was out of work, the working tax credit for which he was eligible was deducted to go towards these payments when he was in work, leaving him unable to contribute to improving the extent of the problematic debt carried by his 'new' family. Mrs Graham also struggled with the additional expenditure associated with Mr Graham's first child, when he came to stay with them each weekend and during school holidays.

Mr Bolton

Mr Bolton's partnership had also broken down. He owned the house that his ex-partner and her daughter had moved into with him, and they built an extension to it when they had a son of their own. When their relationship broke down, his partner wanted him to borrow from his parents or re-mortgage the house to enable her to set up home separately. He was unwilling to do the former and unable to do the latter because he had already done so to build the extension. He therefore exhausted his savings and used his credit cards and overdraft facility to fund the financial settlement. This left him in an even more vulnerable position when he was made redundant for a second time.

As he explained when asked how he would account for his current difficulties, the factors contributing to his problematic debt had not acted in isolation but had been part of a cumulative process: '. . . partially the break-up of the relationship. . . . Getting into the relationship. . . . Getting out of the relationship! . . . Being out of work: the first two times of being made redundant . . . basically, it's a knock-on effect, isn't it?'

Family change

The Rowsons

Finally, the case of the Rowsons, whose original debts had been incurred during the last recession, illustrated the limits of 'interdependence' within close personal relationships, in a situation where efforts to deal with over-indebtedness are not seen to be equally shared. Helen and her husband remained a couple, but the impact of dealing with their debts had left her with a sense of greater independence. Fifteen years earlier her husband had been self-employed and they had been owner-occupiers. But 'late payers' among his customers led the Rowsons to default on their mortgage, get into arrears with bills, and eventually go out of business. The house was re-possessed, they became council tenants, and spent years paying off creditors.

With the benefit of hindsight, Helen wondered whether this had perhaps been the best thing that could have happened; because her husband did get a job, they had more space in their council house than in the house they had owned and their finances were more manageable. At least this had been her thinking until her husband took time off from his new job with fatigue. It was then three years before he returned to work, to a lower paid job, and during that period, Helen reluctantly became the breadwinner, working shifts in two jobs. This led, over time, to her also taking over more of the kind of household activities she saw as traditionally undertaken by men (household repairs, decorating, mowing the lawn), and eventually to assuming single-handed control and management of their finances.

But her taking over responsibility for their household finances was more complex than a simple correspondence between earning the money and claiming 'ownership' and associated control of it. It was to do with 'showing him', as she put it – demonstrating to her husband that if he could not or would not fulfil the traditional male role, she would show that she did not actually need him:

> I used to think 'Well, if he can sit there and let me do this, then I'll do it. I'll show him ... I don't need him' ... because you don't have to be beholden to anybody ... you become independent, don't you? Even in a relationship, I think people can become independent people. ... You know you can walk out the door anytime. And I know I'll still be able to know what's in the bank ... my wages will be fine.

Furthermore, she did not feel she was alone in having made this transition:

> I think if you go along any street, in most houses now there's been a change ... a big turn ... I think the idea of men being providers is out the window now, because there are so many more women that are on their own that are having to do it anyway – and even women that are in relationships have to do it.

Discussion/conclusion

In the depression-era Britain of 1933, the publication of a novel that painted a picture of 'love on the dole' caused quite a stir.[29] Through the notion of interdependency I have tried to show the connections between the complex factors at play in a contemporary version of this narrative: maintaining close personal relationships on a low and insecure income reduced even further by over-indebtedness. By being aware of temporal factors, I have also tried to take into account the idea of change: over the life course of individuals, couples and families; and at the societal level. In contrast to the 1930s, new family forms together with a culture of 'easy' credit followed by a 'credit crunch' characterise the current era. The couples in this research belonged to what Dean[30] refers to as the 'precariat'. They were in a state of constant flux: getting a job, keeping a job, losing a job; buying a house, extending a house, losing a house; making a family, keeping a family together (or apart), losing a family, making a new family; getting into debt, borrowing to get out of debt, getting into greater debt.

Some couples were able to weather the debts brought into a partnership from earlier bouts of spending on credit as single individuals, usually where at least one of them retained a long-term foothold in employment and where they actively managed their household income to reduce their expenditure, or (very occasionally), where they were 'buffered' for a while by modest savings. For some, 'sexually transmitted debt',[31,32,33,34] also referred to

---

29 W Greenwood, *Love on the Dole* (London: Jonathan Cape 1933).
30 H Dean, 'The ethical deficit of the United Kingdom's proposed Universal Credit: pimping the precariat?' (2012) 83(2) *The Political Quarterly* 353.
31 J Dodds Streeton, 'Feminist perspectives on the law of insolvency' in J Dodds Streeton and R Langford (eds), *Aspects of Real Property and Insolvency Law* (Adelaide, Australia: *Adelaide Law Rev Research Paper* 1994).
32 N Howell, 'Sexually transmitted debt: a feminist analysis of laws regulating guarantors and co-borrowers' (1995) *Australian Feminist LJ* 93.
33 S Singh, *For Love Not Money: Women, Information and the Family Business* (Consumer Advocacy and Financial Counselling Association of Victoria 1995).
34 M Kaye, 'Equity's treatment of sexually transmitted debt' (1997) 5(1) *Feminist L Studies* 35.

as 'relationship debt' or 'emotional debt'[35] placed severe strains on the relationship, posing such a strong threat to it in one case, that this was resisted in the short term only by evading the most serious debt altogether; such was the level of investment in the couple relationship. Others were counting the cost of over-indebtedness in terms of loss of more than money – that is, in terms of relationship breakdown, loss of the form of family they had had, or in terms of mental health issues.

How have scholars and the state responded to these changes in families and in society? While its counter to an 'over-determined' analysis of society has been recognised, the individualisation thesis has also been widely critiqued,[36,37] and more recent theorising of the family recognises its diversity and fluidity;[38] utilises much more complex and less linear notions of how families change across generations and in time;[39] and gives what Collier[40] describes as a more complex and multi-layered account of the interconnected nature of the personal lives of women, children and men.

The research reported here supports both continuity and change, illustrated in relation to notions of independence and interdependence. As far as the lone fathers in the study were concerned, there was evidence that they found the need to juggle paid work and parenting as challenging as many lone mothers do; and that when they themselves had to undertake primary responsibility both for the care and welfare of children and the day-to-day management of a low income, they were equally at risk of the associated anxiety and depression as women in these circumstances have frequently reported. Nevertheless, it is still women who tend to be defined in terms of dependency within couple relationships, both economically and emotionally. This research shows a more complex picture than that, however, characterised by tensions between dependence, independence and interdependence.

Halleröd and others[41] suggest that once women feel less of a need to keep open their ability to potentially leave a relationship, they may relax their efforts to remain economically independent – supporting the idea that 'separate economies are not only a way to maintain independence within the relationship but also a way to maintain an exit option'.[42] As we saw, Mrs Hobson did not want to maintain an exit option. Her willingness to allow her partner repeatedly to 'act out' *his* financial dependence on *her* via 'collective' expenditure on her credit cards, even to the extent of her taking responsibility for levels of debt that she was completely unable to service, was a manifestation of their mutual investment in the relationship – autonomy and independence being forfeited in favour of interdependence – she on him for the status and security afforded by an intimate couple relationship and he on her for a (putative) ability to be a 'provider'. They were striving to maintain the traditional 'breadwinner' model of family – but doing so 'on credit'.

---

35 P Baron, 'The free exercise of her will: women and emotionally transmitted debt' (1995) *L in Context* 23.
36 Duncan and Smith (n 20).
37 M Daly and K Scheiwe, 'Individualisation and personal obligations – social policy, family policy and law reform in Germany and the UK' (2010) 24(2) *Intl JL, Policy and the Family* 177.
38 B Neale, 'Theorising family, kinship and social change' (2000) www.leeds.ac.uk/cava/papers/wsp6.pdf [accessed 19 September 2012].
39 C Smart and B Shipman, 'Visions in monochrome: families, marriage and the individualization thesis' (2004) 5(4) *British J Sociology* 491.
40 R Collier, 'Fathers' rights, gender and welfare: some questions for family law' (2009) 31(4) *J Social Welfare and Family L* 357.
41 B Halleröd et al., 'Doing gender while doing couple' in J Stocks, C Diaz and J Stocks (eds), *Modern Couples Sharing Money, Sharing Life* (New York: Palgrave Macmillan 2007).
42 Ibid. 148.

Helen Rowson did not want independence either, but had had it thrust upon her. She too had wanted to maintain a traditional breadwinner model of family, but had been unable to do so. Her marriage and family unit remained intact, and their minimal debts were now more manageable, but she had lost the version of coupledom/family that she had 'signed up for'. She had unwillingly exchanged it for what she saw as an increasingly common but not altogether welcome independence within marriage. She recognised that this gave her an exit option, but it was not one she had sought.

As far as the law is concerned, there are also contradictory trends. Diduck[43] documents a whole raft of legislative changes in the area of family, criminal, employment and common law, as well as laws to do with informal caring, that constitute what she calls a greater 'familiarisation' (or familialisation) of both the private and public sphere. Specifically in relation to debt, she notes recent legal decisions that call for a reconsideration of the traditional view that 'a man's obligation is to pay his debts and pay them promptly, even if discharging this duty affects his duty to maintain his wife and family'.[44] While many of these changes were made for laudable reasons to do with promoting the welfare of children and the furtherance of non-discrimination and equality, Diduck notes, she also sounds a note of caution. She suggests that such familiarisation can also be seen as a 'disciplinary' or regulating trend, absorbing potentially 'risky' subjects and groups back into 'familiar' roles, thereby constituting the privatisation of both human and social welfare: 'The blurring or redrawing of the boundary between public and private responsibilities in this way, so as to extend the space reserved for "family" may be part of a continuing process of privatising social reproduction and social responsibility.'[45]

In line with a new social and political order in which governments take less and less responsibility for the social welfare of citizens by encouraging them to help themselves,[46,47] activation programmes and conditionality, as well as caps on benefits are increasingly being introduced into the provision of UK welfare. Recent research suggests that this may have serious implications for members of the 'precariat'. Proposed changes to the way Local Housing Allowance is to be calculated and proposals to limit the amount of benefit an out of work household can receive, for example, are both likely to impact particularly negatively on households with children living in the privately rented sector, while the proposed move on to Job Seekers Allowance once the youngest child reaches the age of five is likely to make life harder for lone parents who are typically unable to access affordable child care.[48] The nature and level of child care support to be introduced in the Universal Credit will also affect the ability of many families with children to earn an adequate income and will determine

---

43 A Diduck, 'Shifting familiarity' (2005) 58(1) *CLP* 235.
44 *Re Bailey* [1977] 1 *WLR* 278, 284.
45 Diduck (n 43) 252.
46 J Fudge and B Cossman, 'Introduction: privatisation, law and the challenge to feminism' in J Fudge and B Cossman (eds), *Privatisation, Law and the Challenge to Feminism* (Toronto, ON: University of Toronto Press 2002).
47 S Gavigan and D Chunn (eds), *The Legal Tender of Gender: Law, Welfare and the Regulation of Women's Poverty* (Oxford: Hart 2010).
48 S Lister *et al.*, 'The impact of Welfare Reform Bill measures on affordability for low income private renting families' (2011) http://england.shelter.org.uk/professional_resources/policy_and_research/policy_library/policy_library_folder/the_impact_of_welfare_reform_bill_measures_on_affordability_for_low_income_private_renting_families [accessed 19 September 2012].

how far the government succeeds in 'making work pay'.[49] None of the assessments and predictions made so far in relation to these reforms take account of levels of over-indebtedness, however. As the reforms take effect in the UK, therefore, it remains to be seen what they will mean for the close personal relationships of women and men like those in this research, who are still struggling to maintain a foothold in home, family and work life in the face of the problematic personal debt that for them forms part of the aftermath of an earlier era of easy credit.

Bibliography

Baron, P (1995) The free exercise of her will: women and emotionally transmitted debt. *Law in Context*, 23.

Beck, U (1992) *Risk Society: Towards a New Modernity*. London: SAGE.

Burgoyne, CB and Morison, V (1997) Money in remarriage: keeping things simple – and separate. *The Sociological Review*, 45(3): 363–95.

Burgoyne, C and Sonnenberg, S (2009) Financial practices in cohabiting heterosexual couples, in J Miles and R Probert (eds) *Sharing Lives, Dividing Assets*. Oxford: Hart.

Burns, M, Burgoyne, C and Clarke, V (2008) Financial affairs? Money management in same-sex relationships. *Journal of Socio-Economics*, 37(2): 481–501.

Collier, R (2009) Fathers' rights, gender and welfare: some questions for family law. *Journal of Social Welfare and Family Law*, 31(4): 357–71.

Daly, M and Scheiwe, K (2010) Individualisation and personal obligations – social policy, family policy and law reform in Germany and the UK. *International Journal of Law, Policy and the Family*, 24(2): 177–97.

Dean, H (2012) The ethical deficit of the United Kingdom's proposed Universal Credit: pimping the precariat? *The Political Quarterly*, 83(2): 353–59.

Diduck, A (2005) Shifting familiarity. *Current Legal Problems*, 58(1): 235–54.

Diduck, A and Kaganas, F (1999) *Family Law, Gender and the State, Texts, Cases and Materials*. Oxford: Hart.

Dodds Streeton, J (1994) Feminist perspectives on the law of insolvency, in J Dodds Streeton and R Langford, *Aspects of Real Property and Insolvency Law*. Adelaide Law Review Research Paper no. 6.

Duncan, S and Smith, D (2006) Individualisation versus the geography of 'new' families. *21st Century Society*, 1(2): 167–89.

Elizabeth, V (2001) Managing money, managing coupledom. *The Sociological Review*, 49(3): 389–411.

Fudge, J and Cossman, B (2002) Introduction: privatisation, law and the challenge to feminism, in J Fudge and B Cossman (eds) *Privatisation, Law and the Challenge to Feminism*. Toronto, ON: University of Toronto Press.

Finney, A (2009) The role of personal relationships in borrowing, saving and over-indebtedness. In J Miles and R Probert (eds) *Sharing Lives, Dividing Assets*. Oxford: Hart.

Gavigan, S and Chunn, D (eds) (2010) *The Legal Tender of Gender: Law, Welfare and the Regulation of Women's Poverty*. Oñati International Series in Law & Society. Oxford: Hart.

Giddens, A (1992) *The Transformation of Intimacy: Sexuality, Love and Eroticism in Modern Societies*. Cambridge: Polity Press.

Goode, J, Lister, R and Callender, C (1998) *Purse or Wallet? Gender Inequalities and Income Distribution Within Families on Benefits*. London: Policy Studies Institute.

---

49 D Hirsch and J Beckhelling, *Tackling the Adequacy Trap: Earnings, Income and Work Incentives Under the Universal Credit* (London: Resolution Foundation 2011).

Goode, J (2012) Brothers are doing it for themselves? Men's experiences of getting into and getting out of debt. *Journal of Socio-Economics*, 41(3): 327–35.

Halleröd, B, Diaz, C and Stocks, J (2007) Doing gender while doing couple, in J Stocks, C Diaz and B Halleröd (eds) *Modern Couples Sharing Money, Sharing Life*. New York: Palgrave Macmillan.

Hirsch, D and Beckhelling, J (2011) Tackling the adequacy trap: earnings, income and work incentives under the Universal Credit. Resolution Foundation. www.resolutionfoundation.org/publications/tackling-adequacy-trap-earnings-incomes-work-incentives-universal-credit/ [accessed 8 February 2017].

Howell, N (1995) Sexually transmitted debt: a feminist analysis of laws regulating guarantors and co-borrowers. *Australian Feminist Law Journal*, 4: 93–112.

Kaye, M (1997) Equity's treatment of sexually transmitted debt. *Feminist Legal Studies*, 5(1): 35–55.

Kirchler, E, Rodler, C, Holzl, E and Meier, K (2001) *Conflict and Decision-Making in Close Relationships: Love, Money and Daily Routines*. Hove, UK: Psychology Press.

Lister, S, Reynolds, L and Webb, K (2011) The impact of Welfare Reform Bill measures on affordability for low-income private renting families. http://england.shelter.org.uk/professional_resources/policy_and_research/policy_library/policy_library_folder/the_impact_of_welfare_reform_bill_measures_on_affordability_for_low_income_private_renting_families [accessed 8 February 2017].

Molloy, D and Snape, D (1999) *Financial Arrangements of Couples on Benefit: a Review of the Literature*. In-house report 58, GB: Department of Social Security.

Neale, B (2000) Theorising family, kinship and social change. Workshop Paper no. 6, *ESRC Research Group for the Study of Care Values and the Future of Welfare*. www.leeds.ac.uk/cava/papers/wsp6.pdf [accessed 8 February 2017].

Pahl, J (1990) Household spending, personal spending and the control of money in marriage, *Sociology*, 24(1): 119–38.

Pahl, J (2000) Couples and their money: patterns of accounting and accountability in the domestic economy. *Accounting, Auditing & Accountability Journal*, 13(4): 502–17.

Rake, K and Jayatilaka, G (2002) *Home Truths: An Analysis of Financial Decision Making Within the Home*. London: Fawcett Society.

Rowlingson, K and Joseph, R (2010) *Assets and Debts Within Couples: Ownership and Decision-making*. York, UK: Friends Provident Foundation.

Singh, S (1995) *For Love Not Money: Women, Information and the Family Business*. Consumer Advocacy and Financial Counselling Association of Victoria, Melbourne: Australia.

Smart, C and Shipman, B (2004) Visions in monochrome: families, marriage and the individualization thesis. *British Journal of Sociology*, 5(4): 491–509.

Vogler, C (2005) Cohabiting couples: rethinking money in the household at the beginning of the twenty first century. *The Sociological Review*, 53(1): 1–29.

Wilson, G (1987) *Money in the Family: Financial Organisation and Women's Responsibility*. Aldershot, UK: Avebury.

Wilson, V (1999) *The Secret Life of Money*. St. Leonards, NSW, Australia: Allen and Unwin.

2 Intra-household inequality, poverty and well-being

Sara Cantillon and Marie Moran

Introduction

In the aftermath of the 2008 global economic recession, wealth and inequality have become hot topics in academia and policy-making.[1] The extent of economic inequality and the increasing gap in many countries in income distribution between richest and poorest have given rise to a renewal of social protest and other forms of civic engagement. Piketty's focus on wealth and in particular the top 1 per cent of income earners has ensured that talk about the 99 per cent and the 1 per cent is entrenched in public debate. Indeed the slogan 'We are the 99%' formed the basis of the Occupy movement in the US and elsewhere.[2] However, as Atkinson argues, the problem is not simply that the rich are getting much richer but the failure to tackle poverty and the fact that the majority of people are being left behind.[3] Any focus on alleviating poverty must also address the extent of wealth and income inequality and the driving forces behind its sharp rise in recent decades.

Aside from moral arguments against excessive economic inequality made by Solow and others,[4] increasing attention is being paid to the costs of such economic inequality. These costs are evident across political, economic and social contexts in terms of macroeconomic stability, the democratic process and social cohesion. In relation to the costs of societal inequality, there is an established literature on the relationship between societal inequality, and physical and psychological health and well-being on both an inter- and intra-national scale, which demonstrates a significant correlation between the lived experience of inequality and psychological well-being.[5] At the micro level, there is accumulated empirical work on the impact of unemployment and financial strain on psychological well-being.[6] This book is concerned with inequalities of wealth and poverty in close personal relationships and, since the 1990s, the question of the allocation of resources *within* households has attracted a large literature focusing on issues such as income pooling, financial decision-making, and

---

1 J Stiglitz, *The Price of Inequality* (New York: Norton 2012); AB Atkinson, *Inequality: What Can Be Done?* (Cambridge, MA: Harvard University Press 2015).
2 T Piketty, *Capital in the 21st Century* (Cambridge, MA: Harvard University Press 2014).
3 Atkinson (n 1).
4 R Solow, *In Conversation about Inequality* (New York: CUNY Graduate Centre, 1 May 2015).
5 R Putnam, *Bowling Alone: The Collapse and Revival of American Community* (Cambridge, MA: Simon and Schuster 2000); E Diener and R Biswas-Diener, 'Will money increase subjective well-being?' (2002) 57 *Social Indicators Research* 119; M Marmot, 'Social determinants of health inequalities' (2005) 365 *The Lancet* 1099; R Wilkinson and K Pickett, *The Spirit Level* (London: Allen Lane 2009).
6 C Whelan, D Hannon and S Creighton, 'Unemployment, poverty and psychological distress' (1991) ESRI General Research Series Paper no. 150.

expenditure and material outcomes.[7] Social inequality, financial strain and within-household distribution provide the framework for this chapter, which looks at the impact of inequality in material outcomes on individual well-being and coping in heterosexual married couples.

While there are many studies which relate societal inequality to societal psychological well-being, very few have attempted to examine the relationship between intra-household inequality and individual psychological well-being. In particular, there is little research investigating the extent to which differences in living standards and the internal financial arrangements adopted explains variance in the psychological health of individual family members beyond that which is attributable to social class, household income or other socio-economic variables.

Previous research on traditional nuclear households has indicated that, where household resources are unequally distributed, the distribution tends to be weighted in favour of the husband, and that furthermore, where a household is characterised by low income and low resources, the burden of responsibility for stretching scarce resources falls disproportionately on the wife, such that she is more likely to deal with the financial strain of making ends meet.[8] However, even though women typically adopt the role of management of scarce resources, this is not to say that they will experience greater psychological distress as a result. The normalisation of such roles and responsibilities, both within the household and within broader societal discourses could potentially generate a situation where either the psychological distress generated by the uneven division of responsibility is not articulated or recognised as distress by the women involved, or where the women involved actually do experience a disproportionately smaller degree of psychological distress than the situation might suggest, for reasons such as the availability of more sophisticated social networks for women, or the acquisition of coping mechanisms at an early developmental stage.[9] Indeed, research indicates that some women derive peace of mind and a sense of pride from their skills as managers of low income.[10] In any event, the gendered division of resources and power within a household does not exist in a vacuum but is related to the affluence and classed position of that household to begin with – both in terms of the allocative system adopted, and the amount of resources available for intra-household distribution.[11] What matters for the purposes of this analysis is whether, at the level of the household, gender

---

7   C Vogler and J Pahl, 'Money, power and inequality within marriage' (1994) 42 *The Sociological Review* 262; C Nyman and S Dema, 'An overview: research on couples and money' in J Stocks, C Díaz Martínez and B Halleröd (eds), *Modern Couples Sharing Money, Sharing Life* (New York: Palgrave Macmillan 2007); S Sung and F Bennett, 'Dealing with money in low-moderate income couples: insights from individual interviews' in K Clarke, T Maltby and P Kennett (eds) (2007) 19 *Social Policy Review* 151; J Bonke and M Browning, 'The distribution of financial well-being and income within households' (2009) 7 *Review of Economics of the Household* 31; S Cantillon, 'Measuring differences within households' (2013) 75 *Journal of Marriage and Family* 598.

8   J Goode, C Callender and R Lister, *Purse or Wallet: Gender Inequalities and Income Distribution within Families on Benefit* (London: Policy Studies Institute/Athenaeum Press 1998); L Adelman, S Middleton and K Ashworth, 'Intra household distribution of poverty and social exclusion' (2000) *Poverty and Social Exclusion Survey of Britain* Working Paper no. 23; S Cantillon, B Gannon and B Nolan, *Sharing Household Resources* (Dublin: Combat Poverty Agency 2004).

9   C Nathanson, 'Illness and the feminine role: a theoretical review' (1975) 9 *Social Science and Medicine*, 57; WR Gove, 'Gender differences in mental and physical illness: the effects of mixed and nurturant roles' (1984) 19 *Social Science and Medicine* 77.

10 Goode, Callender and Lister (n 8).

11 J Pahl, 'Earning, sharing, spending: married couples and their money' in R Walker and G Parker (eds), *Money Matters* (London: SAGE 1987).

differences in deprivation and experiences of financial strain give rise to gender-differentiated experiences of psychological stress, over and above that level of economic insufficiency and concomitant psychological stress generated by wider economic or labour market forces.

The chapter begins with a brief overview of the literature that demonstrates correlations between relative deprivation and psychological distress, and between financial strain and psychological distress, and those few studies which look at these issues within 'the black box' of the household. It reviews the results of a specially designed individual level study that examined differences between spouses in material deprivation across a broad range of indicators, the management of scarce resources and psychological strain. This chapter then explores the question of whether such differences have a significant and negative psychological impact on the member of the family burdened with this relative deprivation and disproportionate financial responsibility, using data from a special ad hoc module in the 1999 Living in Ireland Survey (LIIS). While dated, it remains the only survey ever done in Ireland that sought responses at an individual level across a broad range of non-monetary deprivation and financial decision-making indicators while also surveying individuals on psychological health. In 2010 the EU Survey of Income and Living Conditions (EU-SILC) included an ad hoc module aimed at investigating outcomes within the household, which focused mainly on income pooling. It included five indicators of material living standards and a few indicators of financial decision-making. An analysis of those responses is provided in this chapter where relevant.

Relative deprivation, financial strain, psychological distress and the lived experience of inequality

As stated previously, there is a substantial body of work which shows a significant correlation between the lived experience of inequality and psychological well-being.[12] What this research demonstrates is that beyond a certain degree of material well-being, it is the psychological strain associated with the experience of inequality, rather than the material or institutional constraints generated by such inequality, which produces detrimental health effects. While these studies do not deny that the experience of poverty itself can also generate psychological distress, they are more concerned with the consequences of living in an unequal society: how the experience of inequality can adversely affect the psychological health, affective well-being and, often as a result, physical health of individuals and nations, in addition to, or over and above, the physical and psychological effects of living in poverty.[13]

Beyond these epidemiological studies which are primarily concerned with the general health of the population, there is a range of studies which are more specifically concerned with the impact of inequality on psychological as opposed to physical well-being. O'Connell found that when controlling for average income, the level of equality in the income distribution of a given country is significantly predictive of the satisfaction level of the population, but that when controlling for the equality level, the average income rates were *not* significantly predictive of satisfaction level.[14] O'Connell's work forms part of a larger

---

12 Putnam (n 4); R Wilkinson, *Unhealthy Societies: The Afflictions of Inequality* (London: Routledge 1996); Wilkinson and Pickett (n 5); Putnam (n 5); Diener and Biswas-Diener (n 5).
13 M Fineman, *The Autonomy Myth: A Theory of Dependence* (New York: The New Press 2004); J Baker, K Lynch, S Cantillon and J Walsh, *Equality from Theory to Action* (2nd edn, Basingstoke, UK: Palgrave 2009).
14 M O'Connell, 'Fairly satisfied: economic equality, wealth and satisfaction' (2003) 25 *Journal of Economic Psychology* 297.

body of research which suggests that beyond a certain cut-off point, societal, and indeed individual, levels of satisfaction are not related to wealth but to perceptions and experiences of one's relative position or affluence within the society.[15]

The role of financial strain in explaining psychological distress

Within the broader body of research which examines the relationship between psychological distress and socio-economic status as it relates to both absolute and relative deprivation, there is a significant subset of research which employs the concept of financial strain to illuminate this relationship. In the literature, and more specifically in this chapter, financial strain is conceptualised as the cognitively experienced component of deprivation or a low-income existence which involves juggling finances, stretching scarce resources and having to 'do without'. While scarce resources also impact on the physical well-being of individuals, the concept of financial strain is helpful insofar as it allows us to differentiate between the stress associated with straightforward physical deprivation, such as a lack of food or warm clothing, and the stress associated with the management of scarce resources – the financial strain of 'making ends meet'. These micro-dynamics of intra-household financial strain are, of course, located within a bigger picture which involves not only individual or household levels of deprivation but also individual or household socio-economic status.

The gendered division of financial control and psychological well-being

Unemployment, poverty and financial strain clearly explain a substantial and significant amount of the variance in psychological stress experienced by household members. A question that these studies have not addressed, however, is how much further variance could be explained by reference to the gendered distribution of resources and control within a given household, and indeed to the financial management systems in place which allocate different degrees of power and responsibility to household members according to gender.

Women's relative position in the household may be considered a central variable in the relationship between women's socio-economic status and psychological health. This is not simply because of its confounding effects on attempts to single out the well-being of women as distinct from the overall well-being of the household but also because of the way in which a woman's relative power and resources within the household must affect the level of strain she experiences on a daily basis.

Few studies of the relationship between women's socio-economic status and their psychological health focus on the gendered division of financial control or gendered experience of financial strain within the household. One such study was carried out by Walters and co-authors that used data from the 1994 Canadian National Population Health Survey (NPHS) to explore the extent to which gender differences in health may be explained by work, household structure and social, personal and material resources.[16] A more recent study

---

15 TR Tyler, R Boeckmann, H Smith and Y Huo, *Social Justice in a Diverse Society* (Boulder, CO: Westview Press 1997); B Buunk and T Mussweiler, 'New directions in social comparison research' (2001) 31 *European Journal of Social Psychology* 467; P Sweeney and D McFarlin, 'Social comparisons and income satisfaction: a cross-national comparison' (2004) 77 *Journal of Occupational and Organizational Psychology* 149.
16 V Walters, P McDonough and L Strohschein, 'The influence of work, household structure, and social, personal and material resources on gender differences in health: an analysis of the 1994 Canadian National Population Health Survey' (2002) 54 *Social Science and Medicine* 677.

explored the relationship between psychological well-being and savings, investments and debts.[17] It found that there was a growing independence in financial arrangements between couples, with investments and debts more likely to be individually held. Savings, on the other hand, were viewed as shared assets. In terms of psychological well-being, the authors found that men's psychological well-being was affected by their own levels of savings, investments and debts rather than their partners, while women's well-being was influenced by both their own levels and that of their partners.[18] We will return to the significance of this finding later in the chapter.

Another attempt to provide a gendered analysis of the relationship between financial strain or management and psychological well-being was carried out by Rottman.[19] In his study of income distribution within Irish households, he looked at the relationship between the financial management system, the degree of sharing of resources and the psychological well-being of men and women, as measured separately from the overall well-being of the household. This study is the closest to what is attempted in this paper and provides a useful benchmark for comparison purposes. In summary, Rottman found that there was a statistically significant relationship between income sharing and levels of psychological distress as well as feelings of fatalism. Sharing of income was associated with lower levels of psychological distress and lower levels of fatalism. The effects were found to be stronger for wives than for husbands. The results clearly signalled that it was the amount of money shared rather than the absolute amount available for common consumption that was the psychological predictor. An identifiable link was also found between the division of expenditure responsibilities and psychological distress. Rottman concluded that:

> The main implication is to reinforce the importance of paying attention to how families organise their finances. How income and expenditure responsibilities are shared affects the material and psychological well-being of family members but the effects are particularly evident for wives.[20]

The special ad hoc module in the living in Ireland survey

We now turn to look at the results in relation to differences between husbands and wives in living standards within households and differences in financial strain or burden of coping in situations of scarce resources as well as results for men's and women's psychological health. In the next section, we examine the relationship between these variables to assess the impact, if any, on psychological distress and inequality within households of married couples.

The analysis is based on two separate modules of the 1999 LIIS. The first was a specially designed module, included as a one-off in the annual LIIS, which investigated intra-household inequality using non-monetary deprivation indicators, including questions on household budgeting and measures of financial strain. The second module, known as the Outlook on Life, is part of the annual LIIS and employed two separate measures of

---

17 MY Kan and H Laurie, 'Savings, investments, debts and psychological well-being in married and cohabiting couples' (2010) Institute for Social and Economic Research Working Paper Series 2010–42.
18 Ibid.
19 D Rottman, *Income Distribution within Irish Households* (Dublin: Combat Poverty Agency 1994).
20 Ibid. 15.

psychological health – namely, the General Health Questionnaire (GHQ) and fatalism measures. The LIIS is a large nationally representative survey, which forms the Irish component of the European Community Household Panel (ECHP) conducted on an annual basis since 1994. The sample size available for analysis was 1,124 couples (2,248 individuals). Since 2003, the LIIS has been replaced by the annual Survey of Income and Living Conditions conducted at the level of the European Union.

Differences in material deprivation between spouses

The analysis of the responses to the set of specially designed indicators focused on the scale and nature of differences between spouses in living standards. The questions related to levels of consumption and material deprivation ranging from basic deprivation items to central heating, car use, family meals and food consumption to access to pastimes/leisure activities, social activities, personal spending money and education and training. The results showed that the majority of husbands and wives reported that they did not have to do without these items due to lack of money.[21]

Where there was disparity (that is, where only one partner was without), there was a consistent, albeit not very dramatic, imbalance in favour of husbands across all the items. This imbalance widened considerably, however, when the non-monetary indicators broadened beyond the very basic deprivation items such as shoes and clothes to areas of social and leisure activity. The greatest differences between husbands and wives showed up in relation to social activities and spending money. Nearly 30 per cent of couples gave different responses in relation to having a regular pastime or leisure activity and, in about two-thirds of these, it was the husband who had, and the wife who did not have, a regular leisure activity. A high proportion of wives who did not have an activity where their husband did cited lack of time (due to household or childcare responsibilities) rather than lack of money as the reason. This was also true in relation to the socialising question (having/not having an afternoon or evening out over the previous fortnight) where childcare is given as the reason by 9.4 per cent of wives compared to 2.9 per cent of husbands.

The results are consistent with the expanding literature on time poverty which indicate that time, particularly time spent on childcare responsibilities, may be a greater constraint for women than money per se.[22] The findings on personal spending money mirror those of Rottman's study[23] and fit into the pattern established by previous national and international research, which show that husbands are more likely than wives to have personal spending money and to have more to spend on themselves.[24]

The information provided by the various non-monetary indicators was used to construct summary measures of the extent of deprivation experienced by husbands and wives, and of

---

21 This is consistent with the rapid increase in general living standards in Ireland during the late 1990s and the simultaneous pronounced fall in consistent poverty measures. In contrast, the 2010 EUSILC showed a rapid decline in living standards of Irish households with large increases in deprivation especially for households with children. This reflects the dramatic change in economic circumstances in Ireland from a period of boom to a period of bust.
22 C Vickery, 'The time poor – a new look at poverty' (1977) 12 *Journal of Human Resources* 27; M Bittmann and J Wajcman, 'The rush hour; the quality of leisure time and gender equity' (1999) SPRC Discussion Paper no. 97.
23 Rottman (n 19).
24 Vogler and Pahl (n 7); C Nyman, 'Gender equality in "the most equal country in the world"? Money and marriage in Sweden' (1999) 47 *The Sociological Review* 466.

the differences between spouses/partners in this regard. Two summary deprivation indices were compiled which reflected 'enforced lack' – that is, a score is added to the index only for those items lacked and regarded as not affordable.[25] The first summary index comprises eight basic items which include a raincoat, two pairs of shoes, a new suit, haircut, dental care, doctor visits, new clothes and having to buy secondhand, rather than new, clothes. The second summary index focuses on the four less basic items (leisure, social, entertainment and educational/training pursuits) that display higher levels of deprivation for both spouses and greater differences in the responses of spouses.

We construct a measure of the difference between spouses in reported deprivation levels by subtracting the husband's score on this summary index from that of his wife. A positive 'gap' measure for the couple thus means that the wife has reported a higher level of deprivation than the husband, while a negative 'gap' measure means the husband has reported greater deprivation. The summary deprivation index reflecting enforced lack for the eight basic items showed a gap in deprivation scores for 13 per cent of couples. This was divided between cases where the wife reported greater deprivation than her husband (8 per cent), and those where it was the husband who reported greater deprivation (5 per cent). The second summary deprivation index, reflecting enforced lack for the four non-basic items, showed a gap in enforced deprivation scores for 29 per cent of couples. Here there is a greater imbalance, with the wife reporting greater deprivation than her husband in 19 per cent of these couples compared to the 9 per cent where it was the husband who reported greater deprivation. We return to these deprivation indices in the multivariate analysis which, as we will see, demonstrates a systematic relationship between male and female deprivation scores, certain household characteristics and psychological well-being.

Differences in management and control over household resources

A second objective of the individual level non-monetary indicators was to assess differences in access to and management of finances within Irish households and, in particular, to assess the extent to which women carried a disproportionate burden of responsibility for stretching scarce resources. The results showed a complex pattern, where management varied not only across households but also across different areas of spending. When asked what they would do when they needed a coat or a pair of shoes, men were more likely than women to say that they would buy the item straight away or budget for it with their partner. Women were more likely than men to say they would save up to buy it. In low-income households, it was more common for both spouses to say that they would save up to buy the item, but women were still more likely to give this response than men. Joint decision-making was common among both low-income and other households for the purchase of most large household items, for borrowing and repaying money and for dealing with large unexpected bills. For example, about three-quarters of both men and women said that, if a large bill unexpectedly arose, the partners would decide together how to meet it. This was also true in low-income households. However, a traditional division in financial responsibility was evident in relation to regular grocery shopping and weekly budgeting. The wife took on

---

25 It is important when constructing scales of this kind to determine how well the set of items measures a single construct. One such measure is Cronbach's alpha coefficient of reliability or consistency in the data. Cronbach's alpha for the male summary index is measured at 0.75, for the female index at 0.77, and for the combined index at 0.86, all indicating a high degree of consistency across these items.

this role in more than half of the couples, with most of the remainder saying that both partners did so.

A similar picture emerged from the 2010 module (EU-SILC) which showed gender 'specialisation' in terms of everyday decisions, but a sharing of responsibility when it came to big decisions and larger expenditures. For instance, decision-making regarding shopping was shared for only 22 per cent of adults but 53 per cent of adults had a role in decisions regarding furniture or large consumer durables. Shared decision-making was also more likely for borrowing and saving in (58 per cent and 53 per cent respectively). Compared to decisions on shopping, shared decision-making was also higher (48 per cent) in the case of expenditure for the children, where there are children in the household.[26]

In relation to the issue of managing scarce resources, the burden of coping falls disproportionately on women. The response to the question 'Who takes the main responsibility for trying to make sure money, when tight, stretches from week to week?' showed that it was seen as a joint responsibility in approximately 56 per cent of couples and as the responsibility of the wife in about 34 per cent. In very low-income households – households below the 40 per cent relative income poverty line – the proportion of wives who said they took sole responsibility for making scarce resources stretch increased to 46 per cent.

Differences in outlook on life

The Outlook on Life section in the LIIS employed two separate measures of psychological stress – the widely used 12-item General Health Questionnaire (GHQ) and a six-item fatalism measure which measures feelings of powerlessness or loss of control. Fatalism has consistently been identified as 'the most important belief in affecting an individual's level of distress'.[27]

The distribution of GHQ scores for husbands and wives across the 12-item scale was markedly skewed with a large proportion of husbands and wives, 73 and 67 per cent respectively, recording a zero score, implying that they were in good psychological health. About 27 per cent of husbands and 33 per cent of wives scored between 1 and 12, indicating the presence of psychological distress, with most of those, for both husbands and wives, in the 1–3 categories. In analyses of the 12-item GHQ score, a threshold score of two or greater is normally used and employing that threshold with this data showed 15 per cent of husbands and 21 per cent of wives of the total sample reporting psychological distress.[28]

The fatalism scores for husbands and wives showed that approximately a third of the sample recorded a zero score, implying high levels of mastery or sense of control. On the other hand, 65 per cent of husbands and 68 per cent of wives scored between 1 and 6 on the fatalism index, although it should be noted that more than half of these scored 1 or 2. As no threshold is commonly used in fatalism scores, the 1–6 results were used as the comparable benchmark in the analyses that follow.

---

26 D Watson, B Maitre and S Cantillon, 'Implications of income pooling and household decision-making for the measurement of poverty and deprivation: an analysis of the SILC 2010 Special Module for Ireland' (2013) Social Inclusion Technical Paper no. 4.
27 Whelan, Hannon and Creighton (n 6).
28 The alpha (reliability) co-efficient for the GHQ scale, computed from the ESRI data, is measured at 0.84 for the male index and 0.87 for the female index, indicating a high degree of consistency across the items in this index.

Psychological distress and fatalism across household income

It is of interest, even if only for the purposes of confirming the literature, to examine the relationship between reported psychological distress and fatalism for spouses/partners and household income.

Table 2.1 shows the relationship between GHQ threshold scores for husbands and wives across equivalised household income. The two extremes of the income distribution, decile 1 and decile 10, showed, as expected, a strong relationship with the GHQ such that the highest probability of psychological distress was in the lowest income decile and, conversely, the lowest probability of psychological distress was in the highest income decile. This held true for both husbands and wives. Thereafter, for husbands, there was no consistent pattern moving up the income distribution. It is, however, noteworthy that 30 per cent of husbands in the poorest decile suffered psychological distress. This figure was almost twice as high as the next highest figure for any other decile and reflects the well-established literature on the relationship for men between unemployment, financial strain and psychological distress.[29] For wives, there appeared to be a much more consistent relationship between GHQ score and household income. For each of the top five equivalised household income deciles (50 per cent of the income distribution), wives had a lower probability of a GHQ score than wives for the sample as a whole.

Table 2.2 examines the relationship between the fatalism measure of psychological distress and household income. There appears to be a significant negative correlation between fatalism and household income for both husbands and wives. For husbands, the fatalism score was much higher than average in the bottom three deciles at 78, 82 and 71 per cent respectively, compared to 65 per cent for the sample as a whole. In the top four income deciles, the fatalism score was lower for husbands than for the sample as a whole. For wives, as with the GHQ measure, the relationship between fatalism and household income was more consistent than for husbands. For the bottom 50 per cent of the income distribution, the

Table 2.1 General Health Questionnaire threshold scores for husbands and wives across household income

Household income Deciles	GHQ threshold score (2–12) % of sample Husbands	Wives
1	29.5	28.7
2	13.7	25.8
3	11.1	20.6
4	15.7	25.0
5	13.0	19.1
6	15.5	18.9
7	14.8	20.3
8	17.2	17.2
9	11.0	17.0
10	9.9	14.3
Average	15	21

---

29 Whelan (n 6).

Table 2.2 Fatalism scores for husbands and wives across household income

Household income	Fatalism score (1–6) % of sample	
Deciles	Husbands	Wives
1	77.8	77.1
2	81.5	84.7
3	70.6	73.0
4	62.0	69.4
5	63.5	72.3
6	67.2	64.7
7	60.9	65.6
8	63.4	60.2
9	40.0	52.0
10	49.5	52.8
Average	65	68

wives' fatalism score was higher than for the sample as a whole while, for the top 50 per cent, the fatalism score was lower. Not surprisingly, this shows that feelings of powerlessness or lack of control are greater than average for the bottom half of the income distribution.

Material deprivation, burden of coping and determinants of psychological distress

We now turn to exploring the factors that influence the psychological health of husbands and wives. The two measures of psychological well-being examined thus far, GHQ and fatalism, were taken as the dependent variables. In each case, ordinary least squares (OLS) estimation was used to estimate the relationship between the GHQ and fatalism indices and the following independent variables (Model A):

- household equivalent income;
- existence, or otherwise, of wife's independent income (excluding child benefit);
- a continuous variable for age;
- ten dummy variables for education (three, with less than leaving certificate education as the benchmark); social class (three, with unskilled as the benchmark); labour force status; geographical location; the presence or absence of children; and, the presence or absence of another adult at the time of interview.

Many of these factors were found to be significant determinants of the variation in material deprivation and the burden of coping across husbands and wives. In order to say more about the sources of psychological health, the extent to which material deprivation and financial strain/burden of coping impact on these well-being measures is considered in the second stage of this analysis.[30]

---

30 Both sets of explanatory factors are considered separately due to the potential for multicollinearity if included as explanatory factors in the same model.

The measures included are:

- dummy variables for the husband's deprivation on both the eight (a raincoat, two pairs of shoes, a new suit, haircut, dental care, doctor visits, new clothes and having to buy second hand, rather than new, clothes) and four-item (leisure, social, entertainment and educational pursuits) indices and for the wife's deprivation on both the eight and four-item indices,
- dummy variables for husbands burdened with coping and for wives burdened with coping.

The regression results for psychological health using the variant GHQ for both husbands and wives are given in Tables 2.3 and 2.4 – the former presents results for the first set of explanatory factors, income and socio-demographic variables while the latter includes summary deprivation and financial burden measures as explanatory variables. Similar models for the fatalism measure of psychological distress are presented in Tables 2.5 and 2.6. In each case the results are presented initially with all independent variables included. The restricted model was produced by retaining only those variables that contribute significantly to the explanatory power of the equation. The significance level for the exclusion of variables was set at 0.10. F-tests confirm the overall statistical significance of all regressions. Increases in the adjusted R^2 values support the validity of the restricted over the full models.

The results in Table 2.3 for the first psychological health measure (GHQ) show that for the husband, three independent variables were statistically significant in terms of being able to explain some of the variation in the dependent variable in the restricted model. These variables were household income, the husband having at least a Leaving Certificate qualification (equivalent to A Levels/High School Diploma) and his employment status. In each case, a significant negative relationship was found, indicating that higher income levels, having at least a Leaving Certificate qualification and being employed reduce psychological distress. In the wife's case, the results for the psychological distress measure (GHQ) revealed that three independent variables were statistically significant in terms of being able to explain some of the variation in the dependent variable. As in the husband's case, higher levels of income and the employment status of husbands led to lower levels of psychological distress. A significant negative relationship was also found between the age of the husband and the wife's GHQ measure, indicating that in younger age groups wives experience greater psychological distress.

The extent to which deprivation and financial burden measures impacted on the GHQ scores is presented in Table 2.4. For husbands, deprivation based on both the eight (basic), and four (social) item index had a significant positive effect on the GHQ measure and, as such, could be considered a source of psychological distress experienced by husbands. In addition, where the wife was deprived on the basis of the eight-item index a significant positive result also emerged. Similarly, for wives, where there was deprivation on both the eight- and four-item index, significantly higher GHQ scores were observed. The husband's deprivation on the eight-item index was also a source of psychological distress for wives. In addition, a significant and positive relationship was also found between wives faced with the burden of managing financial resources and her GHQ scores.

Tables 2.5 and 2.6 contain the regression results for the second measure of psychological distress – fatalism. The first two columns of Table 2.5 show the results for the fatalism measure of psychological health for husbands. Eight income and socio-demographic variables were found to be statistically significant in terms of being able to explain some of the variation

Table 2.3 Determinants of psychological distress: the impact of income and socio-demographic factors

	Husband's GHQ		Wife's GHQ	
	Full model	Restricted model	Full model	Restricted model
Constant	1.0872*** (0.4011)	0.1243*** (0.1162)	2.3581*** (0.5210)	2.0822*** (0.3996)
Household income	−0.0003 (0.0006)	−0.0008* (0.0005)	−0.0006 (0.0008)	−0.0010* (0.0006)
Female has independent income	−0.0004 (0.0005)		−0.0002 (0.0006)	
Age	0.0035 (0.0052)		−0.0125* (0.0067)	−0.0094* (0.0056)
Higher education	0.1827 (0.1671)		−0.2853 (0.2178)	
Leaving Cert education	−0.2203 (0.1404)	−0.2512* (0.1338)	−0.1949 (0.1830)	
Professional	−0.0823 (0.1454)		−0.1680 (0.1894)	
Skilled	−0.0175 (0.1267)		−0.0857 (0.1655)	
Employed	−0.5445*** (0.1495)	−0.4817*** (0.1154)	−0.4152** (0.1958)	−0.4552** (0.1882)
Urban	−0.1324 (0.1086)		0.1784 (0.1407)	
Children	0.2229* (0.1336)		−0.0971 (0.1744)	
Adult present[1]	−0.1523 (0.1037)		−0.0937 (0.1349)	
R-squared	0.0352	0.0295	0.0162	0.0102
Adjusted R-squared	0.0257	0.0260	0.0065	0.0075
F-statistic (P-value)	3.69 (0.0000)	8.50 (0.0000)	1.66 (0.0766)	3.83 (0.0096)

Standard errors given in parenthesis:
*** indicates significance at the 1% level;
** indicates significance at the 5% level;
* indicates significance at the 10% level.
Household characteristics are associated with husbands unless otherwise indicated.

[1] 'Adult present' refers to a wife being present at the time of the husband's interview in the case of the husband and vice versa in the case of the wife.

Table 2.4 Determinants of psychological distress: the impact of deprivation and financial strain

	Husband's GHQ		Wife's GHQ	
	Full model	Restricted model	Full model	Restricted model
Constant	0.4877*** (0.0754)	0.5790*** (0.0550)	0.6538*** (0.0969)	0.7202*** (0.0873)
Deprivation (8) Male	1.0468*** (0.2357)	1.0811*** (0.2338)	1.0118*** (0.3031)	1.0387*** (0.3009)
Deprivation (8) Fem	0.6210*** (0.1938)	0.6903*** (0.1824)	0.8300*** (0.2492)	0.8471*** (0.2486)
Deprivation (4) Male	0.3694** (0.1769)	0.3762** (0.1737)	0.4123** (0.1719)	
Deprivation (4) Fem	0.0250 (0.1337)		0.0738 (0.2274)	0.4121*** (0.1690)
Male burdened	0.1212 (0.1410)		0.2926 (0.1813)	
Female burdened	0.1809* (0.1056)		0.4013*** (0.1358)	0.3577*** (0.1326)
R-squared	0.0381	0.0352	0.0452	0.0429
Adjusted R-squared	0.0329	0.0326	0.0401	0.0395
F-statistic	7.37 (0.0000)	13.63 (0.0000)	8.81 (0.0000)	12.53 (0.0000)

Standard errors given in parenthesis:
*** indicates significance at the 1% level;
** indicates significance at the 5% level;
* indicates significance at the 10% level.

in the dependent variable in the restricted model. The variables of significance were the level of household income, his age, his level of education (two categories), his social class (two categories), his employment status and his geographical location. As with the first measure of psychological well-being, GHQ, the husband's fatalism score declined if he was employed and/or had a leaving certificate. In addition, household income, higher education, social class (either professional or skilled relative to unskilled) and an urban geographical location also had a positive impact on psychological health.

The last two columns in Table 2.5 show the equivalent regression results for the wife. Five variables were statistically significant in terms of being able to explain some of the variation in the dependent variable. These were household income, the wife's independent income, and the age, education level and social status of her husband. As for husbands, there was a negative relationship between household income, higher education and employment status such that the wife's fatalism score declined the higher the household income and in line with the husband's level of education and employment status. In addition, there was a significant negative relationship between the wife having an independent income and her fatalism scores such that an independent income for the wife had a significant beneficial effect on her levels of fatalism or feeling of powerlessness. Finally, a significant

Table 2.5 Determinants of fatalism: the impact of income and socio-demographic factors

	Husband's fatalism		Wife's fatalism	
	Full model	Restricted model	Full model	Restricted model
Constant	1.5496*** (0.3436)	1.7916*** (0.2836)	1.6567*** (0.3641)	1.5723*** (0.2841)
Household income	−0.0007 (0.0005)	−0.0009** (0.0004)	−0.0010** (0.0005)	−0.0014*** (0.0005)
Female has independent income	−0.0001 (0.0004)		−0.0010*** (0.0004)	−0.0010** (0.0004)
Age	0.0180*** (0.0044)	0.0153*** (0.0038)	0.0136*** (0.0047)	0.0139*** (0.0040)
Higher education	−0.4407*** (0.1431)	−0.4382*** (0.1425)	−0.3647** (0.1522)	−0.3664*** (0.1304)
Leaving cert. education	−0.3542*** (0.1203)	−0.3594*** (0.1199)	−0.1725 (0.1279)	
Professional	−0.3731*** (0.1245)	−0.3586*** (0.1239)	−0.2064 (0.1324)	
Skilled	−0.2948*** (0.1086)	−0.2982*** (0.1085)	−0.1300 (0.1157)	
Employed	−0.6292*** (0.1281)	−0.5945*** (0.1252)	−0.2760** (0.1368)	−0.2879** (0.1325)
Urban	−0.2244** (0.0930)	−0.2223*** (0.0914)	−0.0547 (0.0983)	
Children	0.1636 (0.1144)		0.0461 (0.1219)	
Adult present[1]	0.0049 (0.0888)		0.0182 (0.0943)	
R-squared	0.1735	0.1720	0.0995	0.0951
Adjusted R-squared	0.1653	0.1660	0.0906	0.0911
F-statistic (P-value)	21.21 (0.0000)	28.92 (0.0000)	11.16 (0.0000)	23.48 (0.0000)

Standard errors given in parenthesis:
*** indicates significance at the 1% level;
** indicates significance at the 5% level;
* indicates significance at the 10% level.
Household characteristics are associated with husbands unless otherwise indicated.

[1] 'Adult present' refers to a wife being present at the time of the husband's interview in the case of the husband and vice versa in the case of the wife.

Table 2.6 Determinants of fatalism: the impact of deprivation and financial strain

	Husband's fatalism		Wife's fatalism	
	Full model	Restricted model	Full model	Restricted model
Constant	1.2724*** (0.0691)	1.2870*** (0.0610)	1.4066*** (0.0710)	1.4434*** (0.0669)
Deprivation (8) Male	0.7929*** (0.2162)	0.7916*** (0.2147)	0.1101 (0.2219)	
Deprivation (8) Female	0.9685*** (0.1778)	0.9588*** (0.1699)	0.9242*** (0.1825)	
Deprivation (4) Male	0.4942*** (0.1622)	0.5039*** (0.1594)	0.1197 (0.1665)	
Deprivation (4) Female	-0.0352 (0.1226)		0.1719 (0.1258)	0.9885*** (0.1740)
Male burdened	0.0973 (0.1294)		0.3621*** (0.1328)	0.3730*** (0.1325)
Female burdened	0.1847* (0.0969)	0.1682* (0.0945)	0.1828* (0.0994)	0.1979** (0.0988)
R-squared	0.0559	0.0554	0.0431	0.0409
Adjusted R-squared	0.0508	0.520	0.0380	0.0383
F-statistic	11.02 (0.0000)	16.40 (0.0000)	8.39 (0.0000)	15.92 (0.0000)

Standard errors given in parenthesis:
*** indicates significance at the 1% level;
** indicates significance at the 5% level;
* indicates significance at the 10% level.

positive relationship was observed between age and fatalism scores for both husbands and wives, indicating that, in older age groups, feelings of fatalism and powerlessness are more prominent.

Table 2.6 presents regression results capturing the impact of deprivation and burden of coping measures on the measures of fatalism for husbands and wives. Perhaps as expected, for husbands, his level of deprivation (on both indices) and his wife's deprivation on the eight-item index had positive coefficients, indicating that the husband had higher levels of powerlessness or loss of control when deprived, or when his wife was deprived. In addition, where the wife was under financial strain, the husband also experienced a certain element of powerlessness. In the wife's case, financial strain was a greater determinant of the feeling of powerlessness, with significant positive effects found for both the wife's and the husband's measure of financial burden. Interestingly, for wives, neither her own nor her husband's deprivation on the eight-item index appeared to be significant in determining her levels of fatalism. However, where the wife was deprived, based on the four-item index, this was significant at the 1 per cent level. The eight-item index comprised items of basic material deprivation whereas the four-item index comprised items relating to pastimes and leisure activity, social activity, personal spending money and education or training. The significant correlation between deprivation on this index and feelings of control and powerlessness is thus not that surprising.

Conclusions

The relative deprivation hypothesis proposes that individual levels of satisfaction are derived from comparison of the favourability of one's situation to the situations of those around them: that is, what matters in terms of personal satisfaction are subjective assessments of relative rather than absolute income or resources.[31] This chapter focused on the relationship between the relative deprivation and financial strain experienced individually by married couples and their psychological distress and feelings of fatalism. Specifically, it addressed the question of whether inequalities within the household in relation to material standards of living, financial arrangements and expenditure responsibilities have an independent impact on individual levels of psychological distress and feelings of powerlessness. This question was explored by using the results from the module on intra-household inequality along with the responses of the same couples to questions from the Outlook on Life section of the Living in Ireland Survey.

For the GHQ measure, the results showed, first, that a high proportion of husbands and wives were not suffering from psychological distress. This is consistent both with previous studies of psychological distress in Ireland and with the results of the intra-household module on material deprivation which showed that the majority of couples felt that they were not deprived of certain goods or activities due to lack of money. Both sets of results reflect the increase in general living standards in Ireland during the boom time mid- to late 1990s, the pronounced fall in consistent poverty measures and the analogous surveys showing the Irish to be 'the happiest in Europe'.[32] On the other hand, a substantial minority of husbands and wives were shown to experience considerable levels of psychological distress. A third of the women and over a quarter of the men in the sample indicated that they suffered some psychological distress scoring between 1 and 12 on the GHQ, with the majority of those in the 1 to 3 categories.

Using the standard GHQ threshold, the analysis confirmed the presence of a number of expected correlations. There was clearly a positive relationship between the GHQ score and household income, with the stronger correlation for husbands again reflecting and supporting the literature in relation to the links between unemployment, financial strain and psychological distress. The multivariate analysis demonstrated a significant relationship between material deprivation, financial strain and psychological distress. For both husbands and wives, deprivation, based on their own and each other's eight-item indices, and on their own four-item indices, had a significant positive effect on the GHQ measure. That is, relative material deprivation increased their psychological distress.

For wives, but notably not for husbands, a significant and positive relationship was found between financial burden and GHQ scores. Wives faced with the burden of managing scarce financial resources suffered higher levels of psychological distress.

In relation to the fatalism measure, the multivariate analysis showed the importance of household income, age, education and social status for both husbands and wives. In addition, for husbands, employment status was a significant independent variable with the

---

31 Tyler *et al.* (n 15).
32 R Veenhoven, 'The return of inequality in modern society' (2005) 6 *Journal of Happiness Studies* 457.

negative co-efficient implying that a husband's fatalism score declines when employed. This finding corroborates previous studies and perhaps also underscores the continuing ideological significance of the breadwinner role for men. For wives, there is a significant negative relationship between having an independent income and her fatalism scores. An independent income has a significant beneficial effect on her levels of fatalism or feelings of powerlessness. Again, this finding is in line with the emphasis placed on financial independence in the intra-household literature and with previous studies which demonstrated the impact of an independent income in narrowing the gap in deprivation scores between husbands and wives.[33] This study shows that the higher the independent income that accrues to the wife, the greater the positive impact on her psychological health.

Finally, the multivariate analysis showed the impact of deprivation and burden of coping on the measure of fatalism for husbands and wives. Material deprivation was a significant explanatory factor for husbands. For wives, however, it was deprivation in relation to social activities and personal spending money rather than material deprivation per se, that was the significant independent variable in determining her fatalism scores. Financial strain was a significant determinant of the feeling of powerlessness with positive effects found for both husbands and wives on their own and each other's measure of financial burden.

What this chapter shows, then, is that intra-household inequality does impact upon individual psychological well-being. Specifically, differences in living standards, the financial arrangements adopted and the extent of income sharing explains some of the variance in the psychological health of individuals in close personal relationships, beyond that which is attributable to social class, household income or other socio-economic variables. Significantly, these differences are gendered, demonstrating that within the 'black box' of the household, unequal gendered roles are borne with evidential psychological impact.

Bibliography

Adelman L, Middleton S and Ashworth K, 'Intra household distribution of poverty and social exclusion' Poverty and Social Exclusion Survey of Britain Working Paper no. 23 (2000).

Atkinson A, *Inequality: What Can Be Done?* (Cambridge, MA: Harvard University Press 2015).

Baker J, Lynch K, Cantillon S and Walsh J, *Equality from Theory to Action* (2nd edn, London: Palgrave 2009).

Bittman M and Wajcman J, The rush hour: the quality of leisure time and gender equity' SPRC Discussion Paper no. 97 (Middlesex, UK: Social Policy Research Centre 1999).

Bonke J and Browning M, 'The distribution of financial well-being and income within households' (2009) 7(1) *Review of Economics of the Household* 31–42.

Buunk BP and Mussweiler T, 'New directions in social comparison research' (2001) 31(5) *European Journal of Social Psychology* 467–75.

Cantillon S, 'Measuring differences within households' (2013) 75(3) *Journal of Marriage and Family* 598–610.

—— Gannon B and Nolan B, *Sharing Household Resources* (Dublin: Combat Poverty Agency 2004).

—— and Nolan B, 'Are married women more deprived than their husbands?' (1998) 27(2) *Journal of Social Policy* 151.

—— and Nolan B, 'Poverty within households: measuring gender differences using non-monetary indicators' (2001) 7(1) *Feminist Economics* 5.

---

[33] S Cantillon and B Nolan, 'Are married women more deprived than their husbands?' (1998) 27 *Journal of Social Policy* 151; Cantillon, Gannon and Nolan (n 8); Cantillon (n 7).

Diener E and Biswas-Diener R, 'Will money increase subjective well-being?' (2002) 57(2) *Social Indicators Research* 119–69.
Fineman M, *The Autonomy Myth: A Theory of Dependence* (New York: The New Press 2004).
Goode J, Callender C and Lister R, *Purse or Wallet: Gender Inequalities and Income Distribution Within Families on Benefit* (Cambridge, MA: Policy Studies Institute/Athenaeum Press 1998).
Gove WR, 'Gender differences in mental and physical illness: the effects of mixed and nurturant roles' (1984) 19(2) *Social Science and Medicine* 77–84.
Kan MY and Laurie H, *'Savings, investments, debts and psychological well-being in married and cohabiting couples'* Institute for Social and Economic Research Working Paper Series (Colchester, UK: University of Essex 2010) 42.
Marmot M, 'Social determinants of health inequalities' (2005) 365(9464) *The Lancet* 1099–1104.
Nathanson CA, 'Illness and the feminine role: a theoretical review' (1975) 9 *Social Science and Medicine*, 57–62.
Nyman C, 'Gender equality in "the most equal country in the world"? Money and marriage in Sweden' (1999) 47(4) *The Sociological Review* 766–93.
Nyman C and Dema S, 'An overview: research on couples and money' in J Stocks, C Diaz Martínez and B Halleröd (eds), *Modern Couples Sharing Money, Sharing Life* (New York: Palgrave Macmillan 2007).
O'Connell M, 'Fairly satisfied: economic equality, wealth and satisfaction' (2003) 25(3) *Journal of Economic Psychology* 297–305.
Pahl J, 'Earning, sharing, spending: married couples and their money' in R Walker and G Parker (eds), *Money Matters* (London: SAGE 1987).
Piketty T, *Capital in the 21st Century* (Cambridge, MA: Harvard University Press 2014).
Putnam R, *Bowling Alone: The Collapse and Revival of American Community* (London: Simon and Schuster 2000).
Rottman D, *Income Distribution within Irish Households* (Dublin: Combat Poverty Agency 1994).
Solow R, *In Conversation with Inequality* (New York: CUNY Graduate Centre 1 May 2015).
Stiglitz J, *The Price of Inequality* (London: Norton 2012).
Sung S and Bennett F, 'Dealing with money in low-moderate income couples: insights from individual interviews' in K Clarke, T Maltby and P Kennett (eds) (2007) *Social Policy Review 19* (Bristol, UK: Policy Press).
Sweeney P and McFarlin DB, 'Social comparisons and income satisfaction: a cross-national comparison' (2004) 77(2) *Journal of Occupational and Organizational Psychology* 149–54.
Tyler T, Boeckman R, Smith H and Huo Y, *Social Justice in a Diverse Society* (Boulder, CO: USA Westview Press 1997).
Veenhoven R, 'The return of inequality in modern society' (2005) 6(4) *Journal of Happiness Studies* 457–87.
Vickery C, 'The time poor – a new look at poverty' (1977) 12(1) *Journal of Human Resources* 27–48.
Vogler C and Pahl J, 'Money, power and inequality within marriage' (1994) 42(25) *The Sociological Review* 263–88.
Walters V, McDonough P and Strohschein L, 'The influence of work, household structure, and social, personal and material resources on gender differences in health: an analysis of the 1994 Canadian National Population Health Survey' (2002) 54(5) *Social Science and Medicine* 677–92.
Watson D, Maitre B and Cantillon S, 'Implications of income pooling and household decision-making for the measurement of poverty and deprivation: an analysis of the SILC 2010 Special Module for Ireland' (2013) Social Inclusion Technical Paper no. 4, Ireland.
Whelan C, Hannon D and Creighton S, 'Unemployment, poverty and psychological distress' (1991) ESRI General Research Series Paper no. 150.
Wilkinson R, *Unhealthy Societies: The Afflictions of Inequality* (London: Routledge 1996).
Wilkinson R and Pickett K, *The Spirit Level* (London: Allen Lane 2009).

3 The ownership and distribution of money in Spanish dual-income couples

Gender differences and the effects of some public policies[1]

Sandra Dema Moreno and
Capitolina Díaz Martínez

Introduction

In the last 40 years, Spain has experienced important and rapid transformations, both politically and socially, that have changed the country into a society comparable to the rest of the members of the European Union. As the country has moved, since 1975, from dictatorship to democracy, Spanish families have also experienced profound changes, affecting the family's structure, its social functions and its internal dynamics.[2]

Central to these changes have been women's agency in the developments and the transformation of gender relations. Women have gained access to greater educational opportunities, with the younger generations matching and even surpassing the educational level of men, and they have joined the labour market *en masse*, although their rate of employment in 2015 is still below that of Spanish men (52.7 per cent of women have a job, more than 10 percentage points lower than Spanish men, who have an employment rate of 62.9 per cent) and also below the average of the EU28 for women (with an employment rate of 60.4 per cent). If we compare 2008 employment rates (at the beginning of the crisis) with the current ones, it appears that in the case of the EU28 the employment gender gap has been slightly reduced from 13.8 per cent to 10.5 per cent, while in Spain the reduction has been bigger, jumping down from a gender difference of 17.9 percentage points in 2008 to the current 10.2. This data reflect the big job loss suffered in that period, especially of male jobs.

---

1 This study is part of a larger-scale research project, '*Los presupuestos familiares desde la perspectiva de género: Análisis no sexista de la EPF y de la ECV*' ('Family budgets from a gender perspective: non-sexist analysis of HBS and EU-SILC') (CSO2008-05182), financed by the Spanish Ministry of Education and Science (Research and Development National Plan (2008–2011), as well as a contribution from the Department of Education and Science of the Principality of Asturias (FC09COF0922).
2 S del Campo, *La 'nueva' familia española* (Madrid: Eudema 1991); TJ Guerrero and M Naldini 'Is the south so different? Italian and Spanish families in comparative perspective' (1996) 1(3) *South European Society and Politics* 42; I Alberdi, *La nueva familia española* (Madrid: Taurus 1999); G Meil Landwerlin, *La post-modernización de la familia española* (Madrid: Acento Editorial 1999); JJ González and M Requena (eds), *Tres décadas de cambio social en España* (Madrid: Alianza Editorial 2005).

Women's arrival in the labour market has brought with it important changes in the family sphere, such as the postponement of marriage and having children.[3] At the same time, family models have diversified. The traditional type of family with a male breadwinner and a housewife has lost ground to other forms of family organisation, such as dual-income couples, single-parent families or same-sex married couples, and traditional family values have lost their influence especially among young people.[4] In fact, an opinion poll of the Spanish Youth Institute, carried out in 2014, showed that for 84.7 of young people in Spain the ideal family was one in which paid work and family responsibilities were shared equally between men and women, while for 9.5 per cent of young people the ideal home was one in which the woman had a less demanding job and took charge of household tasks. Only 4.1 per cent of young people wanted a home in which only the man had a paid job.[5]

Dual-income couples have increased considerably in recent decades in Spain. In 1992, dual-income couples comprised one-third of the households made up of partners between 20 and 59, while in 2000 they constituted 45 per cent of the total.[6] According to the data of the Statistics on Income and Living Conditions (SILC) for Spain in 2008, 68 per cent of couples were dual-income, while the remaining 30 per cent of couples still followed the traditional model of male breadwinner and housewife. Although we are not doing a longitudinal study and cannot therefore observe the changes in family and economic arrangements, we have taken into account other studies that show how couples' flexibility has also increased enormously over recent decades. Jackie Goode, in Chapter 1 in this book, 'Credit and debt in close personal relationships', refers to a new type of couple as the 'precariat' using the term coined by Ledwith and describes it as being 'in a state of constant flux: getting a job, losing a job; buying a house, extending a house, losing a house; making a family, keeping a family together (or apart), losing a family, making a new family; getting into debt, borrowing to get out of debt, getting into greater debt'.[7]

These changes in the family have led us to centre our analysis on ownership and distribution of money in dual-income couples. Financial issues have been identified by a number of studies from the 1960s onwards as good indicators for understanding gender relations within the family.[8] Gender inequality within traditional couples used to reside mainly in the sexual division of labour between men and women generalised in the family model

---

3 The demographic data also reveal a considerable reduction in the birth rate not only in Spain but also in the majority of countries in Southern Europe. This has been interpreted as a strategy implemented not by society but individually and deliberately by the men and women in these countries in order to improve their lives, by reducing family burdens and increasing the standard of living, I Alberdi 'La transformación de las familias en España' (2006) 49–50 *Ábaco* 29, 31.
4 Gonzalez and Requena (n 2) 67.
5 INJUVE, 'Jóvenes, relaciones familiares e igualdad de género', *Estudio INJUVE EJ166* (2014) www.injuve.es/sites/default/files/2014/47/publicaciones/Sondeo%202013-3b.pdf [accessed 6 February 2015].
6 A Franco and K Winqvist, 'Women and men reconciling work and family life' in *Statistics in Focus. Population and Social Conditions* (European Communities: Eurostat 2002).
7 J Goode, Ch 1 in this book.
8 R Blood and D Wolfe, *Husbands and Wives* (New York: Free Press 1960); J Pahl, *Money and Marriage* (Basingstoke, UK: Macmillan 1989); V Zelizer, *The Social Meaning of Money* (Princeton, NJ: Princeton University Press 1997); V Tichenor, 'Status and income as gendered resources: The case of marital power' (1999) 61(3) *Journal of Marriage and the Family* 638; SD Moreno, *Una pareja, dos salarios: El dinero y las relaciones de poder en las parejas de doble ingreso* (CIS 2006); S Dema Moreno and C Díaz Martínez, 'Gender inequalities and the role of money in Spanish dual-income couples' (2010) 12(1) *European Societies* 65.

of male breadwinner and housewife. The fact that nowadays women contribute more and more to the family's income and have a professional life could, in principle, be considered a basis for more egalitarian relationships; however, our research shows that there are still important gender inequalities related to financial issues in Spanish households.

Methodology

In preparing this paper we have used two types of data, both quantitative and qualitative: the 2008 Spanish data of the Statistics on Income and Living Conditions (EU-SILC), as well as 48 interviews carried out among Spanish couples. We have also conducted a review of major public policies as applied to the family in Spain.

We have used 2008 EU-SILC data in order to understand the way in which resources are distributed among men and women within the households. The EU-SILC is a standardised survey carried out throughout the countries of the European Union, and in 2008 included a sample of 13,014 Spanish households. Gender relations within households do not vary much yearly, owing to the fact that they respond to trends consolidated over time, hence it is not foreseeable that between the studied year and the current one major changes have been experienced. If any, we could find greater gender inequality as a result of the crisis and the cuts on policies that affect especially the situation of women, as explained below. Therefore, it should be noted that we present the snapshot of a year and we do not try to measure historical developments or trends.

From these totals, we have selected for this chapter those households made up of heterosexual couples, with or without dependent children, and including no other adults or economically active members.[9] These households represent 49 per cent of the Spanish Statistics on Income and Living Conditions (hereafter S-SILC). Although we agree with researchers such as Clarke, Burgoyne and Burns, who have shown the interesting comparison and contrast made possible by including same-sex couples in the analysis, this inclusion was not practical because of sample size, only 0.2 per cent.[10]

We have categorised the households analysed into three types according to the ages of its members: young, mature and old. The category 'young couple' includes those where both members are between 16 years old (the legal working age in Spain) and the elder one no more than 34 (in general, leaving home and first marriage take place around 30 for both women and men, and it is the average age for having a first child) and constitutes 15 per cent of Spanish couples. This period of 18 years allows enough time for couples to establish their economic patterns, which potentially offer information about the gender relations involved.

The category 'mature couple' includes those where the elder partner is between 35 and 64 years old, with 64 per cent of couples found in this group. Finally, the category 'old couple', where the elder partner is 65 or over, makes up the remaining 21 per cent. In this range, most people have left the labour market and rely on pensions for their income.

The mentioned qualitative data come from interviews carried out within the international project 'Couples, money and individualization', conducted between 1999 and 2005 by researchers from Spain, Sweden, United States and Germany, using the same qualitative

---

9   Dependent children are taken as persons under the age of 25 who are not economically active.
10 V Clarke, C Burgoyne and M Burns, 'For love or money? Comparing lesbian and gay, and heterosexual relationships' (2005) 18(6) *The Psychologist* 356.

methodology in the four participating countries.[11] The aim of that study was to understand the interrelation of money, couples, and the increasing individualisation among dual-income heterosexual couples, a much broader issue than the main focus of the present chapter. We have used the results of this study in Spain here because in-depth interviews allow insight into the internal dynamics and the processes behind financial patterns and therefore allow us to understand the meaning that couples give to the ownership of money and explain the main patterns of use of money in couples, two issues on which, for the moment, the main surveys on domestic economy provide little information.[12]

The final element in the preparation of this study was the analysis of three types of government policy that have a clear impact on family and gender relations: pensions, work-life balance and fiscal policy.

Distribution of money within Spanish dual-income couples: gender differences

The increase in dual-income couples

The number of Spanish dual-income couples has increased substantially in recent years. 68 per cent of Spanish couples are dual-income, where both partners earn at least a small amount of money, compared to 30 per cent in which the man is only income earner and the remaining 2 per cent in which the woman is the only income earner.

Taking age into account: 85 per cent of young couples (16–34) have a double income, while this is the case in less than 45 per cent of old couples (65 or over). The majority of couples over 65 still follow the traditional model of male breadwinner and housewife, 55 per cent of this group, compared to 13 per cent of young couples (Figure 3.1).

The increase in dual-income couples is related to the improvement of women's educational level in recent decades and their access to the labour market. Over the last few decades, Spanish women and men have gained ever greater access to the educational system and improved their training. It is notable that in 64 per cent of older couples (65 plus) both partners have either no education or only primary level (up to the age of 12 or 13), while in younger couples only 4 per cent have failed to go beyond primary level. In contrast, 26 per cent of the youngest age group (couples 16–34) show both partners with university education, while this is the case for only 4 per cent of the oldest group (Figure 3.2).

There is a clear pattern of homogamy, as almost 60 per cent of couples have the same level of education (Figure 3.3). However, it is worth noting that a greater percentage of women have a level of educational attainment that is higher than their male partners in the younger generations, the opposite of the pattern seen with the older generations.

The increase in dual-earner couples over the past decades is linked to the access of women to the labour market; almost 80 per cent of women in younger couples have a paid job,

---

11 The methodological procedure and the main results of the comparative research were published in J Stocks, C Diaz Martínez and B Halleröd (eds), *Modern Couples, Sharing Money, Sharing Life* (New York: Palgrave Macmillan 2007).
12 Fortunately, the 2010 module of the EU-SILC concerning the distribution of resources within households reveal, for the first time and in a comparative way, some questions related to the main patterns of domestic economy for the 27 EU countries. Yet the information from the survey does not have the depth and richness of in-depth interviews, in order to understand the dynamics within the household, mainly concerning gender issues.

Money in Spanish dual-income couples 43

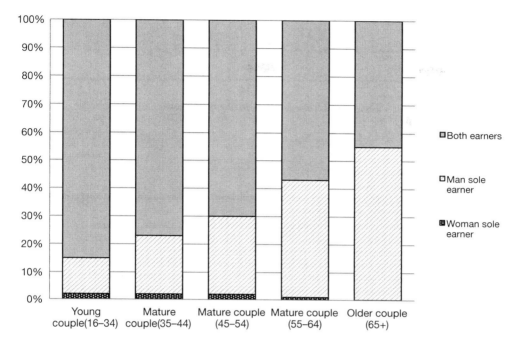

Figure 3.1 Households according to earners.
Prepared by the authors from S-SILC 2008 data.

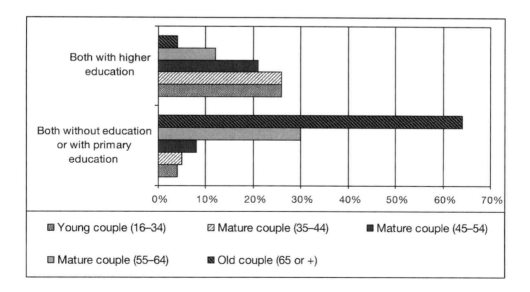

Figure 3.2 Couples by educational attainment.
Prepared by the authors from S-SILC 2008 data.

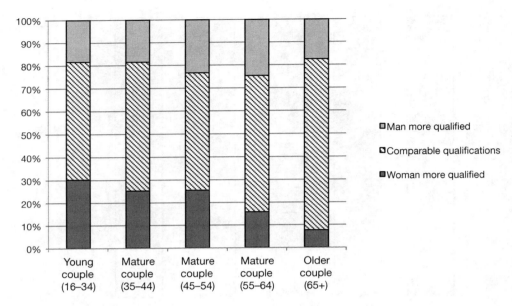

Figure 3.3 Difference in educational level within couples.
Prepared by the authors from S-SILC 2008 data.

a trend that reduces progressively with age. In contrast, the proportion of women who have never been in paid employment increases, mainly for those over 55. It should be underlined that among couples under 55 the percentage of women who have never worked (both 'mature' and 'young') is relatively low, below 6 per cent, while among those over 65 it is 35 per cent (Figure 3.4).

However, women and men have not entered the employment market in the same circumstances and the difference in each partner's participation in the labour market is a very important factor in understanding gender relations and the persistence of division of roles within a couple. Men have a higher employment rate than women, particularly until the age of 54, as is seen from Figure 3.4.

Economic inequalities in dual-income couples

As the difference in men's and women's economic activity would indicate, fewer women than men have income and when we compare women's and men's earnings, there is a clear gender income gap. Following the line of reasoning proposed by Sorensen and McLanahan, we have taken as an index of economic inequality within the couple those instances where the difference between one partner's income and the other's falls outside a range of 15 per cent.[13] Figures 3.5 and 3.6 show that there are very few cases in any age group where the woman's earnings are greater than those of the man and that the number of cases declines with age.

---

13 A Sorensen and S McLanahan, 'Married women's economic dependency: 1950–1980' (1987) 93(3) *American Journal of Sociology* 659.

Money in Spanish dual-income couples 45

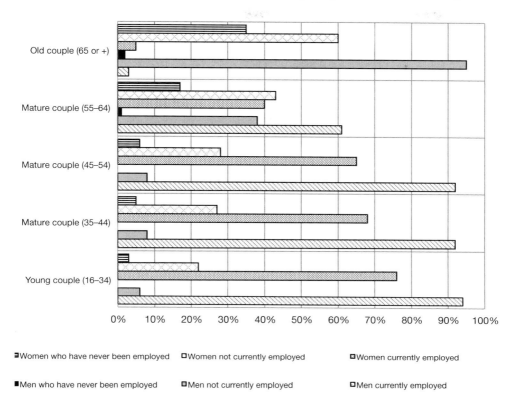

Figure 3.4 Employment activity by age group data.
Prepared by the authors from S-SILC 2008.

The greatest income inequality between men and women is in older couples (65 and over), in which 80 per cent of women earn 15 per cent less than their partner (Figure 3.5). This percentage declines with age so that, for young couples, 61 per cent of women earn 15 per cent or less than their partner.

In contrast, the percentage of couples where women earn over 15 per cent more than their male partners is very small. For those over 65, it is 4 per cent, for those in the mature groups it varies between 10 per cent and 12 per cent and, for the younger couples, it stands at 9 per cent. These data indicate that even today there are few young women who get a job that is better paid than their partner's and that this situation shows little improvement through their economic life.

Couples whose incomes are roughly equal, taking those where there is no more than 15 per cent difference between the man's and the woman's contribution, vary between 17 per cent for older couples (65+) and 29 per cent for younger couples (16–24). Although income inequality between men and women is slightly reduced among the younger generation, in most couples it is still the norm for the man to earn more.

As Figure 3.6 shows, in half of older couples, the difference between the man's contribution and the woman's is more than 90 per cent, which places the woman in a situation of extreme dependence on her partner. In younger couples, although the percentage is

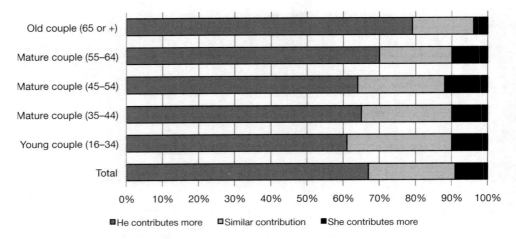

Figure 3.5 Couples with an income differential greater than 15 per cent.
Prepared by the authors from S-SILC 2008 data.

reduced, it still represents 13 per cent and in this generation, households in which men contribute between 16 per cent and 90 per cent more than women are still 45 per cent of the total. By contrast, there are hardly any households in any age group where the contribution of women is greater than 16 per cent of male earnings.

Economic inequality within couples is clearly linked to women's educational level and employment situation (Table 3.1). As educational level rises, so does the likelihood of a couple's economic equality. Of women with only primary or no education 61 per cent earn (over 15 per cent) less than their partners compared with 20 per cent of women with university education, a figure that still remains very high.

As would be expected, if women are or have been employed, there is less economic inequality within the couple, 16 per cent of women employed earn less than their partners and 20 per cent of retired women earn less than their partner, while this difference rises to 48 per cent among the unemployed.

Economic inequalities between men and women depending on the type of household

Once the economic differences in dual-income couples are analysed, it is interesting to compare their situation with the reality of men and women in other types of households. Spanish EU-SILC data show that in all family types there are fewer women receiving income than men. Those with income, whether they live alone or in a couple, earn less than men in a similar position.

Women living in couples receive substantially less income than those who do not live with a partner, and those without children earn more €12,535 annual average) than those who do have children (€11,656 per year). Women of working age who do not live with a partner are the highest earning women, but always earn less than men in the same situation. Women who head single-parent households actually earn most (€17,150 annual average), followed very closely by women in single-person households (€17,097 per year). In contrast,

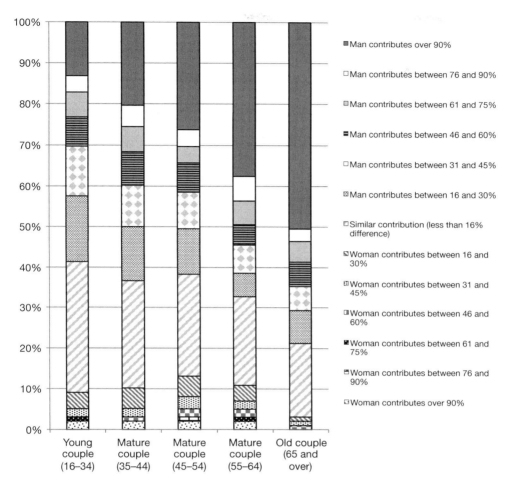

Figure 3.6 Differences in couples' income by sex and age.
Prepared by the authors from S-SILC 2008 data.

the men of working age who live as part of a couple are those with the highest income. Men who have children earn the most (€23,807 on average annually), followed by those without children (annual average €22,416) and then by those living alone (€20,396 annual average).

Despite receiving higher income, single-parent and single-person households headed by women are those at highest risk of poverty (36.7 per cent and 38.9 per cent respectively) compared to 20.9 per cent of households headed by men and to those formed by a couple, with or without dependants, ranging from 12.6 per cent for couples under 65 without dependent children and 25 per cent for couples over 65 (this excludes the case of large families, where the risk of poverty reached a rate of 41.8 per cent). In conclusion, we can say that the economic balance favours men, although men's economic dominance declines when women have higher education, also if they are in employment and their partners are

Table 3.1 Income inequality within couples according to women's educational level and employment activity

	Average (%)
Women's level of education	
Primary or no education	61
Lower secondary education (13–15)	53
Secondary education (15–17+) or post-secondary	38
Higher education	20
Women's employment situation	
Employed	16
Unemployed	48
Retired	20

Prepared by the authors from S-SILC 2008 data

Table 3.2 Income by sex, age and type of household

Person by age, sex and type of household	Annual income (€)
Man of working age living in a couple with children	23,807
Woman of working age living in a couple with children	11,656
Man of working age living in a couple without children	22,416
Woman of working age living in a couple without children	12,535
Man over 65 living in a couple without children	13,624
Woman over 65 living in a couple without children	3,602
Man of working age living in a one-person household	20,396
Woman of working age living in a one-person household	17,097
Man over 65 living in a one-person household	12,854
Woman over 65 living in a one-person household	9,205
Working age woman heading a single-parent household	17,150

Prepared by the authors from S-SILC 2008 data

in the age range of 45–54. In other words, male economic dominance within households is the norm in both the frequency of total cases and their distribution.

Ownership and the meaning of money: common money

These differences between men and women in the distribution of income within households contrast with ownership models and are undoubtedly related to money management patterns found in dual-income households, as well as the use of money by men and women. Pooling of income is quite a common way of allocating money in many countries, as previous research on money and families has shown, and is a typical pattern in the traditional family model of male breadwinner and housewife.[14] What we found in the Spanish interviews with dual-

---

14 C Vogler and J Pahl, 'Money, power, inequality within marriage' (1994) 42(2) *Sociological Review* 263; Pahl (n 8).

income couples is that money and resources are more than pooled. They are considered and treated as 'family money' and, men and women, regardless sex, age or income, rejected the idea of their 'own money' and even found it an alien concept. In fact, the common feature that emerges is not only pooling, but also the commonality of the household money.[15] Spanish couples' high regard for money held in common must be seen and interpreted in the context of the Mediterranean welfare states, where one of the features is familialism, or high 'familialisation' in MacLaughlin and Glendinning's words,[16] meaning that families, sometimes including extended families, act as a micro-solidarity safety net.

In Spain the symbolic link between couple and common money is very strong and is seen as an important aspect of being a couple, a symbol of togetherness. The system of common property is also legally supported, as it is part of the marriage contract by default.[17] But pooling of economic resources is done not merely to comply with the law; on the contrary, the law provides legal status to a long-standing custom in most of the country. Changing such a norm seems to be acceptable only in special circumstances: families of businessmen, millionaires and more recently unconventional couples. This is the case of one of the couples in our research. The only interviewed couple that has separate property feels the need to give us an explanation for it: the man is in charge of the business of his family of origin and they want to avoid any trouble in that business interfering with their domestic economy. In contrast, the rest of the couples, where money is common property, just mention the fact without further explanation, since they follow the norm, both legal and social.

Pooling was also seen in the couples' interviews as a means of guaranteeing equal access to money and thus a way of achieving gender equality. Nevertheless, the fact that the majority of the couples we interviewed think of money as belonging to the shared pool does not mean that men and women use money in the same way.

In many cases, the money is pooled in name only and hides gender inequalities, which vary from couple to couple but are present in all of them. Men's and women's behaviour in relation to money differs, particularly when there is a substantial difference of income and when men and women share a traditional gender ideology. From the interviews, it can be appreciated that, generally, men have more individualised spending patterns. They have more money available than women; they are the ones with more 'pocket money' who usually pay on social occasions involving guests such as dinners, drinks, etc. Women tend to limit their personal spending more than men and, especially when they have children, tend to put the family interests ahead of their own.[18] This fact is also suggested by other research such as that of Coria, Nyman, and Vogler and Pahl.[19]

In couples' economic decision-making processes, we have found patterns that are similar to those seen in the consideration of household money as common money. In the majority

---

15 C Díaz Martínez, S Dema Moreno and MI Pascual, 'The intertwining of money and love in couple relationship' in Stocks, Díaz Martínez and Halleröd (eds) (n 11) 100.
16 E MacLaughlin and C Glendinning, 'Paying for care in Europe: is there a feminist approach?' in L Hantrais and S Mangen (eds), *Family Policy and the Welfare of Women* (Loughborough: Cross-National Research Group, European Research Centre, Loughborough University of Technology 1994) 52.
17 Except in Catalonia, where the predominant marriage contract involves the separation of property.
18 Díaz, Dema and Ibáñez (n 15) 139; S Dema Moreno, 'Behind the negotiations: financial decision-making processes in Spanish dual-income couples' (2009) 15(1) *Feminist Economics* 27, 45.
19 C Coria, *El sexo oculto del dinero* (Barcelona: Paidós 1991); C Nyman, 'Gender equality in "The most equal country in the world"? Money and marriage in Sweden' (1999) 47(4) *Sociological Review* 766, and C Nyman, 'Mine, yours or ours? Sharing in Swedish couples', unpublished dissertation (Umeå, Sweden: Department of Sociology 24, University of Umeå 2002); Vogler and Pahl (n 14).

of couples interviewed, the women found themselves in a subordinate position, which prevented them from considering themselves, and from being considered by their partners, as equal in negotiations. Obstacles such as women's economic dependence, the persistence of men in the role of providers, men's privileged participation in the management of the family money, and the socialisation of gender roles for both men and women were the main difficulties that women encountered in portraying themselves as equal in negotiation processes; these factors also favoured men's greater influence in decision-making.[20] As with common money, common debt can play an important role in sustaining or breaking a couple's relationship, in maintaining or destroying the form of family life they had, and in affecting individual members' mental health as shown in Chapter 1 of this book by Jackie Goode.

The effects of public policies on families

As the data from the Spanish EU-SILC show, the traditional family model, dependent on the breadwinner's income, is losing relevance and, in the case of couples, is increasingly being replaced by a dual-income model. However, it appears that the state has not taken this transformation of family relationships into account in its development of public policy. On the contrary, the Spanish welfare state, in fact, has been built on a public-private dichotomy, on an artificial distinction between productive and domestic work, without regard to inequalities and power relations that are generated inside the home. In addition, the effects of public policy, far from promoting equality of women, reinforces and legitimises inequality. These criticisms of the welfare state are not exclusive to the Spanish model. Many researchers in the field have taken upon themselves to report similar problems caused by various types of welfare state with regard to gender relations.[21] A growing body of research has revealed the effects of some public policies on intra-household gender inequalities. These include Jerome De Henau and Susan Himmelweit, who state that

> Knowing about such effects is important for two reasons: first because intra-household inequality is a significant aspect of gender inequality overall, and second, because any policy will be designed more effectively if account is taken of any effects on intra-household inequalities that may impede or help meet its goals.[22]

With this concern in mind, we have analysed three types of government policy that have a clear impact on families and particularly on the gender relations within them: pensions, conciliation policies and fiscal policies. The pension system is probably one of the most notorious examples of government policy that is not adapted to the new reality of Spanish households and has been especially designed to maintain the status of the male breadwinner in the face of contingencies such as unemployment, illness or invalidity, and old age. In Spain, there is a dual system of pensions, contributory and non-contributory. To be contributory pensioners, people must have contributed over the years they have worked

---

20 Dema (n 18).
21 M Daly and J Lewis, 'The concept of social care and the analysis of contemporary welfare states' (2000) 51(2) *British Journal of Sociology* 281; J Lewis, 'Gender and welfare change' (2012) 4(4) *European Societies* 331; D Sainsbury (ed.), *Gendering Welfare States* (London: SAGE 1994).
22 J de Henau and S Himmelweit, 'Examining public policy from a gendered intra-household perspective: changes in family-related policies in the UK, Australia and Germany since the mid-nineties' (2013) 3(7) *Oñati Socio-Legal Series* 1222–48.

and the amount of pension depends on the wages received. Those who do not reach a minimum number of years will receive a non-contributory pension of lesser value. Those who have never contributed, such as housewives, are left without the right to a pension.

In the case of retirement, ownership of so basic a social right is not universal, and is not conferred by our status as citizens, but is contingent upon the path of our professional life. Only those who have worked a good number of years in full-time employment will have the right to a contributory pension. Those who do not qualify for a contributory pension acquire their rights in a secondary way, by means of a pension that either the state decides to grant as a form of assistance, or in a way linked to being the partner of a contributory-pension holder, or having carried out caregiving for the deceased holder of such a pension (widow's or family member's pension).

This system is clearly prejudicial to women, who have less access to contributory pensions for disability or retirement (34.72 per cent and 36.26 per cent respectively, compared to 65.28 per cent and 63.74 per cent of men). In contrast, they are the main recipients of non-contributory retirement pensions (80.41 per cent) and of almost all widows' pensions (92.86 per cent).[23]

These differences in the types of benefits result in significant gender differences in the income available for elderly people to live on (see Table 4). For contributory retirement pensions, women receive on average €692 per month, about 40 per cent less than men (who receive €1,143), a similar gap to the women widow's pension (€629). The widow's pension for men is even lower (€469), as it is dependent on the years of contributions and

Table 3.3 Recipients of contributory and non-contributory pensions

Type of pension	Men (%)	Women (%)
Permanent disability (contributory)	65.28	34.72
Retirement (contributory)	63.74	36.26
Widowhood	7.14	92.86
Family member	23.95	76.05
Disability (non-contributory)	45.41	54.59
Retirement (non-contributory)	19.59	80.41

Prepared by the authors from Boletín Mensual de Estadística (INE) and Fichero Técnico de Pensionistas no Contributivos del IMSERSO, 2013

Table 3.4 Average amount of pensions per month, in euros

Type of pension	Men (€)	Women (€)
Permanent disability (contributory)	975.20	780.60
Retirement (contributory)	1,143.32	691.61
Widowhood	469.26	629.01
Family member's	461.55	513.24

Prepared by the authors from Boletín Mensual de Estadística (INE) and Fichero Técnico de Pensionistas no Contributivos del IMSERSO, 2013

23 The differences in the percentages of men and women beneficiaries of the various types of pensions between 2008 and 2013, as well as the corresponding amounts of the benefits, are barely noticeable, so we have decided to include only those of 2013, the last year available when writing this chapter.

earnings made by the wives of the men receiving it, but, as seen in Table 3, the number of men receiving a widower's/survivor's pension is very small. Recipients of the type of pension designated as *favor familiar* (for a family member), meanwhile, received on average around €500 a month.[24]

The average amount for a non-contributory retirement pension is €353.39 and for a disability pension €392.89. If we compare the amounts for the equivalents in terms of contributory pensions, whether disability or retirement, there is a substantial difference between those, mainly men, receiving the contributory ones and those, mainly women, receiving the non-contributory ones. The income of those receiving a non-contributory retirement pension is around 70 per cent less than that of men on a contributory pension and almost 60 per cent less than men on a disability pension (see Table 4). As is evident here, this area of government policy is based on the idea that retirement rights do not have to be the same for those who have worked full time and for those who have not been in that situation, so this model simply means that the labour inequalities between men and women are reproduced once they have left the labour market. This creates a clear situation of vulnerability and dependence for women who have not entered the labour market, have not remained on it a sufficient number of years or have not done so full time.

In the analysis of government policy and its effects on gender relations, another interesting area is those policies targeted at the care of dependants, particularly those aimed at work-life balance, including maternity and paternity leave, leave of absence for care and measures to make working hours more flexible. For a long time, the Spanish welfare system rolled out very few public policies of this type, based on the idea that caring is a female responsibility, not a responsibility that belongs to the whole of society and therefore a public issue to be addressed by the state. Although this conception has changed and, in recent years, some efforts have been made to help workers balance work and family life and to implement measures to facilitate care for dependent persons, the data show that women still assume most of the responsibility for the care of children and dependent family members.[25]

In Spain, there are two types of leave for birth or adoption. The first one, maternity leave, is a 16-week licence, of which only six weeks – the period closest to the childbirth – are compulsory for mothers in order to facilitate the recover from childbirth. The remaining 10 weeks can be taken either in whole by the mother or the father, or divided between them. Only 1.7 per cent of men enjoy some of those weeks. This is a massively feminised leave of absence, designed for women to take care of their children, as its name suggests. The second, called

Table 3.5 Maternity and paternity leave

Type	Total	Men (%)	Women (%)
Maternity leave (10 weeks can be shared by men and women)	288,842	1.7	98.30
Paternity leave (only for men)	237,988	100	–

Prepared by the authors from Instituto Nacional de la Seguridad Social, 2013

24 The Spanish phrase *'favor familiar'* denotes a type of pension which is given to those who have cared for a relative other than their spouse, after that person's death, as long as the deceased held a paid job with title to a contributory pension.
25 See INE Enaestz de Empleo del Tiempo 2009–2010 (Spanish Time Use Survey).

paternity leave, is a 13-day licence for fathers, neither mandatory nor transferable to the mother. Despite this, and even though the percentage of parents who enjoy them is growing, fathers only take the licence in 57 per cent of total births. In any case, there is a gap of 11 points between women and men who take maternity and paternity leave, respectively.

When women and men are entitled to unpaid leave of absence for childcare or relatives care, we can see a massive female availability (95 per cent and 85 per cent of the permissions for childcare and for other relatives care, respectively). The same happens with part-time jobs that allow people to undertake the care of relatives (97.8 per cent of women versus 2.2 per cent of men). It appears that child and other relatives' care is an individual and almost exclusive responsibility of women and not a social responsibility to share.

In the approach that guides this type of policy, it is actually very important that states incorporate the issue of care into their political agenda and address it in public policy, implying a substantial change in the understanding of who holds responsibility for care. In theory at least, understanding that care is a public issue that must be addressed by the state makes it possible to stop conceiving of it as an exclusively female responsibility and it becomes a matter for the whole of society, requiring public funds to be dedicated to its provision.

Even so, flexibility of timetable, where much work-life balance policy is focused, comes to mean in practice that women adapt their working hours to the needs of their dependent family members. This adaptation tends to consist of reducing their hours and being less flexible in their availability to their employer's demands. Both of these options tend to act as a brake on professional development, and often lead to dismissal (as those who are not clearly and wholly committed to the company are more likely to be dismissed first). This is what happens on the work side. On the side of family relations, it means a crystallisation of women's role as carers, as their flexible working hours mean that they are better able to give more to the family. Both elements produce a negative synergy for any move towards equality or for women's professional self-fulfilment[26] and, as Cristina Carrasco and Arantxa Rodríguez point out, women do not withdraw from the responsibility for caring for others when they are employed.[27] In short, the system that we have is far from guaranteeing that men and women will share domestic chores and provision of care equally.

The measures adopted to combat the crisis in recent labour reforms may mean a worsening of the situation for women.[28] On the one hand, it makes dismissal easier and cheaper, and

Table 3.6 Other leave and part-time job for caring

Type	Men (%)	Women (%)
Unpaid parental leave	5.5	94.50
Unpaid family care leave	14.78	85.22
Part-time job for caring children, sick adults or elderly people	2.21	97.79

Prepared by the authors from Instituto Nacional de la Seguridad Social, 2013

26 C Díaz Martínez and S Dema Moreno, 'Vivir la igualdad, compartir la vida: Las políticas de acción positiva y las medidas para la conciliación' (2006) 49 *Ábaco* 147.
27 C Carrasco and A Rodríguez, 'Women, families, and work in Spain: structural changes and new demands' (2000) 6(1) *Feminist Economics* 45.
28 Law 3/2012, of February 10, on urgent measures to reform the labour market.

on the other, it allows businesses to modify the working day in line with their production and organisational needs, which may well collide even more with the rights aimed at improving work-life balance, mentioned earlier. Furthermore, the period designated for maternity leave is assigned to only one parent if both are employed, thus removing the possibility of sharing it between the two, which in practice reinforces traditional gender roles even further. In fact, this pattern of care does not guarantee that it is shared equally between men and women within households. It penalises women, who suffer in their careers the negative consequences of motherhood and it also generates a negative impact on the birth rate in the country (1.32 children per woman of childbearing age, as average, which is one of the lowest fertility rates in the EU28, which stands at 1.58).

There is, lastly, a third type of policy that interests us: tax policy. When a government through its tax policies privatises responsibility for the economic security of its citizens, instead of assuring it, it always has a negative impact on women. Tax policies could, among other things, help to reduce the pay gap between men and women within a household, but this is not usually the case. Experts on the matter explain how the reason for this lies in the fact that the model of direct taxation on income was created with the traditional family of male breadwinner and female housewife in mind, and therefore reinforces inequality.[29] Until 1989, married couples were forced to pay taxes jointly and many still do so today, so that the woman's pay is added to that of the man. As the tax is progressive and as the total income rises, the woman's income is taxed in terms of the man's marginal rate, so that, especially when the woman's pay is low and the man's high, the cost of working outside the home is made very high. As María Pazos indicates, married women have to pay a significant percentage of their wages in taxes, an inequality that is aggravated if there are children or other dependants at home.[30]

Other researchers have highlighted the effect of indirect taxes on women, since these taxes have a disproportionate impact on those groups with the lowest incomes, women and the poor, who are forced to hand over a far higher proportion of their income in taxes.[31]

Discussion and conclusions

The analysis carried out here on both the ownership and the income distribution of money in Spanish dual-income couples has revealed some trends towards greater equality between men and women, especially in the younger generations; however, we have also observed how certain elements tied to gender inequalities persist. On the one hand, the vast majority of young couples are dual-income compared to the traditional model of male breadwinner and housewife, still dominant in the older generation's households but with a declining presence in Spanish society. This phenomenon is related to the improvement of women's educational level in recent decades and their greater integration into the labour market. Indeed, in a context where educational levels for the whole of the Spanish population have risen, women have made a greater advance than men so that for the first time in history, we find among the younger households couples where the woman has a higher level of education than her partner. Another factor that favours equality in gender relations is women's integration into paid employment. Young women have high levels of labour activity, and

---

29 M Pazos Morán, 'Roles de género y políticas públicas' (2011) 73 *Sociología del Trabajo* 5.
30 Ibid. 15.
31 I Bakker (ed.), *The Strategic Silence* (London: Zed Books 1994).

the percentage of women who have never had paid employment continues to decline, which points to a dramatic shift in women's work situation compared with earlier generations.

However, we have also observed some elements that persist in all generations and which obstruct egalitarian relationships, even for the youngest couples, and one is the income gap between women and men. Although there has been a rise in the number of dual-income couples, women earn less than their male partners in all age groups, a phenomenon that points to the fact that women seldom find jobs that are better paid than their partners; this is so even for the youngest, who, as noted earlier, tend to be better educated than the men. These income differences place women in a dependent situation when using money, both for their personal expenses and in negotiating family expenses with their partners.

Government policy is a mechanism that can transform families' situations and break or indeed reinforce traditional gender roles. As we have tried to show, current family policies were constructed around models based on men's lives and to meet their needs so that they do not benefit women in the same way. In order to guarantee full citizenship for women, it is necessary to rethink relations between state, market and the family when it comes to providing goods and services, when it comes to ensuring equitable sharing of the overall workload and allowing everybody access to comparable standards of welfare throughout their lives.

In an economic crisis like the current one there is a serious risk that the crisis's consequences could be worse for women, as well as leading to an increase in poverty and social inequality. This is what happened in previous crises, such as those of the 1970s and 1980s of the twentieth century, and today some writers are warning of similar negative effects from the containment measures and deficit cuts recommended by the EU and being followed in the approaches of most European governments.[32] They are concerned that in Spain for example, the cuts have impacted on the social policies that the government implemented earlier, and they advocate that the strategy needed to avoid an increase in inequality should be the opposite: that is, the promotion of social policies, which would in turn generate jobs and boost the economy out of recession.[33]

Perhaps this is a good moment to propose a reflection on which economic and social model we want for the future, and in this sense, feminist ideas offer suggestive approaches. One of them is the need to understand work, both productive and reproductive, as an activity intrinsic to the welfare of individuals and of society, not an activity to serve the interests of the market.[34] From this perspective, both paid and unpaid work should be shared on equal terms, ensuring that people regardless of gender can perform a quality job that gives them financial independence. This distribution would also allow them to assume their domestic and caring responsibilities as well as to develop their potential as human beings. Considering the high rates of unemployment in Spain, one of the highest in the European Union, a measure such as reducing working hours could allow these goals to be pursued.[35]

There are those who suggest reforming the financial policy model to guarantee the maintenance of the welfare state, as well as wealth redistribution so that those who have

---

32 I Palmer, 'Public finance from a gender perspective' (1995) 23(11) *World Development* 1981; Bakker (n 32); D Elson (ed.), *Male Bias in the Development Process* (Manchester, UK: Manchester University Press 1995).
33 L Gálvez and J Torres, *Desiguales. Mujeres y hombres en la crisis financiera* (Barcelona: Icaria 2010).
34 C Carrasco, 'La sostenibilidad de la vida humana: ¿un asunto de mujeres?' (2003) 195 *Utopías* 151.
35 A Coote, J Franklin and A Simms, *21 hours. Why a Shorter Working Week Can Help Us All to Flourish in the 21st Century* (London: New Economics Foundation 2010).

more pay more, avoiding gender discrimination.[36] Other authors advocate establishing a reproduction tax. According to the economist Ingrid Palmer, women pay a reproductive tax as their workload focused on the home and care takes place within the home so that they are placed in an unequal position relative to men when it comes to participation in the labour market.[37] This is a situation that can only be reversed if the state takes on the caregiving through public services or if business pays a tax to meet the cost of reproduction/care for the workforce that they save by having it carried out by women.

Whatever approach is taken, it is vital that government and voters recognise that all policy has a gender dimension and that it can and must be harnessed for the benefit of society as a whole. As several aspects of this study indicate, the broad trend of change in society and in gender relations progresses from a complex of causes at a scale that is both individual and generational, and is to some degree independent of government intervention, yet government policy does much to foster or retard this change and impacts the form it takes. It is important, therefore, that the effects of policy should be planned and monitored rather than emerging as unintended consequences from programmes that neglect or ignore the gender dimension.

Bibliography

Alberdi I, 'La transformación de las familias en España' (2006) *Ábaco* 49–50, 29–65.
Bakker I (ed.), *The Strategic Silence* (London: Zed Books 1994).
Blood R and Wolfe D, *Husbands and Wives* (New York: Free Press 1960).
Carrasco C, 'La sostenibilidad de la vida humana: ¿un asunto de mujeres?' (2003) 195 *Utopías* 151–73.
Carrasco C and Rodríguez A, 'Women, families, and work in Spain: structural changes and new demands' (2000) 6(1) *Feminist Economics* 45–57.
Clarke V, Burgoyne C and Burns M, 'For love or money? Comparing lesbian and gay, and heterosexual relationships' (2005) 18(6) *The Psychologist* 356–8.
Coote A, Franklin J and Simms A, *21 Hours. Why a Shorter Working Week Can Help Us All to Flourish in the 21st Century* (London: New Economics Foundation 2010).
Coria C, *El sexo oculto del dinero* (Barcelona: Paidós 1991).
Daly M and Lewis J, 'The concept of social care and the analysis of contemporary welfare states' (2000) 51(2) *British Journal of Sociology* 281–98. http://dx.doi.org/10.1111/j.1468-4446.2000.00281.x
del Campo S, *La 'nueva' familia española* (Madrid: Eudema 1991).
Dema Moreno S, *Una pareja, dos salarios: el dinero y las relaciones de poder en las parejas de doble ingreso* (Madrid: CIS 2006).
Dema Moreno S, 'Behind the negotiations: financial decision-making processes in Spanish dual-income couples' (2009) 15(1) *Feminist Economics* 27–56.
Dema Moreno S and Díaz Martínez C, 'Gender inequalities and the role of money in Spanish dual-income couples' (2010) 12(1) *European Societies* 65–84.
Díaz Martínez C and Dema Moreno S, 'Vivir la igualdad, compartir la vida: las políticas de acción positiva y las medidas para la conciliación' (2006) 49 *Ábaco* 147–57.
Díaz Martínez C, Dema Moreno S and Ibáñez Pascual M, 'The intertwining of money and love in couple relationship' in J Stocks, C Díaz Martínez and B Halleröd (eds), *Modern Couples, Sharing Money, Sharing Life* (New York: Palgrave Macmillan 2007) 100–42.
Elson D (ed.), *Male Bias in the Development Process* (Manchester: Manchester University Press 1995).
Franco A and Winqvist K, 'Women and men reconciling work and family life' in *Statistics in Focus. Population and Social Conditions* (Luxemburg: European Communities, Eurostat 2002).

---

36 Pazos (n 30).
37 Palmer (n 33).

Gálvez L and Torres J, *Desiguales. Mujeres y hombres en la crisis financiera* (Barcelona: Icaria 2010).

González, JJ and Requena M, *Tres décadas de cambio social en España* (Madrid: Alianza Editorial 2005).

Henau J and Himmelweit S, 'Examining public policy from a gendered intra-household perspective: changes in family-related policies in the UK, Australia and Germany since the mid-nineties' (2013) 3(7) *Oñati Socio-Legal Series* 1222–48.

INE, *Enaestz de Empleo del Tiempo* 2009–2010. www.ine.es/prodyser/miao_emptiem.html [accessed 8 February 2013).

INJUVE 'Jóvenes, relaciones familiares e igualdad de género'. *Estudio INJUVE EJ166* (2014) www.injuve.es/sites/default/files/2014/47/publicaciones/Sondeo%202013-3b.pdf [accessed 8 February 2017].

Jurado Guerrero T and Naldini M, 'Is the South so different? Italian and Spanish families in comparative perspective' (1996) 1(3) *South European Society and Politics* 42–66. http://dx.doi.org/10.1080/13608749608539482.

Lewis J, 'Gender and welfare change' (2012) 4(4) *European Societies* 331–57.

MacLaughlin E and Glendinning C, 'Paying for care in Europe: is there a feminist approach?' in L Hantrais and S Mangen (eds), *Family Policy and the Welfare of Women* (Cross-National Research Group, European Research Centre, Loughborough: University of Technology, UK 1994) 52–69.

Meil Landwerlin G, *La postmodernización de la familia española* (Madrid: Acento Editorial 1999).

Nyman C, 'Gender equality in "the most equal country in the world"? Money and marriage in Sweden' (1999) 47(4) *The Sociological Review* 766–93.

Nyman C, *Mine, yours or ours? Sharing in Swedish couples* (2002). Dissertation, Department of Sociology 24, University of Umeå, Sweden.

Pahl J, *Money and Marriage* (Basingstoke, UK: Macmillan 1989).

Palmer I, 'Public finance from a gender perspective' (1995) 23(11) *World Development* 1981–6.

Pazos Morán M, 'Roles de género y políticas públicas' (2011) 73 *Sociología del Trabajo* 5–23.

Sainsbury D (ed.), *Gendering Welfare States* (London: SAGE 1994).

Sorensen A and McLanahan S, 'Married women's economic dependency: 1950–1980' (1987) 93(3) *American Journal of Sociology* 659–87.

Stocks J, Díaz Martínez C and Halleröd B (eds), *Modern Couples, Sharing Money, Sharing Life* (New York: Palgrave Macmillan 2007).

Tichenor V, 'Status and income as gendered resources: The case of marital power' (1999) 61(3) *Journal of Marriage and the Family* 638–50.

Vogler C and Pahl J, 'Money, power, and inequality within marriage' (1994) 42(2) *The Sociological Review* 263–88.

Zelizer V, *The Social Meaning of Money* (Princeton, NJ: Princeton University Press 1997).

4 Money practices among older couples: patterns of continuity, change, conflict and resistance[1]

Debora Price, Dinah Bisdee and Tom Daly

Introduction

How do older couples view, manage and negotiate about money? Knowing this is important for our understanding of social life in a number of spheres including social stratification, inequality, poverty and social exclusion in later life; the effects of ageing and the life-course on inter- and intra-household inequality; hidden poverty within older households; the management of assets and debts over the life-course; control of household resources among older couples; ageing and couple relationships; intergenerational financial exchanges; and the impacts of social security, savings, debt and pensions policies on individuals within older households.

It is surprising then that, despite a wealth of sociological enquiry into money management within households for couples of working age,[2] there is little investigation of these issues for older people when, behind the closed doors of the household, traditional gender divisions of labour may no longer apply, yet individual resources are rarely equal.[3] Considering the dimensions of time and age is important since money management and the meaning of money within couples is not static, but is shaped by time, social class and economic status, family, culture, gendered identities, generation, individual experience and circumstance, and is also an important manifestation of power and conflict within households.[4]

---

1 We are very grateful to the Economic and Social Research Council for funding the project *Behind Closed Doors: Older Couples and the Management of Household Money*, Research Grant RES-061–25-0090. We also express our gratitude to the men and women who participated in this study.
2 See recent reviews in: SR Lauer and C Yodanis, 'Money Management, Gender and Households' in J Treas, J Scott and M Richards (eds), *The Wiley Blackwell Companion to the Sociology of Families* (Oxford: John Wiley & Sons 2014); F Bennett, 'Researching within-household distribution: overview, developments, debates, and methodological challenges' (2013) 75 *Journal of Marriage and Family* 582; S Himmelweit et al., 'Sharing of resources within the family and the economics of household decision making' (2013) 75 *Journal of Marriage and Family* 625; C Nyman, L Reinikainen and J Stocks, 'Reflections on a cross-national qualitative study of within-household finances' (2013) 75 *Journal of Marriage and Family* 640; C Vogler, 'Managing money in intimate relationships: similarities and differences between cohabiting and married couples' in J Miles and R Probert (eds), *Sharing Lives, Dividing Assets* (Oxford: Hart 2009).
3 S Arber and J Ginn, 'Ageing and gender. diversity and change' (2004) 34 *Social Trends* 14; D Price and J Ginn, 'The future of inequalities in retirement income' in J Vincent, C Phillipson and M Downs (eds), *The Futures of Old Age* (London: SAGE Publications 2006); D Price, 'Why are older women in the UK poor?' (2006) 7 *Quality in Ageing and Older Adults* 9.
4 J Pahl, *Money and Marriage* (Basingstoke, UK: Macmillan 1989); C Vogler, C Lyonette and RD Wiggins, 'Money, power and spending decisions in intimate relationships' (2008) 56 *The Sociological Review* 117; C Vogler,

An ageing perspective exemplifies and develops our empirical and theoretical understanding in each of these areas.[5]

In this chapter, we present findings from the 'Behind Closed Doors' project, a qualitative study investigating cultural, social and life-course influences on how older couples manage their money, and the implications for autonomy and well-being in later life. We examine here the ways in which ageing couples cope with major financial transitions such as retirement, where we find an unanticipated stickiness about financial practices. We go on to consider conflict, change and subversive behaviour, before concluding with a discussion of our findings.

Background

In the world of social policy and economics, the household, rather than the individual, is usually considered to be the unit of production and consumption. An assumption is made of equal sharing of resources within partnerships, to the extent that much government and academic analysis takes place at the household level only, and many benefits (such as pension credit) are paid at the level of the couple.[6] Sociological research has revealed that this is a crude assumption, and that within households, financial inequality is an important matter for the autonomy and well-being of the individual.[7] Men and women do not share money equally and even when they do share, they do not have equal control. Moreover, access to money management does not imply control over spending. Many women are required

---

'Money in the household: some underlying issues of power' (1998) 46 *The Sociological Review* 687; C Nyman, 'Gender equality in "the most equal country in the world"? Money and marriage in Sweden'; KR Heimdal and SK Houseknecht, 'Cohabiting and married couple's income organization: approaches in Sweden and the United States' (2003) 65 *Journal of Marriage and the Family* 525; C Nyman, 'The social nature of money: meanings of money in Swedish families' (2003) 26 *Women's Studies International Forum* 79; C Yodanis and S Lauer, 'Economic inequality in and outside of marriage: individual resources and institutional context' (2007) 23 *European Sociological Review* 573; S Dema-Moreno and C Díaz-Martínez, 'Gender inequalities and the role of money in Spanish dual-income couples' (2010) 12 *European Societies* 65; Bennett (n 2); V Tichenor, 'Maintaining men's dominance: negotiating identity and power when she earns more' (2005) 53 *Sex Roles* 191.

5 J Ginn and S Arber, *Connecting Gender and Ageing: A Sociological Approach* (Buckingham, UK: Open University Press 1995); S Arber and J Ginn, 'The invisibility of age: gender and class in later life' (1991) 39 *The Sociological Review* 260.

6 F Bennett and S Sung, 'Dimensions of financial autonomy in low-/moderate-income couples from a gender perspective and implications for welfare reform' (2013) 42 *Journal of Social Policy* 701; S Cantillon, 'Measuring differences in living standards within households' (2013) 75 Journal of Marriage and Family 598; Bennett (n 2); F Bennett and S Sung, 'Money matters: using qualitative research for policy influencing on gender and welfare reform' (2013) 27 *Innovation: The European Journal of Social Science Research* 5.

7 Bennett (n 2); SJ Lundberg, RA Pollak and TJ Wales, 'Do husbands and wives pool their resources? Evidence from the United Kingdom Child Benefit' (1997) 32 *Journal of Human Resources* 463; C Nyman, 'Gender equality in "the most equal country in the world?" Money and marriage in Sweden' (1999) 47 *The Sociological Review* 766; FM Deutsch, J Roksa and C Meeske, 'How gender counts when couples count their money' (2003) 48 *Sex Roles* 291; I Dasgupta, 'Gender-biased redistribution and intra-household distribution' (2001) 45 *European Economic Review* 1711; J de Henau and S Himmelweit, 'Unpacking within-household gender differences in partners' subjective benefits from household income' (2013) 75 *Journal of Marriage and Family* 61; I Hardill, AE Green, AC Ludleston and DW Owen 'Who decides what? Decision making in dual-career households' (1997) 11 *Work, Employment & Society* 313.

to manage household accounts (a considerable burden if resources are limited) but have little say in how resources are spent.[8]

Unequal access to money has been shown to affect power over household decision-making but it has also been shown that men's earnings and women's earnings are viewed differently within households, because of the powerful construction of breadwinner versus homemaker identities. Because economic resources are given meaning by cultural and social settings, a wife's income is seen as being earmarked for different purposes, and therefore different, and arguably less important than a husband's income.[9] Mothers' incomes are often spent on children, and child-care costs tend to be paid for out of mothers' income.[10] Even where both partners consider that equal sharing of money is appropriate, in practice the partner contributing less may feel constrained in and will seek permission for personal spending.[11] Thus the acceptance of the male-breadwinner role is a source of hierarchy within a partnership that has ramifications beyond the mere allocation of financial resources.

Life-course transitions such as retirement, bereavement and re-partnering, ill-health and pension receipt are potential triggers for changes in financial management and access to resources, or may reinforce the resilience of patterns of financial control within households. Similarly, breadwinner and homemaker identities may be challenged by the impact of retirement from paid work and the receipt of pension, social security and disability benefits in old age, or despite these structural changes couples may find ways through their handling of money to reinforce gender identities forged over time. As cultural and social factors

---

8   CB Burgoyne, 'Heart-strings and purse-strings: money in heterosexual marriage' (2004) 14 *Feminism & Psychology* 165; CB Burgoyne, 'Money in marriage: how patterns of allocation both reflect and conceal power' (1990) 38 *The Sociological Review* 634; H Laurie and J Gershuny, '"Couples, work and money"' in R Berthoud and J Gershuny (eds), *Seven Years in the Lives of British Families: Evidence on the Dynamics of Change from the British Household Panel Survey* (Bristol, UK: The Policy Press 2000); Vogler, 'Money in the household: some underlying issues of power' (n 4); C Vogler and J Pahl, 'Social and economic change and the organisation of money within marriage' (1993) 7 Work, Employment and Society 71; Pahl, *Money and Marriage* (n4); C Vogler and J Pahl, 'Money, power and inequality within marriage' (1994) 42 *The Sociological Review* 263; R Fleming and S Kell Easting, *The Common Purse: Income Sharing in New Zealand Families* (Auckland, New Zealand: Auckland University Press 1997); K Rake and G Jayatilaka, 'Home truths: an analysis of financial decision making within the home' (London: Fawcett Society 2002); F Bennett, J de Henau and S Sung, 'Within-household inequalities across classes? Management and control of money' in J Scott, R Crompton and C Lyonette (eds), *Gender Inequalities in the 21st Century: New Barriers and Continuing Constraints* (Cheltenham, UK: Edward Elgar Publishing 2010); G Wilson, *Money in the Family: Financial Organization and Women's Responsibilities* (Aldershot, UK: Avebury 1987).

9   Vogler, 'Money in the household: some underlying issues of power' (n 4); Pahl, *Money and Marriage* (n 4); Burgoyne, 'Heart-strings and purse-strings: money in heterosexual marriage' (n 8); CB Burgoyne, V Clarke, J Reibstein and A Edmonds '"All my worldly goods I share with you?" Managing money at the transition to heterosexual marriage' (2006) 54 *The Sociological Review* 619; Nyman, 'The social nature of money: meanings of money in Swedish Families' (n 4); J Stocks, C Diaz and B Halleröd, *Modern Couples Sharing Money, Sharing Life* (New York: Palgrave Macmillan 2007); Cantillon (n 6).

10 Dasgupta; Lundberg, Pollak and Wales; J Pahl, 'Couples and their money: patterns of accounting and accountability in the domestic economy' 502; J Pahl, 'Gender, power and the household' (2001) 30 *Journal of Social Policy* 157; SA Phipps and PS Burton, 'What's mine is yours? The influence of male and female incomes on patterns of household expenditure' (1998) 65 *Economica* 599; Saba Waseem, *Household Monies and Decision-Making*, Policy Research Paper no. 23 (Australian Government Department of Family and Community Services 2004); J Pahl, 'Individualisation in couple finances: who pays for the children?' (2005) 4 *Social Policy and Society* 38; Deutsch, Roksa and Meeske (n 7).

11 Burgoyne, 'Heart-strings and purse-strings: money in heterosexual marriage' (n 8); Burgoyne, 'Money in marriage: how patterns of allocation both reflect and conceal power' (n 8); Burgoyne *et al.*; Nyman, 'Gender equality in "the most equal country in the world"? Money and marriage in Sweden' (n 4).

influence the uses, meanings and ownership of money,[12] variation in arrangements for money management are also likely to be embedded in local and ethnic cultures, in different social class structures, and among different age groups, each with different financial status, monetary ideologies and partnering and inter-generational norms.

How these issues persist, resolve and develop as people and couples age has been little researched. Because of the assumption of equal sharing behind closed doors, very little is known about inequality of income among older couples, but we do know that married older women have few financial resources in their own right.[13] The parlous financial resources of married women are a direct cause of the poverty of lone women in later life, as most of these married women will become widowed,[14] yet we do not know the extent to which older couples are conscious of and manage this risk.

Through this research, we therefore aim to gain insight into the meanings of money for older people, in particular how money is integrated into relationships and life-views, by what mechanisms older couples manage money, and how these daily practices reflect gendered identities and imbalances within the relationship. We are particularly interested in how these might have changed over time and with circumstances, and how the ageing process impacts on these financial arrangements. We explore how transitions such as retirement and failing health impact on financial arrangements within the home

Methods

Money always represents something other than itself.[15] It has affective, symbolic and behavioural components and is therefore imbued with complex meanings. To gain understanding of the meanings attached to money by older couples and the implications for everyday life, we conducted an in-depth qualitative study. We interviewed 45 couples (89 respondents, since one man was too unwell to be interviewed) both jointly and alone, each supplying different understandings and knowledge: couple interviews result in a jointly constructed and negotiated response, while lone interviews elicited personal and private perspectives.[16]

Our respondents were purposively sampled to represent maximum variation in life-course, age, health, social class, local environment, ethnicity and socio-economic status. Couples were drawn from three contrasting areas in the South-East of England selected for occupying

---

12 VA Zelizer, *The Social Meaning of Money*, vol 95 (New York: Basic Books 1994); V Zelizer, *The Purchase of Intimacy* (Princetown, NJ: Princeton University Press 2005); VA Zelizer, *Economic Lives: How Culture Shapes the Economy* (Princetown, NJ: Princeton University Press 2011).
13 D Price and J Ginn, 'Sharing the crust? Gender, partnership status and inequalities in pension accumulation' in S Arber, K Davidson and J Ginn (eds), *Gender and Ageing: Changing Roles and Relationships* (Maidenhead, UK: Open University Press 2003); Price (n 3); J Ginn, *Gender, Pensions and the Life Course* (Bristol, UK: The Policy Press 2003); Arber and Ginn, 'ageing and gender. Diversity and Change' (n 3).
14 Price (n 3).
15 P Webley, CB Burgoyne, S Lea and B Young, *The Economic Psychology of Everyday Life* (Hove, UK: Psychology Press 2001); A Furnham and M Argyle, *The Psychology of Money* (London: Routledge 1998); Zelizer, *The Purchase of Intimacy* (n 12).
16 H Arskey, 'Collecting data through joint interviews' (1996) 15 *Social Research Update* 1; F Racher, J Kaufert and B Havens, 'Conjoint research interviews with frail, elderly couples: methodological implications' (2000) 6 *Journal of Family Nursing* 367; G Valentine, 'Doing household research: interviewing couples apart and together' (1999) 31 *Area* 67; L Polak and J Green, 'Using joint interviews to add analytic value' (2015) *FirstView*, *Qualitative Health Research*.

diverse positions on the Index of Deprivation.[17] Couples were heterosexual, and married, re-married or cohabiting, with at least one member of the couple over the age of 65, with as wide an age range as practicable within that constraint. Qualitative data was analysed through constant comparative methods derived from a grounded theory approach, with the assistance of NVivo(r). All names have been changed to protect identities.

While we draw on theories of power, money and marriage,[18] we critically assess power related to financial production, which may ignore the changing financial position of men as they age, and of men and women who are no longer involved with the paid labour market. The life-course perspective holds that later life outcomes are a result of dynamic and cumulative processes and events. The essential and structuring dimensions of gender and class[19] are necessarily incorporated within the use of this perspective.[20]

Transitions to retirement

Contrary to widespread expectation, the transition from the social status of 'work' to that of 'retirement' was not a time for couples to renegotiate or reorganise money practices, which were deeply embedded in the day to day lives of couples. This was the case even where retirement was a planned event, for example, associated with taking financial advice, going on a pre-retirement course, or downsizing. Among all those in our study, only one couple[21] had opened a joint account after downsizing for unspecified 'tax' reasons. It seemed that maintenance of the status quo was important through this important life-course transition, and that the prior gender hierarchies, gender identities and couple identities exemplified by money arrangements were preserved.

This is illustrated by the case of Elizabeth and Pryce [Couple 33]. They had been married 54 years and were from the higher professional classes. Elizabeth was aged 70–75 and Pryce was over 75; they were both in good health. Typical of the way that retirement was dealt with:

INT: No, no, no. So you didn't have to sit down and say, 'We will have to adjust to this or to adjust that'
ELIZABETH: Can't remember.
PRYCE: No, we never brought it up. Tom I think we were thinking that, when we started, that errr . . . People might actually sit down on their retirement and sort of reorganise things. But that doesn't seem to have happened.

---

17 ODPM, *Indices of Deprivation 2004* (Office of the Deputy Prime Minister ed., 2007).
18 CB Burgoyne, 'Money in marriage: how patterns of allocation both reflect and conceal power' (1990) 38 *The Sociological Review* 634; JF Zipp, A Prohaska and M Bemiller, 'Wives, husbands, and hidden power in marriage' (2004) 25 *Journal of Family Issues* 933; C Vogler and J Pahl, 'Money, power and inequality within marriage' (1994) 42 *The Sociological Review* 263; Vogler, 'Money in the household: some underlying issues of power' (n 4); SJ Sonnenberg, 'Household financial organisation and discursive practice: managing money and identity' (2008) 37 *Journal of Socio-Economics* 533.
19 (and ethnicity, although we do not discuss ethnicity in this chapter). For discussion of some of the ethnic dimensions of this research, see D Bisdee, T Daly and D Price, 'Behind closed doors: older couples and the gendered management of household money' (2013) 12 *Social Policy and Society* 163.
20 Ginn *et al.* (n 5); S Arber, K Davidson and J Ginn, 'Changing approaches to gender and later life' in Arber, Davidson and Ginn (n 13).
21 Couple 40, married for 40 years.

PRYCE: We sat down and discussed everything, but at the end of the day we didn't change much because . . . Things were working all right. It didn't . . .

However, on examination, it seemed that the couple had not 'done nothing' as they thought, but gone to quite some lengths to maintain as far as possible the exact arrangements that pertained prior to retirement, even though this led to some convoluted dealings between them, as Elizabeth revealed in her sole interview. In fact they had arranged for Pryce to top up her income to its exact pre-retirement level, with Elizabeth giving Pryce little choice, saying that he should supplement her income to its original level before she would allow him access to her pension.

ELIZABETH: I suppose I did. He gave me what I earnt, to start with . . . So I really, it wasn't that much difference, to me . . . You know, it was in my account once a month, while I earned.
INT: That's interesting, yeah.

This kind of manoeuvring was commonplace to retain the status quo, although it played out in different ways. In the following example, Bill [Couple 25] explains that since his wife had always paid her wages into the bank account that he controlled, she had to continue doing this with her pension. They had been married for 44 years, manual workers, both aged 65–70 with severe health problems. Theirs was a traditional marriage where Bill controlled the money management, and his wife still works as a cleaner for 'pin money', mostly to buy herself cigarettes.

BILL: . . . I said, 'Well, you're going to have to stick your pension,' because she was drawing her pension for a few years, you know, and, em, because they draw it at 60, don't they? I said 'You'll have to stick yours into' – [laughter] – 'the bank,' you know, like I'll just get it paid into the bank, you know . . .
INT: Straight in.
BILL: . . . And she wasn't too happy about that. [Laughter]
INT: Did she do it?
BILL: Oh yeah, you know . . .
INT: What would have happened if she said 'No I won't'?
BILL: [Laughter] Well I'd say, 'Well you can't, we'll have to sell the house.'

Where one partner (usually, but not always, the man) had always managed the finances, this simply continued as Rory and Violet illustrate. Rory and Violet had been married for 41 years, from higher professional and managerial classes both aged 75–80 with some health problems:

RORY: Well we're both, both inclined to carry on doing our own thing, without thinking too much ahead, quite honest. . . . now we're getting older and older and still in this house, and our families are miles away.
INT: So when Rory retired or . . . nothing really changed, in terms of joint accounts or . . . ?
VIOLET: Money, no not really. Not that I noticed, no . . . And pensions. So that's . . . he manages all the finances. I . . . I really am very ignorant about our finances. I've no idea, vague idea what we've got. And I've no idea how to pay any of the bills.

All in all, we encountered many, sometimes perverse, strategies for couples to maintain the money practices status quo ante, including a wife's pension being handed over to her husband so that he could continue to pay her the housekeeping that she had always been paid, or a wife keeping her pension but this amount now being deducted from her housekeeping, or money being handed over from the husband to the wife so that she continues to have her 'income' replacing her wages.

Change and resistance

It therefore seems that financial arrangements leading to day-to-day money practices are quite intransigent. How do couples cope with conflict, and what does lead to change? If things do not change, do individuals find strategies to resist these long-standing arrangements? We begin this section with a discussion of conflict over money.

Money often features large in relationship breakdown, but among our older couples, even if unhappy or unhappily married, these are intact couples, and generally they accept that they will now be married until death. With a few exceptions (discussed below), as daily money practices become embedded in couple behaviour over time, such battles over money as there were or had been are no longer fought. We witnessed a large degree of resignation about arrangements that often reflected longstanding differences in power and access to money, generally from the women in the sample. This is illustrated here by Cathy [Couple 30]. They were both aged 75–80, and Cathy's health was moderate whereas her husband has severe heart problems. Married for 50 years, from professional/managerial backgrounds, the couple had fallen on hard times as a result of litigation with the Inland Revenue. Sidney had been declared bankrupt and so Cathy manages the money in the household. They are dependent on her small pension.

CATHY: Yes, yes, I can't change it. Em, maybe I could have done things differently, em, but, I, I don't know what, em, because there's, em, I said wine, women, and cigarettes might be . . . *[Laughter]* em, all three . . . have been a problem, so, er, it's . . . one follows the other. Yes. And then he would, em, seek refuge and take . . . a consolation, he would find somebody else who would, er, be sympathetic and, you know, was obviously going to be fun when I wasn't, you know. *[Laughter]*
INT: Oh dear, that's very . . .
CATHY: No, no, it's all right, I just got, you know, you get resigned to it because what are the options? You know, there's, I can't walk away from . . . this, it's too late. It's too late.

And later in her interview:

INT: Yes, yeah. You said you still felt a bit resentful, I mean . . .
CATHY: Mm.
INT: . . . do you feel it's sort of unfair what's happening, or . . .?
CATHY: Oh, yes, I've got resigned to it now. . .
INT: Mm.
CATHY: . . . you know, things won't change, so. . . . They won't change . . .

And here from Sharon [Couple 12]. Married for 49 years, she and her husband were manual workers. Sharon was aged 65–70, her husband 71–75; he has severe health problems, she has some, and they rent their property from a Housing Association.

INT: Ok. So just finally then, looking back over your life and your life with Tony, is there anything you would change, with hindsight, is there anything you'd change about the way you managed your finances?
SHARON: Not really, 'cos I've always coped, d'you know what I mean? I suppose really you would wish he would've been more fair. D'you know what I mean?

We observed among these couples a stasis in money practices that appears to make change virtually impossible for them. Often, even if one partner is, and has been, very unhappy with the way that the finances are arranged, they will live with this rather than discuss it. Interestingly, all respondents who have been married before had taken the opportunity in the *new relationships* to change the way money was handled, and this was the case whether the new relationship was after divorce or widowhood. While interesting in itself, what appeared equally remarkable was that this reflected a deep dissatisfaction with the way that money had been handled in their old relationships, but within that earlier relationship they had perceived themselves as powerless to change it.

Thus, where they had been divorced or widowed, problems with money management arrangements encountered in the first relationship were avoided or rectified from the outset as part of the bargaining for the terms of the new relationship. Some women who had dysfunctional or controlling husbands in the past made sure that this was not reproduced in the current relationship. In the main, the women in second marriages or relationships who had been particularly disempowered had sought and achieved a greater degree of independence, or men in second relationships had wanted more equal sharing of day to day finances.

Regrets over household money management in the current relationship were therefore a reflection of deep seated barriers to change. Some expressed regret over, for example, a house remaining in the sole name of one partner, not necessarily the man – we saw this for both husband and wife. Yet, there was apparently no reason why, if the parties regret this, they could not simply execute the relevant deed to change ownership, yet this seems not to occur to them. The barriers, while in practice minor and relatively inexpensive, in the minds of the couple are substantial, and it takes something substantial to shift them. In the following example, we see Jennifer [Couple 36] discussing changing their house ownership from John's sole name to their joint names. Jennifer and John had been married for 46 years, they were both aged 75–79, with minor health difficulties.

INT: Is it jointly owned or . . .?
JENNIFER: It wasn't until last year.
INT: Oh really?
JENNIFER: Yeah, it was always in John's name. And last year, when he was going to Australia last year, ummmm, I thought I ought to get it. . . . 'cos he's always, 'Oh it doesn't matter, you'll get it anyway.' And I decided. So I went up to [lawyer], up the road, cost me three hundred and odd quid actually, to get it done, but we've got it in joint names now.

We therefore see in this account the remnants of a long running discussion whereby Jennifer seems to have over time raised this issue with John who told her that, as she would inherit the house, there was no need to change the ownership. Something about a trip to Australia, unexplored in the interview but possibly about a fear that he might die during the trip, finally made Jennifer take the step, in their late 70s, to have the house transferred into joint names When it actually happened, it did not cause conflict between them and was not difficult to effect. Change in money practices and arrangement appears to require a great deal of effort or determination when it is not forced.

Sites of ongoing conflict

In general then, old conflicts over money that are unresolved are buried, and the couple stop arguing and get on with living with the arrangements. However the issue of housing remains a site of conflict between couples even into later life, since unlike contribution, access and control, this is an arena where the couple must continue actively to negotiate their current position, since this is subject to ongoing change. This is one of the few remaining spaces where power imbalances over money can be directly observed.

In the following extract, Pryce [Couple 33] explains how he and his wife chose their current property. As noted above, they have been married for 54 years, from professional/managerial backgrounds; he is over 75 and she is between 70 and 75. They are both in good health.

PRYCE: . . . I turned around and said 'We're moving' and that was it.
INT: It was instant.
PRYCE: It wasn't so much. . . . She did not want to go. . . . But I put my foot down and said I have done enough . . . at [place] we looked at several places and we saw this and she agreed . . . and so . . . we are here . . . it is nice and quiet . . .

We see similar discussion between Gervais and Caroline [Couple 38]. Married for 28 years, Gervais left his first wife for Caroline. She is 65–70, and he is over 80; he has had a heart attack and health is a concern. Caroline had made longstanding plans to retire to a seaside town, where she had hoped to be nearer to her family. They were a relatively wealthy couple, having fortuitously been able to purchase their flat in a prestigious area in London under the government's 'right to buy' scheme.

GERVAIS: So. . . . One day, I took a separate decision to purchase this flat under the Thatcher Right to Buy Scheme. Because I know that Caroline was thinking, well [coastal town], when I'll retire I'll move there. But I did feel this was a very good invest . . . investment.
CAROLINE: And then we thought we would retire down in [coastal town], and we bought another flat on mortgage in the same block.
INT: Right.
CAROLINE: . . . so we could look after parents . . .
INT: Right.
CAROLINE: And Gervais' dad moved down there as well, Ok. From [place]. So that was gonna be the centre of things. Errr. But then you bought this.

It transpired that Gervais had made the purchase without Caroline knowing, as he had been the tenant of the flat entitled to the purchase. In purchasing the flat that they were living in, it became impossible for them to move to the seaside town. Caroline had been presented with a fait accompli, and required to accept the situation.

Strategies for resistance: subversive behaviour

We know from research among younger couples that there are great gender imbalances in access to money and resources, and financial decision making within couples. This research has revealed that where these power imbalances exist, they persist into old age in ways that seem resistant to change. As a counterfoil to this power, research on younger couples has also revealed strategies for resistance, such as the existence of 'secret accounts' by women who are in other respects disempowered. We also observed subversive behaviour around finances among our older couples.

In this example, Ruth [Couple 39] explains how she resists the imposition of power by her husband over their housing decision. They have been married for 52 years. She is in her early 70s but he is in his late 70s with serious health problems.

RUTH: Yes, I mean he was. . . . Last year he was thinking of moving to a flat, which I don't want to do. I went with him, to humour him, to see all these flats, etc. etc. And some of them are so lovely, you know, and. . . . But I don't think I could, I'm ready, or. . . . And also they're further out, 'cos our children live further out now. And he was saying we should go back nearer them. But then we'd need two cars. Errr. So that defeats the object of trying to save and money. And errrm. . . . I'm quite happy where I am.

INT: Yes. I see what you mean. So in a case like that, I mean, how would you handle that? Would you have a discussion?

RUTH: Well, I go, no, I go with him to see it, and then I find faults with everything. Because I'd say, errr, 'It has to be on a ground floor', because he could . . ., if the lift wasn't working how would he get up the stairs? And I don't want to be burdened with going up and down stairs, because he can't do it.

Thus Ruth pretends to be acceding to the request and her husband thinks that they will be moving, but it instead will be a war of attrition, which, because of her husband's rapidly failing health, she may well win. If he dies, she would not want to be left living in a place she is unhappy with, although this is never said, and remains implicit.

Strategies for resistance are also employed around intergenerational transfers, most often in the form of secret behaviour. This may be as benign as slipping 10 or 20 pounds to a grandchild, or more serious, and while most often seen in the context of stepfamilies, also observed with adult children of the couple. Here, Violet [Couple 27] tells of her 'secret' transfers to their daughter. Violet and Rory, from professional/managerial background, both in their late 70s with some health problems, have been married for 41 years. In their joint interview, Violet explains that they helped their daughter with the deposit for her flat:

VIOLET: She owns her own flat, we helped her buy her flat too. I mean we only gave her about five, six thousand, or what was it?

But in her sole interview, she adds that she sends her daughter money for airfares to visit from where she lives in South America:

VIOLET: [Whispers.] Yes. Rory doesn't know, but I do give her some. Her fare over is a thousand pounds, you see, she makes hardly anything in English lessons.

However in this example, as we saw in another case in our sample, the wives may think that they are doing something subversive, giving them the illusion of having power and control over some money, but in his sole interview, Rory reveals that he knows about this:

RORY: And quite frankly, she's so broke in South America that we often pay her fare when she comes over here.

Secretive behaviour from the men is common too, but when men do it, it is from a position of power rather than resistance – they have control over the money and do not need to tell their wives or have a discussion that might lead to conflict. Thus, here we see Joseph [Couple 36], explaining that he often spends without his wife's knowledge or input. They have been married for 46 years, are both in their late 70s, and have some health difficulties.

INT: Yeah. Ummm. May I ask this question now Joseph? To what extent does your wife know how you spend your money?
JOSEPH: Errr. . . . I would say seventy five per cent of the time she knows what I'm buying.
INT: What's the twenty five?
JOSEPH: The twenty five is probably odd items I buy and she disapproves!
INT: Would that be tools or gadgets or . . .?
JOSEPH: Ummmm . . . Well actu . . . Actually, to give an example. I err . . . This electric organ in the corner, at [son's house].

Catalysts for change

It appears to be the case, therefore, that money practices among couples are difficult to change and it requires something substantial to shift long established and practised financial arrangements, as well as gendered identities and power imbalances. While social changes in gender relations were keenly noticed by the couples in our study, not least in the money practices of their own children and grandchildren, these did not impact on their private relations with each other.

What then might act as a catalyst for change? As noted above, new relationships are the main way that individuals change these dynamics, by starting over in a new way with a new partner. The second life event which may cause money management, power and control to shift (usually from husband to wife) is catastrophic ill health. We have written about this elsewhere,[22] but even in this instance, we found that when problems of ageing, such as poor health and cognitive decline, threaten a partner's ability to fulfil a money management role identity, the other partner may try to protect their spouse's role identity from being undermined, using various covert strategies. This might be done to shore up their spouse's self-esteem in the face of such age-related threats to role identity; to 'keep up appearances' to the outside world; or to maintain their identity as a couple at a time of life when there may be multiple difficulties to deal with. Couples thus are shown to go to some lengths to preserve money practices, even where a shift of power and control over money is possible or has already happened.

---

22 D Bisdee, D Price and T Daly, 'Coping with age-related threats to role identity: older couples and the management of household money' (2013) 23 *Journal of Community & Applied Social Psychology* 505.

Discussion

In this chapter, we have presented findings about money management in long marriages and among older couples, an area that has received very little research attention. We find that patterns established early on in the relationship are of prime importance, these persist often through thick and thin, and are often only changed by a cataclysmic event such as breakdown and re-partnering, or very serious ill-health such as the onset of dementia or suffering a stroke. Furthermore, money practices are maintained despite substantial external changes in society and gender relations. While it was not always the case among our couples that men organised the finances, as is apparent throughout these data, money management in later life remains highly gendered, encompassing cultural, personal and gendered factors, longstanding within these long relationships.

Via their money practices, couples maintain to themselves and externally their own and their couple identity, and money management becomes incorporated in their daily work of gender management. As this happens, over time, the symbolic power of money to signify affection, trust, accommodation and stability are important, and we witness women often engaging in long term sacrifice of consumption and wants as a mechanism for maintaining equilibrium, coping and adapting to financial inequalities over time.

In this context, conflict over money reduces or disappears from relationships as old battles are no longer fought and old conversations are no longer had, since things generally do not change and there seems little point. However, the underlying power imbalances continue, and this is most clearly observed in the discussion of issues that of necessity must remain open for discussion. We see this most evidently in ongoing discussions of housing, where many decisions must be made in later life, whether related to downsizing, moving, adaptations and so on, but also in matters of intergenerational transfers. Resistance occurs, but may take place subtly or secretly so that it does not become a site of open conflict, not only in the form of resistance to plans, but also secret shopping and secret inter-generational or family transfers. However, we find that sometimes the husbands know, but do not reveal this knowledge to their wives, or they both really know that he knows, but maintain the pretence that she is exercising some autonomy in the relationship. When men practice secret financial behaviour, this is from a position of power and financial strength, rather than an attempt to subvert the status quo. All of these patterns would appear to be longstanding within the relationship.

It is thus rare for the balance of financial power to be transferred, although gendered inequalities reduce with health, care and the reduced income associated with old age, as men are compelled to give up some of their discretionary spending on hobbies, smoking, gambling and general consumption due to lack of resources. While failing health in men often leads to a transfer of financial control and power to women, we witness that some women will engage in complex emotional work to maintain the breadwinner role identity in their partners.

Ageing and money practice among couples

Our research reveals that age and time do not of themselves change money management practices between couples; rather practices become embedded over time and are remarkably resistant to change. Contrary to expectations, retirement and pension transitions were only rarely catalysts for change in financial arrangements or practices. Rather, we observe that couples can strive to maintain money practices, which are generally determined early in the relationship and viewed as immutable. As is well known from the large body of research referred to in this chapter, these are highly gendered; we add here that these power imbalances remain well into later life.

Apart from the formation of new relationships, failing health is the main catalyst for change in gendered household money management. However, in long relationships, this is often accompanied by the distress associated with a partner's potentially devastating ill-health or cognitive decline, and money practices seem to play an important part in maintaining the identities of both individuals and the couple.[23]

These gendered imbalances have important implications for the well-being of older women in later life. For women who live with little power and unequal access to resources through long marriages, there is a basic issue of fairness and equality, which has long been the subject of feminist comment. However, when considering these issues in the context of ageing, it is important to note that most married and cohabiting women will become widows,[24] often living in widowhood for a long time, and possibly in ill-health and disability, before they die. Not only are the resources of the couple sometimes diminished by the lifelong unequal access to financial resources, leaving less for their later years of life, but women often have less say in decisions that may affect their widowhood severely, for example, pension annuitisation and housing, since they may be left without widows' pensions, and living in housing that they do not want, yet possibly unable to move to their desired location when the time comes. Many women will also have little experience of taking control of financial decisions and may be ill-equipped in terms of human and social capital, to begin this in later life. Couples who are more resilient to these gendered imbalances are those where women have truly exercised or equally shared the power and control over money in later life. This applied to only a few of the older couples in our study,[25] but as contemporary research reveals, gendered imbalances of power persist through modern forms of relationships even among younger couples.[26] Our research suggests that these patterns may well prove resistant to change, even into old age.

Bibliography

Arber S, Davidson K and Ginn J, 'Changing approaches to gender and later life' in S Arber, K Davidson and J Ginn (eds), *Gender and Ageing: Changing Roles and Relationships* (Maidenhead, UK: Open University Press 2003).

Arber S and Ginn J, 'The invisibility of age: gender and class in later life' (1991) 39 *The Sociological Review* 260.

Arber S and Ginn J, 'Ageing and gender. Diversity and change' (2004) 34 *Social Trends* 14.

Arskey H, 'Collecting data through joint interviews' (1996) 15 *Social Research Update* 1.

Ashby KJ and Burgoyne CB, 'Separate financial entities? Beyond categories of money management' (2008) 37 *Journal of Socio-Economics* 458.

---

23 ibid.
24 Price (n 3).
25 See Bisdee, Daly and Price (n 19).
26 Pahl, 'Individualisation in couple finances: who pays for the children?' (n 10); V Elizabeth, 'Managing money, managing coupledom: a critical examination of cohabitants' money management practices' (2001) 49 *The Sociological Review* 389; Burgoyne et al.; KJ Ashby and CB Burgoyne, 'Separate financial entities? Beyond categories of money management' (2008) 37 *Journal of Socio-Economics* 458; C Vogler, M Brockmann and RD Wiggins, 'Managing money in new heterosexual forms of intimate relationships' (2008) 37 *Journal of Socio-Economics* 552; Stocks, Diaz and Halleröd (n 9).

Bennett F, 'Researching within-household distribution: overview, developments, debates, and methodological challenges' (2013) 75 *Journal of Marriage and Family* 582.

Bennett, F and Daly, M, 'Poverty through a gender lens: Evidence and policy review on gender and poverty' (2014) Working Paper supported by the Joseph Rowntree Foundation, Department of Social Policy and Intervention, University of Oxford.

Bennett F, Henau J De and Sung S, 'Within-household inequalities across classes? Management and control of money' in J Scott, R Crompton and C Lyonette (eds), *Gender Inequalities in the 21st century: New Barriers and Continuing Constraints* (Cheltenham, UK: Edward Elgar 2010).

Bennett F and Sung S, 'Dimensions of financial autonomy in low-/moderate-income couples from a gender perspective and implications for welfare reform' (2013) 42 *Journal of Social Policy* 701.

Bennett F and Sung S, 'Money matters: Using qualitative research for policy influencing on gender and welfare reform' (2013) 27 *Innovation: The European Journal of Social Science Research* 5.

Bisdee D, Daly T and Price D, 'Behind closed doors: older couples and the gendered management of household money' (2013) 12 *Social Policy and Society* 163.

Bisdee D, Price D and Daly T, 'Coping with age-related threats to role identity: older couples and the management of household money' (2013) 23 *Journal of Community & Applied Social Psychology* 505.

Burgoyne CB, 'Money in marriage: how patterns of allocation both reflect and conceal power' (1990) 38 *The Sociological Review* 634.

——, 'Heart-strings and purse-strings: money in heterosexual marriage.' (2004) 14 *Feminism & Psychology* 165.

Burgoyne CB, Clarke V, Reibstein J and Edmonds A, '"All my worldly goods I share with you"? Managing money at the transition to heterosexual marriage' (2006) 54 *The Sociological Review* 619.

Cantillon S, 'Measuring differences in living standards within households' (2013) 75 *Journal of Marriage and Family* 598.

Dasgupta I, 'Gender-biased redistribution and intra-household distribution' (2001) 45 *European Economic Review* 1711.

De Henau J and Himmelweit S, 'Unpacking within-household gender differences in partners' subjective benefits from household income' (2013) 75 *Journal of Marriage and Family* 611.

Dema Moreno S and Díaz Martínez C, 'Gender inequalities and the role of money in Spanish dual-income couples' (2010) 12 *European Societies* 65.

Deutsch FM, Roksa J and Meeske C, 'How gender counts when couples count their money' (2003) 48 *Sex Roles* 291.

Elizabeth V, 'Managing money, managing coupledom: a critical examination of cohabitants' money management practices' (2001) 49 *The Sociological Review* 389.

Fleming R and Easting SK, *The Common Purse: Income Sharing in New Zealand Families* (Auckland, New Zealand: Auckland University Press 1997).

Furnham A and Argyle M, *The Psychology of Money* (London: Routledge 1998).

Ginn J, *Gender, Pensions and the Lifecourse* (Bristol, UK: The Policy Press 2003).

Ginn J and Arber S, *Connecting Gender and Ageing: A Sociological Approach* (Buckingham, UK: Open University Press 1995)

Hardill I, Green AE, Dudleston AC and Owen DW, 'Who decides what? Decision making in dual-career households' (1997) 11 *Work, Employment & Society* 313.

Heimdal KR and Houseknecht SK, 'Cohabiting and married couple's income organization: Approaches in Sweden and the United States' (2003) 65 *Journal of Marriage and the Family* 525.

Himmelweit S, Santos C, Sevilla A and Sofer C, 'Sharing of resources within the family and the economics of household decision making' (2013) 75 *Journal of Marriage and Family* 625.

Lauer SR and Yodanis C, 'Money management, gender and households' in Judith Treas, Jacqueline Scott and Martin Richards (eds), *The Wiley Blackwell Companion to the Sociology of Families* (Oxford: John Wiley & Sons 2014).

Laurie H and Gershuny J, '"Couples, work and money"' in R Berthoud and J Gershuny (eds), *Seven Years in the Lives of British Families: Evidence on the Dynamics of Change from the British Household Panel Survey* (Bristol, UK: The Policy Press 2000).

Lundberg SJ, Pollak RA and Wales TJ, 'Do husbands and wives pool their resources? Evidence from the United Kingdom Child Benefit' (1997) 32 *Journal of Human Resources* 463.

Nyman C, 'Gender equality in "the most equal country in the world"? Money and marriage in Sweden' (1999) 47 *The Sociological Review* 766.

Nyman C, 'The social nature of money: meanings of money in Swedish families' (2003) 26 *Women's Studies International Forum* 79.

Nyman C, Reinikainen L and Stocks J, 'Reflections on a cross-national qualitative study of within-household finances' (2013) 75 *Journal of Marriage and Family* 640.

ODPM, *Indices of Deprivation 2004* (Office of the Deputy Prime Minister ed., 2007).

Pahl J, *Money and Marriage* (London: Macmillan 1989).

Pahl J, 'Couples and their money: patterns of accounting and accountability in the domestic economy' (2000) 13 *Accounting, Auditing and Accountability Journal* 502.

Pahl J, 'Gender, power and the household' (2001) 30 *Journal of Social Policy* 157.

Pahl J, 'Individualisation in couple finances: who pays for the children?' (2005) 4 *Social Policy and Society* 381.

Phipps SA and Burton PS, 'What's mine is yours? The influence of male and female incomes on patterns of household expenditure' (1998) 65 *Economica* 599.

Polak L and Green J, 'Using joint interviews to add analytic value.' (2015) 26 *FirstView Qualitative Health Research* 1638.

Price D, 'Why are older women in the UK poor?' (2006) 7 *Quality in Ageing and Older Adults* 9.

Price D and Ginn J, 'Sharing the crust? Gender, partnership status and inequalities in pension accumulation' in S Arber, K Davidson and J Ginn (eds), *Gender and Ageing – Changing Roles and Relationships* (Buckingham, UK: Open University Press 2003).

——, 'The future of inequalities in retirement income' in J Vincent, C Phillipson and M Downs (eds), *The Futures of Old Age* (London: SAGE 2006).

Racher F, Kaufert J and Havens B, 'Conjoint research interviews with frail, elderly couples: Methodological implications' (2000) 6 *Journal of Family Nursing* 367.

Rake K and Jayatilaka G, 'Home truths: an analysis of financial decision making within the home' (London: Fawcett Society 2002).

Sonnenberg SJ, 'Household financial organisation and discursive practice: Managing money and identity' (2008) 37 *The Journal of Socio-Economics* 533.

Stocks J, Diaz C and Halleröd B, *Modern Couples Sharing Money, Sharing Life* (London: Palgrave Macmillan 2007).

Tichenor V, 'Maintaining men's dominance: negotiating identity and power when she earns more' (2005) 53 *Sex Roles* 191.

Valentine G, 'Doing household research: interviewing couples apart and together' (1999) 31 *Area* 67.

Vogler C, 'Money in the household: some underlying issues of power' (1998) 46 *The Sociological Review* 687.

Vogler C, 'Managing money in intimate relationships: similarities and differences between cohabiting and married couples' in J Miles and R Probert (eds), *Sharing Lives, Dividing Assets* (Oxford: Hart 2009).

Vogler C, Brockmann M and Wiggins RD, 'Managing money in new heterosexual forms of intimate relationships' (2008) 37 *Journal of Socio-Economics* 552.

Vogler C, Lyonette C and Wiggins RD, 'Money, power and spending decisions in intimate relationships' (2008) 56 *The Sociological Review* 117.

Vogler C and Pahl J, 'Social and economic change and the organisation of money within marriage' (1993) 7 *Work, Employment and Society* 71.

——, 'Money, power and inequality within marriage' (1994) 42 *The Sociological Review* 263.

Waseem S, *Household Monies and Decision-Making*, Policy Research Paper no. 23 (Australian Government Department of Family and Community Services 2004).

Webley P, Burgoyne CB, Lea SEG and Young BM, *The Economic Psychology of Everyday Life* (Hove, UK: Psychology Press 2001).

Wilson G, *Money in the Family: Financial Organization and Women's Responsibilities* (Aldershot, UK: Avebury 1987).

Yodanis C and Lauer S, 'Economic inequality in and outside of marriage: Individual resources and institutional context' (2007) 23 *European Sociological Review* 573.

Zelizer VA, *The Social Meaning of Money*, vol 95 (New York: Basic Books 1994).

Zelizer VA, *Economic Lives: How Culture Shapes the Economy* (Princeton, NJ: Princeton University Press 2011).

Zelizer V, *The Purchase of Intimacy* (Princeton, NJ: Princeton University Press 2005).

Zipp JF, Prohaska A and Bemiller M, 'Wives, husbands, and hidden power in marriage' (2004) 25 *Journal of Family Issues* 933.

5 Austerity, solidarity and equality

A European Union perspective on gender and wealth

Susan Millns

The impact of austerity and economic hardship for families can be severe and keenly felt. The aim of this chapter is to examine the effects of the economic and financial crisis in Europe[1] and its implications for the acquisition and distribution of wealth in families. This examination is conducted through the lenses of solidarity and equality. Solidarity between European states, between generations, between members of different economic and social classes in society, has been advocated as a justification for the introduction of measures to combat the crisis.[2] The political rhetoric, that 'we are all in this together',[3] suggests that everyone should shoulder their part of the burden in remedying the deficit in public finances. This chapter extends the idea of solidarity in the public space to a consideration of the solidarity that might be required within personal relationships in order to address the challenges of economic austerity measures. Does the burden of solidarity fall equally on everybody? Or are some expected to shoulder a greater part of this burden than others? How does the public sphere impact upon the private in times of hardship and what are the gender implications of austerity measures within domestic relationships? Do women pay a higher price than men in the face of public sector unemployment, and cuts to public spending and welfare? What is the effect of austerity upon the developing notion of a European social citizenship?[4]

The chapter begins with a presentation of the economic and financial crisis and measures taken to address the crisis in Europe. These measures are linked to the call for solidarity at the European level. The EU's commitment to gender equality is then examined through its relationship to the acquisition of EU social citizenship rights and the inclusion or otherwise of women's domestic labour and care work as an appropriate contribution to trigger the application of European citizenship rights. Finally, using the example of the UK, the effects

---

1 The financial crisis took hold in 2007 and its effects were felt on a global level although they were magnified in the EU owing to the flawed design of the EU's policy on the Economic and Monetary Union. For discussion of the history of EMU and the impact of the crisis see A Hinarejos, 'Economic and monetary union' in C Barnard and S Peers (eds), *European Union Law* (Oxford: Oxford University Press 2014) 567. See also F Serricchio, M Tsakatika, and L Quaglia (2013) 'Euroscepticism and the global financial crisis' (2013) 51/1 *Journal of Common Market Studies* 51.
2 H van Rompuy, President of the European Council, 'A test of solidarity', Abrosetti Forum, 8 September 2012, EUCO 162/12.
3 *Conservative Party*, Invitation to Join the Government of Britain: Manifesto 2010 *(2010)*. See further K Veitch, 'Social solidarity and the power of contract' (2011) 38/2 *Journal of Law and Society* 189.
4 For the history of the development of a European Social Citizenship see L Magnusson and B Stråt (eds), *A European Social Citizenship? Preconditions for Future Policies in Historical Light* (Bern, Switzerland: Peter Lang 2004).

of austerity will be reviewed in order to ascertain the gendered nature of solidarity in private relationships. Both at the national and European levels, it will be suggested, the impact of austerity upon women and men is different and this affects women's position and their access to resources and rights in both the public and private spheres.

Austerity and solidarity

The Eurozone sovereign debt crisis that has rocked the European Union over the past few years has had many implications of a financial, economic and even constitutional nature.[5] The crisis has also effectively become a crisis of European solidarity. The crisis has been testing, in the Greek case almost to breaking point, of the extent to which Eurozone member states are prepared and able to come to the rescue of a member state facing a catastrophic sovereign debt default, which would then have forced it out of the single European currency.

Solidarity between the EU's member states, its citizens and between generations, is regarded as one of the core constitutional principles of EU law. It is one of the core aspirations or values of the European Union. Indeed, Article 2 of the Treaty on European Union provides:

> The Union is founded on the values of respect for human dignity, freedom, democracy, equality, the rule of law and respect for human rights, including the rights of persons belonging to minorities. These values are common to the Member States in a society in which pluralism, non-discrimination, tolerance, justice, solidarity and equality between women and men prevail.

'Solidarity' has also over time been included more and more in the primary legislation of the EU with five references in the post-Maastricht Treaties (three in the Treaty on European Union and two in the European Community Treaty), seven in the post-Amsterdam Treaties (five in the Treaty on European Union and two in the European Community Treaty), and now 19 references in the post-Lisbon Treaty framework (11 in the Treaty on the European Union and eight in the Treaty on the Functioning of the EU (TFEU[6]).

As a core EU value, the Treaty on European Union in Article 7 makes it perfectly clear that solidarity, along with the other values named in Article 2 would, in the case of a 'clear risk of a serious breach by a member state', trigger the initiation of the procedure for alerting and sanctioning that member state. Importantly this could occur even if the risk of a breach concerns a field of the member state's autonomous action and thus lies outside the sphere of the Union's activities. Hence a breach of solidarity could trigger a sanction against the offending member state.

The issue of sanction for breach of the values in Article 2 demonstrates the extreme importance of the *content* of that Article for the member states. Given that the Union's foundational values are habitually referred to as 'common' or 'universal' to its members,

---

5 AJ Menéndez, 'The existential crisis of the European Union' (2013) 14/5 *German Law Journal* 453; JE Fossum and AJ Menéndez, 'The European Union in crises or the European Union as crises?' *ARENA Report* No. 2/14 (2014).
6 The Treaty on the Functioning of the EU has replaced the European Community Treaty as following the Treaty of Lisbon, which came into force in December 2009, all European Community Law has been subsumed within European Union Law.

suggesting that they emerge from below, there should be little prospect of a state inadvertently violating one of these European core values without at the same time violating one of its own domestic values. This does presuppose, however, a degree of congruence between EU and national values and that the EU has sought inspiration for its set of values from the constitutional traditions of *all* of its present member states and, as the inclusion of a reference to minority rights protection in Article 2 illustrates, also from its latterly admitted member states.[7]

Yet, there is something about the idea of solidarity that is not quite the same as the other values mentioned in Article 2 TEU. The first sentence of Article 2 mentions a set of what might be broadly described as core democratic values. Alongside these is a second set of values which feature predominantly in national Constitutions but which have received a rather more nuanced transposition in Article 2 TEU. This second set is comprised of claims of a more inspirational, dare one say, utopian, nature. The values posited offer a vision of how society and social relations should be organised, governed and further developed, a key element of this being the appeal to a form of *social justice*. In this regard, inspiration may be gleaned from the constitutional traditions of a number of the member states, including Finland, whose Constitution states that the constitutional regime contributes to the promotion of social justice (Art. 1), the Irish Republic with its commitment to the realization of social order (preamble), the description of the French Republic as social in character (Art. 1), Portugal's commitment to the construction of a society founded upon solidarity (Art. 1) and Spain's constitution as a social democratic state (Art. 1). Italy too embraces this value implicitly with the recognition that the Republic is founded on labour (Art. 1). These provisions in national constitutions represent a long held European belief in the value of collective endeavour. Ross, in a collection of essays on *Promoting Solidarity in the European Union*, suggests that the idea of solidarity in Western Europe may even be traced back for more than two centuries, the term being associated with well cherished notions of *fraternité* at the time of the French Revolution and explicitly incorporated in the Napoleonic French Civil Code of 1804.[8]

Article 2 of the TEU takes these national values on board to the extent that it invokes a view of European society characterized, *inter alia*, as one in which 'solidarity' prevails. This enigmatic response reflects, of course, an acknowledgement that the constitutionalization of solidarity at the European level was one of the very 'hard choices' in the construction of the new Constitution for Europe.[9] On the one hand, to constitutionalize a form of solidarity might ensure that a unique feature of the European social democratic tradition is enshrined at the highest legal level thereby demonstrating a particularity of Europe's commitment to social justice. On the other hand, despite the above mentioned references to the social life of the nation in domestic Constitutions, it is by no means clear that the welfare state is any

---

[7] Minority rights protection was a key feature of the conditionality applied in Accession Agreements with the wave of central and Eastern European states joining the EU in 2004 and lobbying for its inclusion in what ultimately became Article 2 of the TEU was vigorously conducted by the Hungarian government.

[8] M Ross 'Solidarity – a new constitutional paradigm for the EU?' in M Ross and Y Borgmann-Prebil (eds) *Promoting Solidarity in the European Union* (Oxford: Oxford University Press 2010) p. 23. See also S Stjernø, *Solidarity in Europe: The History of an Idea* (Cambridge: Cambridge University Press 2005). It should be noted that the concept of *fraternité*, or brotherhood, explicitly carries with it a gendered dimension which is not unimportant when considering the link between the values of solidarity and equality below.

[9] JHH Weiler, 'A constitution for Europe? Some hard choices' (2002) 40/4 *Journal of Common Market Studies* 563.

longer at the heart of some national policy agendas (such as those of the UK, Italy and Spain). The constitutionalization of solidarity at the European level might, therefore, be an inaccurate representation of a 'common' concern. It might also have the effect of requiring individual member states to address and perhaps even improve their level of welfare provision in order to avoid triggering the sanction mechanism for breach of the EU value of respect for fundamental rights, in the event that this should be interpreted broadly to include social and economic rights.

That said, the concept of solidarity is not only codified in the EU Treaties. It became the core rhetoric of European political leaders as the economic and financial crisis deepened. The former European Council President Van Rompuy in September 2012 said that the crisis represented the first real test of solidarity in the history of the Union and that the very future of the Union was dependent upon it.[10] Solidarity was not a virtue in this sense but a matter of survival. As a matter of compulsion and necessity, the debate around solidarity has led perhaps inevitably to the counterpart of solidarity on the part of its beneficiaries. Countries such as Greece and Ireland, which have benefitted from European financial solidarity, are then required to accept conditions and adopt measures in response to this assistance.

The EU's Financial Framework for 2014–2020 has been presented as being governed by the principle of solidarity[11] and of course the EU budget itself is arguably the most important instrument of solidarity involving all the member states. With a projected guarantee ceiling of 780 billion euro, the European Financial Stability Facility (EFSF), which comes on top of the 110 billion euro bailout granted to Greece in 2010 as a bilateral commitment between the Eurozone countries, could be seen as the single biggest solidarity instrument ever created in the context of the European integration process.[12] Yet it should be remembered that this instrument did not emerge out of a sudden feeling of unselfish generosity by member states but rather out of sheer necessity in order to avoid a collapse of the single currency with all the political and economic consequences that would follow. It is telling that, according to a 2012 Eurobarometer survey, while a large majority of Europeans (84 per cent) believed that, as a consequence of the crisis, EU countries would have to work more closely together (84 per cent), just over half the respondents (51 per cent) said that they did not feel closer to citizens in other EU countries.[13]

Values such as solidarity are, therefore, inevitably malleable by their nature. Solidarity means many things to many different people. As Ross identifies, it has been both declaimed and decried along a spectrum from being *the* problem of the 21st century to a largely empty feel-good slogan.[14] However, it is apparent that in times of crisis the threat to the maintenance of core values is made more acute. Solidarity, dignity, equality, freedom, tolerance and non-discrimination may all be at risk of being compromised when times are hard and citizens are asked to pay the price of economic and financial crisis.

---

10 H Van Rompuy, President of the European Council, 'A test of solidarity', Abrosetti Forum, 8 September 2012, EUCO 162/12.
11 JM Barroso, former European Commission President, 'European renewal – State of the Union Address 2011', 28 September 2011, SPEECH/11/607.
12 For a detailed explanation of the EFSF, see A Hinarejos, *supra* n 1, 'Economic and monetary union' in C Barnard and S Peers (eds), *European Union Law* (Oxford: Oxford University Press 2014) 567, pp. 576–85.
13 European Commission Standard Eurobarometer 77, Public Opinion in the European Union, First Results, spring 2012.
14 M Ross (n 8), p. 23.

It is important therefore to adopt a critical evaluation of the response of the EU and of states and citizens to crisis and its consequences as these present challenges to the EU's value system. The economic and financial crisis in Europe has caused debt, austerity and a dent to living standards for many. It is inevitable that citizens should react, resist and build resilience to the harsh consequences that follow in order to try to protect and maintain their personal situations along with core values and principles. The implications for citizens of the sovereign debt crisis and the crisis in Eurozone economic governance, plans for economic recovery and the broader growth, jobs and competitiveness agenda in Europe, while presented as an exercise in solidarity, may yet destabilise other core values such as equality, non-discrimination and tolerance. A key challenge in understanding the implications of crisis for European citizens is to understand the extent to which Europe's core values are negotiable and their core content fixed or otherwise. Implicit within this question is a further question as to whether values have a gendered application.

Gender equality in the European Union

While the discourse on solidarity is relatively recent within the EU and its primary legislation, developing in the post-Maastricht era of the 1990s, the issue of gender equality has, on the other hand, long been on its agenda. In the post-World War II period, demographic changes and the entry of large numbers of women into paid employment in Europe brought about fundamental transformations in traditional gender roles and this has been reflected in the development of European Economic Community, and subsequent European Union policies on gender equality.[15]

The development and evolution of European Community law on sex equality from 1957 onwards was founded upon a Treaty provision stating that men and women must receive equal pay for equal work (Article 119 of the Treaty of Rome – now Article 157 of the Treaty on the Functioning of the EU). This provision provided the sole basis upon which all subsequent policy in this area was founded. While, originally, the provision was intended to curb unfair competition created by existing wage disparities across member states and responded to demands made by the French government, which had already introduced the principle of equal pay, it went on to became a source of justification for advancing a variety of equality demands for working women.

On the basis of the equal treatment principle now embodied in Article 157 TFEU, the European Economic Community in the 1970s adopted two Directives that would become the bedrock of the Union's gender equality policy over the next decades. The 1975 Equal Pay Directive provided for the elimination of discrimination in all aspects of remuneration between men and women for work of equal value[16] and the 1976 Equal Treatment Directive required member states to ensure equal treatment in access to employment and working conditions.[17]

---

15 C Barnard, 'Gender equality in the EU: a balance sheet', in P Alston *et al.* (eds), *The EU and Human Rights* (Oxford: Oxford University Press 1999) 215; D Anagnostou and S Millns, 'Gender equality, legal mobilization and feminism in a multi-level European system' (2013) 28/2 *Canadian Journal of Law and Society* 115. M Rönnmar, 'Labour and equality law', in C Barnard and S Peers (eds), *European Union Law* (Oxford: Oxford University Press 2014) 591.
16 Council Directive 75/117/EEC Equal Pay, OJ L45/19.
17 Council Directive 76/207/EEC Equal Treatment OJ L39/40.

The Court of Justice of the European Union saw the opportunity created by the development of the principle of gender equality within European law to expand the narrow textual framework of Article 157 around the particular issue of equal pay in order to apply it more generally to issues of equal treatment within the labour market and to the pursuit of a more general social policy objective of equality for women.[18] In the landmark *Defrenne II* judgement of 1976, the Court of Justice stated famously that Article 157 comprises twin objectives:

> First, in the light of the different stages of the development of social legislation in the various Member States, the aim of Article 119 [now 157] is to avoid a situation in which undertakings established in States which have actually implemented the principle of equal pay suffer a competitive disadvantage in intra-Community competition as compared with undertakings established in States which have not yet eliminated discrimination against women workers as regards pay. Secondly, this provision forms part of the social objectives of the Community, which is not merely an economic union, but is at the same time intended, by common action, to ensure social progress.[19]

The Court went on to say that Article 157 provided a directly effective right for individuals, enabling them to enforce the principle of equal pay in domestic courts and irrespective of whether or not national implementing legislation had been passed.[20]

In 2002, as a way of codifying the relevant case law of the ECJ but also the secondary legislation that had been put in place over the previous 20 years, the EU adopted the Equal Treatment in Employment Directive[21] and two years later, it also extended the prohibition against sex discrimination to access to and supply of goods and services.[22] Substantial amendments of the 1976 Equal Treatment Directive have added definitions of indirect discrimination and sexual harassment to the various forms of sex discrimination.

With a view to consolidating legislation and tidying up existing provisions, the EU adopted its 'Recast' Equal Treatment Directive in 2006.[23] This measure systematizes the existing legislation on equal pay, equal treatment, occupational social security and the burden of proof and incorporates relevant rulings of the Court of Justice into legislation.[24] As such, the Recast Directive now governs equal treatment in access to employment and promotion, vocational training, working conditions, including pay, and occupational social security. It includes provisions on remedies and enforcement, adequate compensation, recourse to judicial and conciliation procedures and the burden of proof, and comprehensively sets out member state obligations to ensure the adoption of appropriate penalties, prevention of discrimination, protection against victimization, gender mainstreaming and dissemination of information.

However, it is apparent from the outline above of the EU's approach to gender equality that its scope is very much limited to the public sphere of employment and access to goods

---

18   R Cichowski, 'Women's Rights, the European Court, and Supranational Constitutionalism' (2004) 38/3 *Law and Society Review* 489.
19   Case 43/75 *Defrenne v SABENA (No. 2)* [1976] ECR 455, paras. 9–10.
20   Case 43/75, *Defrenne v SABENA (No. 2)* [1976] ECR 455.
21   Council Directive 2002/73/EC, Equal Treatment Amendment Directive [2002] OJ L269/15.
22   Council Directive 2004/113/EC Access to and Supply of Goods and Services [2004] OJ L373/37.
23   Council Directive 2002/73/EC, Equal Treatment Amendment Directive [2002] OJ L269/15.
24   N Burrows and M Robinson, 'An assessment of the recast of community equality laws' (2007) 13/2 *European Law Journal* 186.

and services where the EU enjoys competence. Within these areas the EU takes an anti-discrimination approach, looking for comparators to ensure equal treatment within this narrow field of EU competence. This does, though, leave many areas of policy-making untouched by the gender equality principle and in particular the commitment to gender equality in the sector of employment masks the reality of the instances of gender inequality in many other areas.

The European Union has attempted, within the limit of its competences, to broaden its approach to equality and its focus on gender equality in employment towards a more holistic view of equality as a core value of the EU and as a fundamental right.[25] This was not without some controversy. The principle of equality was omitted from early drafts of the Constitution for Europe (which went on to provide the basic building blocks for the Treaty of Lisbon and the list of core values in Article 2 TEU),[26] an omission that provoked stringent critique, particularly by those concerned with gender equality in the EU.[27] Its inclusion in the final version of Article 2 TEU, alongside the expression of a commitment to a society in which non-discrimination and equality between women and men prevail, represents a resounding victory for those social and political actors who campaigned vociferously to this end and was wholly justified by the clear and frequent references to this notion in the Constitutions of the member states.[28] At last there was some recognition that oblique references to 'tolerance' and 'non-discrimination', would do little to assist the positive promotion of equality within the EU in the absence of its inclusion as a fundamental value.

Furthermore, the EU made its Charter of Fundamental Rights legally binding with the introduction of the Treaty of Lisbon, coming into force in December 2009. The Charter (which was originally drawn up in 1999/2000) contains a basic equality before the law guarantee (Article 20), as well as a provision setting out a framework for the institutions to pass legislation to combat discrimination on a number of different grounds (Article 21) and a reference to positive action provisions in the field of gender equality (Article 23). The adoption of the Charter itself was a significant development and despite criticisms of its content it marks a step forward for the legitimacy, identity and human rights commitments of the EU.

Equality, solidarity and European social citizenship

The values of equality and solidarity are, thus, linchpins of the EU's constitutional order. However, as has been noted above, their application is linked primarily to the public sphere and thus may fail to penetrate the private domain of personal relationships. Nevertheless, the reality of austerity and financial crisis measures has been the expectation that individuals

---

25 See A Massolot, 'The state of gender equality law in the European Union' (2007) 13/2 *European Law Journal* 152.
26 For discussion of the process of drafting the Constitution for Europe, see G de Búrca (2001), 'The drafting of the EU Charter of Fundamental Rights' (2000) 26/2 *European Law Review* 126.
27 C Hoskyns, Gender Equality and the Convention: A Comment (The Federal Trust for Education and Research, 2003); V Reding, Conclusions: Jean Monnet Conference on 'Gender equality and the New European Union' (European Commission 2003); Working Group XI on Social Europe, Final Report, 4 February 2003, *Conv* 516: 1 March 2003.
28 The concept appears in a number of forms: as a value in and of itself (Spain, Art. 2), in the guise of equality before the law (France, Art. 1; Austria, Art. 7; Finland, Art. 6; Italy, Art. 3), the equal value of all persons (Sweden, Art. 2; The Netherlands, Art. 1), the respect for all beliefs (France, Art. 1) and as a general and key component of the catalogues of rights which are part of the various national constitutional traditions.

will contribute to alleviate the deficit and this inevitably affects their personal situations, given the overlap between employment, welfare and domestic relationships.

A complicated relationship between equality and solidarity has started to emerge in a significant line of case law of the Court of Justice of the EU in the context of European citizenship rights.[29] Following the example of the development of the equal treatment and equal pay principles by the Court of Justice, a similar judicial creativity may be noted with regard to the concept of EU citizenship (bound, like the equal pay principle before it, to predominantly economic parameters) which has important implications for women's equality and citizenship rights, and for the development of solidarity in the EU.

Initially, just as in the sphere of gender equality, where the equal pay provision was first designed to enhance the liberalization of the internal market (and so was motivated by considerations of economy and competition rather than gender justice per se), the Treaty provisions on EU citizenship, which came into force in 1993 with the Treaty on European Union, tend to take a predominantly market-based form rather than conferring a substantial package of social citizenship rights upon women and men.[30]

However, the development of the Treaty provisions by the Court of Justice has, as with the equality principle, enabled a certain broadening of the textual provision away from its economic premise and promising the development of a form of European social solidarity which had an early positive impact for women. For example, in the first significant EU citizenship case of *Martinez Sala*[31] a Spanish national resident in Germany, who had not worked there for many years owing to her childcare responsibilities, was able to rely upon a combination of the non-discrimination principle contained in what is now Article 18 TFEU and the citizenship provisions in the now Article 20 TFEU to gain equal access to a German child-raising benefit. Hence, as a Union citizen she was able to claim equality of treatment on the grounds of nationality even though not economically active in the public sphere and solely dependent on welfare. Such a ruling has a great impact on women as they move between the public and private spheres especially when having children or other caring responsibilities.

Subsequent developments in this line of case law gave hope for an increasingly wide interpretation of the citizenship provisions to include those who are not economically active within their remit and to recognise potentially the extent of women's labour outside of the traditional market place. As Shaw has argued, one interpretation of this combined application of the non-discrimination principle and citizenship provisions is that 'it gives something close to a universal right of access to all manner of welfare benefits to all those who are Union citizens and who are lawfully resident in a member state.'[32]

This novel interpretation of EU citizenship has gone some way to address the otherwise lack of recognition of the care work undertaken by women in the family as 'proper' work for the purposes of the application of EU law. Women's unpaid labour is worth billions to national economies every year and, in particular, unpaid carers – the vast majority of whom

---

29 For a discussion of the early development of EU citizenship rights by the Court of Justice, see S O'Leary, 'Putting flesh on the bones of European Union citizenship' (1999) 24 *European Law Review* 68. See further S Giubboni, 'A certain degree of solidarity? Free movement of Persons and Access to Social Protection in the Case Law of the European Court of Justice', in M Ross and Y Borgmann-Prebil (n 8), 166.
30 The citizenship provisions are now contained within Article 9 TEU and Articles 20-24 TFEU.
31 Case C-85/96 *Martinez Sala v Freistaat Bayern* [1998] ECR I-2691.
32 J Shaw, 'The European Union and gender mainstreaming: constitutionally embedded or comprehensively marginalised?' (2002) 10/3 *Feminist Legal Studies* 213, at p. 222.

are women looking after children or older or sick family members – contribute a huge amount to the personal well-being of the citizens of the EU every year.[33]

Beyond the specific EU citizenship provisions though, the bulk of EU single market law still presupposes an understanding of the notion of 'workers' as including only those engaged in 'economic' activity.[34] As such, and in other respects, women's domestic work is excluded from the single market and this has clear implications for women as they may seek to move between states of the EU either independently or with their families.

Welfare states and social policy in Europe, together with the notion of social citizenship derived from these provisions, have traditionally evolved around the relationship between paid work and welfare. However, that relationship has in turn been heavily influenced by another relationship that links men's waged labour to women's unpaid domestic work. Traditionally, the organization of these 'social models' around the 'male breadwinner' typology implied that those outside the labour market were not included in social protection and social rights on an independent basis (as they are not wage earners) but on the basis of family dependency. The role of women as carers in the private domain was a key part of the construction of this model and, at the same time, operated as an obstacle to their integration in the labour force and the public sphere.

That said, the Court of Justice of the EU sought to build upon the early development of EU social citizenship rights for those who were not economically active through its case law and in the face of growing opposition from member states concerned about the impact of this new form of social solidarity upon their national welfare systems. In the case of *Grzelczyk*[35] it was decided that Grzelczyk, a French national studying in Belgium, was entitled, in the same way as a Belgian student, to the payment of the minimex (a non-contributory minimum subsistence allowance).

Approaching the case on the basis that Grzelczyk was not a worker, the Court found, as in *Martinez Sala*, that there was discrimination on the grounds of nationality contrary to what is now Article 18 TFEU and that Grzelczyk fell within the personal scope of this prohibition as an EU citizen lawfully residing in Belgium. The Court specifically emphasized its findings in this case as being based on the solidarity owed by member states to those EU citizens who would not be an 'unreasonable' burden on their welfare systems.

Later, in the case of *Baumbast*[36] (a case about the refusal to renew the residency permit of a German national and his family who had moved to the UK), the Court of Justice went further still in decoupling EU citizenship rights from the internal market rules by finding that the Treaty provisions on citizenship are directly effective, that is to say they may be relied upon directly by individuals who would otherwise struggle to benefit from the rights granted by the other provisions of EU single market law. The subtext of the development in *Baumbast* was that the refusal to renew the residence permit of Mr Baumbast's Colombian wife in the UK where the family were living would effectively leave their children without their primary carer. In this regard, the Court said, European law had to be read in the light of the requirement of the respect for family life under Article 8 of the ECHR meaning that a child has the right to be accompanied by the person who is his or her primary carer

---

33 Fawcett Society, 'Cutting Women Out', Report 8 March 2013. www.fawcettsociety.org.uk/2013/03/cutting-women-out/ (accessed 19 November 2016).
34 I Moebius and E Szyszczak, 'Of raising pigs and children' (1998) 18/1 *Yearbook of European Law* 125.
35 Case C-184/99 *Grzelczyk v Centre Public d'Aide Sociale d'Ottignes-Louvain-la-Neuve* (CPAS) [2001] ECR I-6193.
36 *Baumbast and R v Secretary of State for the Home Department* [2002] ECR I-7091.

notwithstanding the fact that the carer (as a third country national) may not enjoy independent rights under EU law.

A further example of the recognition of the work of mothers outside the sphere of the market lies in the decision of the Court of Justice in the *Chen* case.[37] In this decision, the UK Secretary of State for the Home Department had refused to grant a long term residence permit to either Catherine Chen (a minor aged eight months of Irish nationality) or her mother (of Chinese nationality) on the grounds that Catherine was not exercising any free movement rights arising from EU law and that her mother was not entitled to reside in the UK under domestic law. The Court of Justice stated, however, that Catherine's right of residence derived from her status as an EU citizen and, furthermore, that 'a refusal to allow the parent, whether a national of a Member State or a national of a non-member country, who is the carer of a child to whom Article 18 EC and Directive 90/364 grant a right of residence, to reside with that child in the host Member State would deprive the child's right of residence of any useful effect.'[38]

In other words, the mother of an EU citizen must be able to invoke a right of residence derived from that of her young child in order to allow the EU national child herself to exercise her EU rights, irrespective of the age of that child. The explicit recognition of the role of the primary carer of an EU citizen and the consequent granting of rights on that basis is an important step towards valuing the care work that women and mothers do despite the fact that this typically falls outside of the EU's market framework and would not normally be recognised as a basis for according legal rights under EU law. Yet, as the Court noted:

> It is clear that enjoyment by a young child of a right of residence necessarily implies that the child is entitled to be accompanied by the person who is his or her primary carer and accordingly that the carer must be in a position to reside with the child in the host Member State for the duration of such residence.[39]

Thus the *Chen* decision is an important example of the increased visibility and recognition of women's role in the care work associated with family life and shows the impact that domestic work can have on the exercise of citizenship rights in the public sphere.

Chen is perhaps an easy case in some respects as the family was self-sufficient financially and unlikely to be a burden, reasonable or otherwise, upon the host state. Additionally in *Chen*, despite member state claims that this was purely a domestic, internal affair, the matter was found to be one that fell within the scope of EU law since Catherine Chen was an Irish citizen (having been born in Northern Ireland) who sought to reside in the UK. However, in later cases, the principle established in *Chen* that third country national parents of EU citizen children may derive residency rights on the back of their children's EU citizenship has been tested to its limits where there were stronger arguments that the issue was purely an internal, national matter and where the financial resource implications for the host state were greater. Yet the case of *Zambrano* brought rights for third country national parents of two EU citizen children living in Belgium despite there being no question of movement and no link to the internal market.[40] Once more in the *Zambrano* case, the Court of Justice

---

37 Case C-200/02 *Zhu and Chen v Secretary of State for the Home Department* [2004] ECR I-9925.
38 Ibid., para. 45.
39 Ibid., para. 45.
40 Case C-34/09 *Ruiz Zambrano v ONEM* [2010] ECR I-1177.

reiterated that without their primary carers being granted a rights of residency and a work permit, the right of the children as EU citizens to reside in Europe would be meaningless.[41]

Zambrano probably represents the high water mark of European social solidarity. In the wake of the economic and financial crisis, when public resources, welfare and social assistance are being cut by member states, equality of access for EU citizens to such welfare and support has proved a testing subject. Member states have long been anxious about the impact of social solidarity and free movement of EU citizens, as developed by the Court of Justice, upon their national welfare systems. In some member states, such as the United Kingdom, the peoples of Europe have also begun to react negatively to free movement and the perceived draw that this has on national welfare resources.[42] Austerity thus appears to have brought a different approach to the Court's thinking and, in the light of national anxieties about 'welfare tourism' across Europe, the Court of Justice has of late begun to take a more restrictive approach which suggests a step backwards for women's EU citizenship rights.[43] The lack of recognition of women's work as carers is explicit in the recent case of *Dano*[44] in which a Romanian national, Ms Dano, who lived in Germany with her infant son, sought unsuccessfully to claim basic social assistance benefits for herself and her son. Since she had not undertaken any professional activity either in Romania or Germany, the Court rejected her claim that she was discriminated against on the grounds of her nationality. Unlike Martinez Sala before her, as an economically inactive citizen without sufficient resources, she could not invoke the non-discrimination principle.[45]

It could be, therefore, that at least for the moment we have seen the highpoint of the interpretation of EU citizenship rights as inclusive and non-discriminatory in terms of valuing the contribution that women make, and the work that they do, within domestic relationships but outside of the public sphere and falling short of 'professional' activity. The *Dano* judgement will impact negatively upon those women who do not have the resources to become economically active, mobile citizens and will mark a return to a more gendered division of labour and inequality of resources in which unpaid care work is, as before, less valued than economically productive labour.

The UK, austerity and gender equality

The distrust of, and lack of social solidarity shown towards, migrants (from the EU and elsewhere) has been a key factor in debates in the United Kingdom that have ultimately led to the so-called 'Brexit' decision. Following a referendum on 23 June 2016, the UK voted to leave the European Union (51.9 per cent to 48.1 per cent). The Brexit debate brings with it extremely important considerations for women, both in the public and private realms, not least the loss of EU citizenship and legal rights that women in the UK, and those from

---

41 *Ibid.*, para. 44.
42 The image of a procession of migrants ostensibly queuing to enter the United Kingdom was a populist image circulated by the UK Independence Party at the time of the UK's referendum on membership of the European Union on 23 June 2016.
43 The Court began to take a more restrictive approach in cases where there was no free movement and where the applicant was not dependent on the EU citizen family member for subsistence rights in Case C-434/09 *McCarthy* [2011] ECR I-3375 and Case C-256/11 *Dereci* [2011] ECR I-11315.
44 Case C-333/13 *Dano v Jobcenter Leipzig* 11 November 2014. EU:C:2014:2358.
45 See further D Thym, 'The elusive limits of solidarity: residence rights of and social benefits for economically inactive Union citizens' (2015) 52/1 *Common Market Law Review* 17.

other member states seeking to move to and reside in the UK, will now face. The deprivation of EU citizenship comes at a price and it is likely that women will pay a higher price than men. The ability to move around Europe to access opportunities to work, to study, to engage in vocational activities, to seek social support, has been invaluable to women as a means to improve their lives and gain economic power. Equally, the EU has provided a necessary supra-national platform or lever through which to secure equality guarantees for women at the domestic level. Without this security, and in a climate of economic uncertainty and continued austerity, there is a serious risk that the achievements of the last half century will be undermined. For those who are outside the EU, the Brexit vote is a stark reminder that European social rights are not universal but are based on citizenship of the Union, and they can be lost just as easily as they can be acquired.

The potential loss of rights for women in the UK, however, is not a result solely of the Brexit decision. This has been a trend that has been growing over recent years and follows on from the economic and financial crisis and the austerity measures that were introduced to tackle this and reduce the national deficit. As a result women's economic inequality remains high. Even prior to the recent economic crisis women were much more likely to be working in low paid, part-time work and more likely to be part of a single parent household and to have fewer financial assets than their male counterparts.[46] Measures taken after the crisis have exemplified this as women face a new 'triple jeopardy' of cuts to jobs, social welfare and public services.[47] Additionally, the Conservative/Liberal Democrat coalition government, which came into power in 2010, oversaw a series of funding cuts that have had a serious impact on the women's movement more generally and its ability to campaign against the austerity measures that would negatively impact upon women and their families. For example, in June 2010 the Wales Women's National Coalition, which represented over 50 women's groups, was closed when the Welsh Assembly said it could no longer fund it and in December 2010 the Women's National Commission, a UK umbrella group representing women's groups in England, Scotland, Wales and Northern Ireland and which had been established since 1969, was forced to close.

Despite these closures, women have mobilized to challenge government measures with mixed results using equality legislation that has been passed partly in response to EU initiatives to extend the principle of equality in the member states. Section 149 of the Equality Act 2010 requires public sector bodies to comply with an equality duty[48] that applies to public authorities, including central and local government bodies, when making budgetary and policy decisions. Challenges to decisions made by the Treasury, Birmingham City Council and Lancashire County Council sought to remind public bodies of this duty.[49]

---

46 Fawcett Society, 'Cutting Women Out', Report 8 March 2013. www.fawcettsociety.org.uk/2013/03/cutting-women-out/ (accessed 19 November 2016).
47 Ibid.
48 Section 149(1) of the Equality Act 2010 provides: 'A public authority must, in the exercise of its functions, have due regard to the need to – (a) Eliminate discrimination, harassment, victimisation and any other conduct that is prohibited by or under this Act; (b) Advance equality of opportunity between persons who share a relevant protected characteristic and persons who do not share it; (c) Foster good relations between persons who share a relevant protected characteristic and persons who do not share it.' The relevant protected characteristics are age, disability, gender reassignment, pregnancy and maternity, race, religion or belief, sex, sexual orientation.
49 *R (Rahman) v Birmingham City Council* [2011] EWHC 944; *R (WM et al.) v Birmingham City Council* [2011] EWHC 1147; *R (JG and MB) v Lancashire County Council* [2011] EWHC 2295.

Forty-one of these decisions concluded, however, that s.149 does not require public bodies to achieve a particular result in terms of equality because the duty is merely to have 'due regard' (i.e. regard that is appropriate in all the circumstances) to equality. Hence, opposing factors must also be considered and in some cases may actually outweigh the equality duty. So, while an equality impact assessment may be helpful in showing that due regard has been had to the duty, such an assessment is not essential, although such an assessment that fails objectively to assess the impact will not be adequate. A failure to make explicit reference to the equality duty was also found not to be fatal to any decision and a 'provisional' budgetary or policy decision may be made before exploring the impact of that decision on equality issues. It is, however, important that any assessment is thorough and that there is scope for change of the budget or policy in the light of the assessment.

The Fawcett Society (one of the UK's leading charities promoting women's equality) used the equality duty to argue that the Conservative and Liberal Democrat Coalition's first budget was illegal because women bore the brunt of service and benefit cuts.[50] It was claimed that the 2010 emergency budget would do little to help those who were already the worst off in the face of drastic public spending cuts and rising unemployment, and above all that this risked widening gender inequalities in the UK. In the case, the government admitted that it had not carried out an assessment of how the budget would impact upon women and men and this was described as 'regrettable'. The judge, Justice Ouseley, found that policies set to have such a dramatically different impact on women and men merit further scrutiny and said that the UK's Equality and Human Rights Commission was best placed to conduct this kind of analysis. The judge did not, however, go on to grant judicial review of the budget. Nevertheless, when drawing up the subsequent Comprehensive Spending Review, the government produced the first ever equalities statement to accompany its financial policy.

In its report on the impact of the 2011 budget and the spending cuts, the Fawcett Society highlighted a number of worrying implications for women of the austerity measures that have been translated from the public sphere down to the private, and inevitably into the distribution of wealth within personal relationships. The Society reported that the government was set to cut around 929,000 jobs in the public sector and, given that women make up 65 per cent of the public sector work force and account for an even higher number in certain sectors (accounting for 75 per cent of local government employees, 77 per cent of National Health Service workers and 80 per cent of the adult social care workers), it was inevitable that women would be the hardest hit by these public sector job cuts.[51] It was expected that around twice as many women as men would lose their jobs in public sector employment as a result of austerity cuts.[52] Inevitably the impact of these job losses will be felt upon families.

Feminist research has long shown the processes of the feminization of female poverty and the way in which this can affect households.[53] Social benefits tend to make up one-fifth of

---

50 R (Fawcett Society) v Chancellor of the Exchequer [2010] EWHC 3522.
51 Fawcett Society, Jobs – 'The triple jeopardy: the impact of job cuts on women', Report, 28 February 2013 www.fawcettsociety.org.uk/2013/02/jobs/ (accessed 19 November 2016).
52 Ibid.
53 See, for example, J Pahl, *Money and Marriage* (London: Macmillan, 1989); J Pahl, *Invisible Money: Family Finances in the Electronic Economy* (Basingstoke, UK: Policy Press 1999). M Daly and K Rake, *Gender and the Welfare State* (Cambridge: Polity Press 2003). F Bennett and M Daly, 'Poverty through a gender lens: evidence and policy review on gender and poverty', Report for the Joseph Rowntree Foundation (Oxford: University of Oxford, May 2014).

the average woman's income in the UK as opposed to one-tenth of men's and women are more likely to be the users of frontline public services.[54] So when women lose their financial independence through the loss of their employment or through the loss of welfare they are being increasingly placed in vulnerable and financially dependent positions within the family. It is in this sense that equality is being compromised and the degree of solidarity expected of women in times of austerity is particularly high. Women's economic independence is key to fighting for women's equality in both the public and private spheres and yet this is one of the first things to be sacrificed in times of crisis.

In conclusion, it is apparent that both the values of solidarity and equality are promoted at the European level as representing the core values of the type of European society that we want to be. However, these values have been shown to be affected by the economic and financial crisis that has hit the European Union and its member states over the past few years. This crisis has led to a hardening of approach and a weakening of solidarity by the peoples of Europe, member states and even the Court of Justice with important implications for those seeking social solidarity in Europe. In turn this has affected perceptions of the type of work that women do and the merit of their contribution to the single market in terms of an increasing failure to recognize and value in economic terms the domestic care work that women provide within family units. Linked to the hardening of approach, at the national level, austerity has provided a justification for cuts to public spending and the impact of these cuts is felt particularly by women who engage in public sector employment and require social assistance more often than men. The consequence of these changes within close personal relationships marks a return to female poverty and dependence within the domestic sphere.

Bibliography

Anagnostou D, and Millns S, 'Gender Equality, Legal Mobilization and Feminism in a Multi-level European System' (2013) 28/2 *Canadian Journal of Law and Society* 115–31.

Barnard C, 'Gender Equality in the EU: A Balance Sheet', in Alston P, *et al.* (eds), *The EU and Human Rights* (Oxford University Press, Oxford 1999) 215–79.

Barroso JM, 'European Renewal – State of the Union Address 2011', 28 September 2011, Strasbourg, SPEECH/11/607.

Bennett F and Daly M, 'Poverty through a Gender Lens: Evidence and Policy Review on Gender and Poverty', Report for the Joseph Rowntree Foundation (University of Oxford, Oxford May 2014).

Burrows N and Robinson M, 'An Assessment of the Recast of Community Equality Laws' (2007) 13/2 *European Law Journal* 186–203.

Cichowski R, 'Women's Rights, the European Court, and Supranational Constitutionalism' (2004) 38/3 *Law and Society Review* 489–512.

Daly M and Rake K, *Gender and the Welfare State* (Polity Press, Cambridge 2003).

de Búrca G, 'The Drafting of the EU Charter of Fundamental Rights' (2001) 26/2 *European Law Review* 126–38.

Fawcett Society, 'Cutting Women Out', Report, 8 March 2013. www.fawcettsociety.org.uk/2013/03/cutting-women-out/ London (accessed 19 November 2016).

Fawcett Society, 'The Triple Jeopardy: The Impact of Job Cuts on Women', Report, 28 February 2013 www.fawcettsociety.org.uk/2013/02/jobs/ London (accessed 19 November 2016).

Fossum JE and Menéndez AJ, 'The European Union in Crises or the European Union as Crises?' *ARENA Report* No. 2/14, Oslo, Norway (2014).

---

54 Fawcett Society, 'Cutting Women Out', Report 8 March 2013. www.fawcettsociety.org.uk/2013/03/cutting-women-out/ (accessed 19 Nov. 2016).

Giubboni S, 'A Certain Degree of Solidarity? Free Movement of Persons and Access to Social Protection in the Case Law of the European Court of Justice', in Ross M and Borgmann-Prebil Y (eds), *Promoting Solidarity in the European Union* (Oxford Online).

Hinarejos A, 'Economic and Monetary Union' in Barnard C and Peers S (eds), *European Union Law* (Oxford University Press, Oxford 2014) 567–90.

Hoskyns C, *Gender Equality and the Convention: A Comment* (The Federal Trust for Education and Research, London 2003).

Magnusson L and Strat B (eds), *A European Social Citizenship? Preconditions for Future Policies in Historical Light* (Peter Lang, Brussels 2004).

Massolot A, 'The State of Gender Equality Law in the European Union' (2007) 13/2 *European Law Journal* 152–68.

Menéndez AJ, 'The Existential Crisis of the European Union (2013) 14/5 *German Law Journal* 453–526.

Moebius I and Szyszczak E, 'Of Raising Pigs and Children' (1998) 18/1 *Yearbook of European Law* 125–56.

O'Leary S, 'Putting Flesh on the Bones of European Union Citizenship' (1999) 24/1 *European Law Review* 68–79.

Pahl J, *Money and Marriage* (Macmillan, London 1989).

Pahl J, *Invisible Money: Family Finances in the Electronic Economy* (Policy Press, Bristol, UK 1999).

Reding V, *Conclusions: Jean Monnet Conference on 'Gender Equality and the New European Union'* (European Commission, Brussels 2003).

Rönnmar M, 'Labour and Equality Law' in Barnard C and Peers S (eds), *European Union Law* (Oxford University Press, Oxford, 2014) 591–620.

Ross M, 'Solidarity – A New Constitutional Paradigm for the EU?' in Ross M and Borgmann-Prebil Y (eds), *Promoting Solidarity in the European Union* (Oxford University Press, Oxford 2010) 23–45.

Serricchio F, Tsakatika M, Quaglia L (2013) 'Euroscepticism and the Global Financial Crisis' (2013) 51/1 *Journal of Common Market Studies* 51–64.

Shaw J, 'The European Union and Gender Mainstreaming: Constitutionally Embedded or Comprehensively Marginalised?' (2002) 10/3 *Feminist Legal Studies* 213–26.

Stjernø S, *Solidarity in Europe: The History of an Idea* (Cambridge University Press, Cambridge 2005).

Thym D, 'The Elusive Limits of Solidarity: Residence Rights of and Social Benefits for Economically Inactive Union Citizens' (2015) 52/1 *Common Market Law Review* 17–50.

Van Rompuy H, 'A Test of Solidarity', Abrosetti Forum, 8 September 2012, Cernobbio, EUCO 162/12.

Veitch K, 'Social Solidarity and the Power of Contract' (2011) 38/2 *Journal of Law and Society* 189–214.

Weiler JHH, 'A Constitution for Europe? Some Hard Choices' (2002) 40/4 *Journal of Common Market Studies* 563–80.

6 Contractual thinking in couple relationships

Tone Sverdrup

Introduction

In both market relationships and couple relationships (marriage and unmarried cohabitation), services are transferred between two legally independent entities but the similarity stops there. In the market, transactions occur in which one receives nothing without providing something in return. Reciprocity between service and counter-service is the fundamental way of thinking in contract law. This contractual way of thinking, where the parties' performances are compared and balanced, leaves its mark on the entire private law – including family law. In family relationships, however, the transfers of assets, goods or services are normally not mutually conditioned. Rather than being contractually conditioned, in a number of cases, the service would lose value if it were conditionally dependent on a counter-service. These differences do not necessarily imply that the logic of private law is inappropriate or unsuitable in intimate relationships. However, due to the fact that cohabitants and spouses tend to live as interdependent entities, there is reason to question how well it this logic fits.

Even if the concept of the lifelong housewife is a thing of the past, in many Western countries, a large number of women still assume the main responsibility for childcare. As a result, they often work only part-time outside the home, meaning they earn less than their partner and have little surplus income to invest. Spouses and cohabitants with these characteristics tend to end up with few assets upon relationship breakdown. This chapter shows how contractual thinking in both legal doctrine and legal policy contributes to these negative outcomes.

Labour: the valuation of childcare

In divorce proceedings in the majority of European countries, property is divided equally according to fixed rules, and the value of inheritance, gifts and premarital assets is excluded from the property subject to division in many of these countries.[1] In England and Wales, Ireland and other common-law countries, the court has discretionary power to divide all property, however defined, on the termination of marriage. There are, however, tendencies

---

1 This is the case in many countries in Southern and Eastern Europe (community property regime) as well as in Germany, Greece and Switzerland (community of accrued gains). In the Nordic countries all property is subject to equal division (deferred community property) except for Norway where premarital assets, gifts and inheritance are exempted from division, cf. K Boele-Woelki, B Braat and I Curry-Sumner (eds), *European Family Law in Action. Volume IV – Property Relations between Spouses* (Mortsel, Belgium: Intersentia 2009).

towards excluding inheritance, gifts and premarital assets from division in English law,[2] as well as in the United States.[3] The common feature of assets not subject to division is that the other spouse is presumed not to have contributed to the acquisition. In other words, *contribution* appears to be the essence of the justification.[4] Naturally, other justifications for equal division might be advanced as well. However, along with rising divorce figures, remarriage and women's increasing participation in the labour force, the trend in legal policy is to replace the broader terms of solidarity, community, partnership, need and so forth, with more explicit economic justifications, such as compensation for contributions made during marriage and for losses suffered. In cohabiting relationships, the parties' gains and losses are emphasised as well, as discussed below.

The rationale for the allocation of assets upon relationship breakdown is not without importance. It is significant in determining whether a certain division of property should be viewed as an entitlement or a charitable transfer and can thus determine the specific content of property regimes both in marriage and cohabiting relationships. In the following, I do not address potential differences between married and unmarried couples with regard to economic vulnerability and types of commitment.[5]

Example A: The American Law Institute

In 2002, the American Law Institute (ALI) proposed new principles of the law of family dissolution.[6] The Institute rejects any justification for equal division of assets that is linked to the spouses' contributions – financial or non-financial.[7] The ALI states that spouses often do not make equal financial contributions and maintains that the factual premise of an 'equal contribution' rationale does not become more plausible by redefining contribution to include contributions of domestic as well as market labour. The drafters reason as follows:[8]

> Much of the spousal earnings during marriage are consumed, and only the surplus remaining is available for division at divorce. For domestic labors to contribute to that surplus, they must not only enhance the financial capacity of the other spouse or the value of marital property but do so by an amount that exceeds the consumption attributable to the spouse performing those labors. For domestic labors to contribute equally to that surplus would require, further, that this excess enhancement equal the excess of the higher-earning spouse's income over that spouse's consumption. Neither data nor intuition support such inferences. (emphasis added)

---

2 *White v White* [2001] 1 AC 596. *Miller v Miller, McFarlane v McFarlane* [2006] UKHL 24.
3 American Law Institute, *Principles of the Law of Family Dissolution: Analysis and Recommendations* (Bender 2002) § 1, Topic 1, Overview of Chapter 4, at 22–3.
4 T Sverdrup, 'Maintenance as a separate issue – the relationship between maintenance and matrimonial property', in K Boele-Woelki (ed.) *Common Core and Better Law in European Family Law*, EFL Series, No. 10 (Mortsel, Belgium: Intersentia 2005) at 119–34.
5 In this field, there is a need for more research, see S Wong, 'Shared commitment, interdependency and property relations: a socio-legal project for cohabitation' (2012) 24/1 *Child and Family Law Quarterly* 60.
6 ALI (n 3).
7 Accordingly, the ALI maintains that it 'makes far more sense to ground an equal-division presumption on the spouses' contribution to the entire marital relationship, not just to the accumulation of financial assets'. One spouse may, for example, 'have contributed more than the other in emotional stability, optimism or social skills, and thereby enriched the marital life', cf. ALI (n 3) § 4.09 comment c, at 735.
8 ALI (n 3) § 4.09 comment c, at 735.

I disagree that neither 'data nor intuition' supports a result where the contributions are considered approximately equal. Let us suppose that the wife takes care of small children below compulsory school age and performs household chores. The husband is employed, earning 40,000 euros per year after taxes. Out of his income, he pays the family's total expenses including principal payments on a mortgage, which amount constitutes the 'surplus' subject to division on divorce. The husband would have had to reduce his working hours by one-half, and consequently halve his income, if he were to take responsibility for his half of the domestic work and childcare, as the children are below school age and therefore need round-the-clock care. Thus, the wife has made half of his earnings possible. Naturally, the total of this sum cannot be regarded as her yearly investments in the house. Part of this enabled income must also be deemed to have been spent to cover consumption expenses.

In our case, it is reasonable to assume that the wife has contributed towards paying *half* of the total consumption expenses and *half* of the total investment in the house. In other words, she has contributed on an equal footing to the surplus subject to division on divorce, as well as to the consumption expenses. The consumption attributable to the spouse performing domestic labour is thus taken into account. If the children are of compulsory school age and the wife still works full-time at home, she will normally enable less than half of his earnings. In modern marriages, however, women assume paid work after a brief period of time at home, and they normally contribute directly to property acquisitions, or indirectly by covering consumption expenses. Thus, in the great majority of marriages, spouses could be regarded as equal contributors to the surplus created during marriage.

What is the difference between this method of evaluation and ALI's method? The emphasised passage in the quote above indicates that the drafters take the value of domestic work as a basic premise and deduct consumption costs attributable to the housewife. The net result equals her contribution to the surplus. In such an account, domestic work is often deemed to be of lesser value than work outside the home – as long as it is valued on the basis of market value. The valuation method is however not mentioned by ALI, thus it seems to be taken for granted that market value should apply.

In ALI's reasoning, the spouses' efforts are regarded as autonomous entities. Before the drafters start their calculation, the spouses have already been assigned their respective work – domestic labour and income. This, however, does not conform to reality in intimate relationships. Services in the family are not rendered independently of one other, as they are in the market. In marriage and domestic cohabitation both partners have an initial responsibility to provide child care and financial support. Thus they constitute a working community with regard to their children, in the sense that if one of the parents does not perform his or her part of the child care for common children, the responsibility has to be assumed by the other party.

In my reasoning, a given amount of domestic work has to be done in the family – if one of the spouses (or cohabitants) performs less, the other must perform more. When a spouse covers more than her share of childcare, she has enabled her partner to earn more, and thus she has contributed to her own consumption. If this enabled income is invested or saved, she has contributed to the derived gain. This valuation method considers the separate efforts of two spouses as mutually dependent.

The fundamental thinking behind this line of reasoning is that if the spouses had performed equal shares of work inside the home, the husband would have had to reduce his working hours – and would have earned proportionately less. On the other hand, the homemaker would have had free time to take on a paid job and thus would have made a direct contribution to the acquisition or an indirect contribution in the form of covering more than her share of consumption expenses. It is worth noting that the spouses' work efforts may be equal at any given moment, yet inequality is generated over time because one work performance is consumed and the other is invested. Consequently, the homemaker does not need to perform extraordinarily much in order to contribute equally to the surplus – an effort at a normal level will suffice.[9] The idea is that the chosen division of labour shall not in itself entail that the homemaker acquires ownership of less than she would otherwise have had: where equal distribution of effort between the spouses both inside and outside the home would have given her a right of co-ownership; a skewed distribution should not lead to a different result.

A broad doctrine acknowledging domestic work as a form of indirect contribution within the framework of a remedial constructive trust, has been adopted in several common law jurisdictions, such as Canada,[10] Australia,[11] and New Zealand,[12] but not in England.[13] It is no surprise that the question of indirect contribution to the acquisition of property was raised in the 1960s and 1970s. Before occupational work became a realistic alternative for many married women, gender or 'the natural order of things' appeared to explain why the housewife could not invest directly in capital accumulation. The idea that a random or unjust benefit or enrichment arises where the right of ownership is determined by who happens to go out to work and who happens to be at home, appears more likely when work outside the home is a viable alternative for women. It is now more plausible to consider both the full-time and part-time homemaker as having enabled portions of the husband's income, and thus as having contributed indirectly to his acquisitions

In the example above, one could however argue that the husband would have earned just as much even if she had not performed 'his' share of the childcare duties; instead he would have paid for a nanny or placed the children in a childcare centre. Therefore the homemaker has not facilitated half of his earnings, but only freed a smaller amount of capital for the wage earner. The Law Commission for England and Wales argues along these lines as discussed in example B below.

Example B: The Law Commission for England and Wales

In 2007, the Law Commission of England and Wales proposed new provisions regulating the financial consequences of relationship breakdown among cohabitants.[14] According to this proposal, a qualifying contribution from one of the cohabitants could give rise to relief if the contribution had resulted in a retained benefit or an economic disadvantage. The Law Commission argues that it is unlikely that the non-owning party (the applicant) would be

---

9   T Sverdrup, 'Compensating gain and loss in marriage: a Scandinavian comment on the ALI principles', in RF Wilson (ed.), *Reconceiving the Family. Critique on the American Law Institute's Principles of the Law of Family Dissolution* (Cambridge: Cambridge University Press 2006) 472.
10 W Holland, 'Legal status of cohabitants in Canada' in JM Scherpe/N Yassari (eds) *Die Rechtsstellung nichtehelicher Lebensgemeinschaften* (Tübingen, Germany: Mohr Siebeck, 2005) 501; J Mee, *The Property Rights of Cohabitees* (Oxford: Hart 1999) 184.
11 Mee (n 10) at 235–38.
12 Ibid. 278.
13 SM Cretney, JM Masson and R Bailey-Harris, *Principles of Family Law* (7th edn, London: Sweet & Maxwell 2002) 112–23.
14 Law Commission for England and Wales, *Cohabitation: The Financial Consequences of Relationship Breakdown* Law Com No 307 (London: Law Commission 2007).

able to show that work done in the home had been a cause of a retained benefit in the other party's hands:

> It would theoretically be possible for an applicant to claim that his or her domestic contributions have conferred a retained benefit on the respondent in the form of savings or increased earning capacity. The applicant might, for example, contend that, by looking after the family, he or she had enabled the respondent to build up savings or to advance a career. However, such a contention would be very difficult to uphold because of the need to establish causation. *The applicant would have to prove what the respondent would have achieved had the applicant not made his or her contribution.* This would be extremely difficult as there are so many variables: for example, *the respondent could argue that he or she would have been able to deal with household tasks by engaging professional domestic help.* Accordingly, it would only be in exceptional circumstances that domestic contributions could be shown to have conferred a retained benefit, and we expect that they would more often give rise to claims of economic disadvantage. (emphasis added)[15]

In this quote, the Law Commission assumes that the domestic work should be evaluated by market price. The issue of whether this is an appropriate evaluation method is not addressed whatsoever. Thus, the Law Commission ignores the fact that the parents are in a shared living relationship.[16] If the father and mother in the above example had been two disassociated stakeholders in the market, the most obvious option would have been to find out what would most probably have happened in the alternative instance, without adding any further preconditions. The father has then gained what it would cost to buy equivalent services in the market. However, this case is about two parties who have joined forces to start a family: neither party is a replaceable stakeholder.

The purpose of the causal reasoning is to trace the economic significance of domestic labour for the acquisition of assets, and in this calculation, the care of parents and others is not fully replaceable. A central characteristic of the market is lacking in the shared living relationship. In marriages and domestic cohabitation, services are not mutually conditioned upon a counter-service during the relationship. The transition of values in the shared living relationship follows a different logic to that of the market. When one service is not conditioned by a counter-service, it has, per definition, no market price. In my view, when the homemaker's contributions are under evaluation, the goggles of the market ought to be taken off.

In the market, the exchange of services is established by the contract. In the shared living relationship, the closest parallel would be the agreed division of labour between the parties. In the absence of any evidence to the contrary, we must assume that the parties agreed upon the division of labour they have actually practised. When one is home with small children (whether part-time or full-time) while the other is the full-time breadwinner, the parties have chosen a division of labour where the children are taken care of by the parents, as opposed to a third party. The fact that the children are taken care of by the parents, should lie there as a constant factor in the causal reasoning, that is, as a premise in the

---

15 Ibid. para 4.48.
16 T Sverdrup, 'An ill-fitting garment: Why the logic of private law falls short between cohabitants', in B Verschraegen (ed.) *Family Finances* (Vienna: Jan Sramek Verlag 2009) 360.

assessment of how great a retained benefit her domestic contributions have conferred on the breadwinner.

Marriage and unmarried cohabitation consist of two equal parties, where neither is employed by the other; therefore it seems foreign to measure the domestic work at the value of the amount it would cost to purchase the equivalent services in the market. From a legal standpoint, it is a random matter who undertakes the unprofitable part of the double task (domestic and outside work), random in the sense that the parties normally do not choose their task by considering who will be the owner of the items acquired during the relationship. The choice is usually based on other factors like wage level, gender roles, commitment, interests, etc. The person who undertakes the domestic work should therefore not *only for that reason* be the owner of less than the other party. In order to achieve this, the parents' choice of childcare mode is taken as a given basis. Thus, when the Law Commission states: 'The applicant would have to prove what the respondent would have achieved had the applicant not made his or her contribution,'[17] the precondition should be that the parents are responsible for the childcare in the hypothetical comparative case. The reason is not that one kind of childcare is necessarily better than another.

There are divergent opinions on this matter in society, and the legal system should – also for this reason – take the parents' choice of childcare as a given point of departure. Thus, the amount of contact between children and their parents should be kept constant in the comparative situation.[18] Furthermore, it must be presupposed that the person working outside the home should have just as much *spare time* in the hypothetical situation where work outside and inside the home is divided equally. If leisure is kept constant, one sees that the respondent (father) would have had to reduce his working hours if the mother had not performed some of his half share of the childcare. From this point of view, she has enabled a portion of his earnings, and if these additional earnings result in savings or greater pension benefits or earning capacity, there is a causal connection *sine qua non* between the domestic work and the retained benefit.

A different result could occur with household chores as such work can be substituted more easily by market services without significantly changing the character of the service. The housewife's labour could therefore be regarded as a freeing of capital for the respondent, which in most cases would entail a lower retained benefit. However, if most of the household chores were to be substituted over a longer period of time, the distinctive character of that particular relationship would change substantially, and freeing of capital is not an obvious alternative.[19]

The conclusion so far is that in the great majority of marriages, a spouse's indirect contribution to the assets acquired during marriage equals the real contribution of the direct contributor. By taking more than her or his share of domestic work and/or consumption expenses, one spouse has enabled part of the other's income and is therefore entitled to

---

17 Law Commission (n 14) para 4.48.
18 This is also the position of the Norwegian Supreme Court when establishing co-ownership on the basis of indirect contributions in the form of childcare. The Court speaks of the freeing of time and not of the freeing of capital when children are concerned, *Norwegian Supreme Court Reports* 1975 at 220, 1976 at 694, 1980 at 1403 and Rt. 1983 at 1146.
19 The Norwegian Supreme Court has regarded household chores in both when establishing co-ownership, cf. *Norwegian Supreme Court Reports* 1978 at 1352 (both time and capital) and 1979 at 1463 (time).

an equal share of the surplus created during marriage. According to this reasoning, losses sustained and contributions made during marriage are two sides of the same coin. The wife's childcare and home-making has enabled the husband to pursue his own career and earn more money. The 'coin' is the childcare and household work, which constitutes on one side an indirect contribution to the breadwinner's acquisitions and on the other side, an obstacle for the homemaker to seek paid work which results in a loss of income. The parties are not replaceable market actors. In my view, the Law Commission falls back on rationales that are not germane to the specific communal relationships in which cohabitants live.[20]

Big money cases

Even though loss and gain are two sides of the same coin, they are not always equal. There may be differences in the quantification, depending on whether one sees things from the gain side or the loss side. However, apart from a small percentage of high-income cases, these two methods of calculation lead more or less to the same result. In the hypothetical assessment, one must take it as established that the full-time or part-time homemaker could have had a more lucrative career if the roles were reversed from the beginning. Therefore, what she has lost and he has gained usually amounts more or less to the same.

In cases where one of the spouses has an extraordinarily high income and has built up a considerable fortune during marriage, it could be argued that these assets are primarily related to the higher-earning spouse's personal abilities, and that such assets should not be divided equally. On the other hand, it may be claimed that the homemaker has freed time for the person to earn high as well as low pay and, consequently, all assets acquired during marriage should be credited to both spouses equally. In these cases, the spouses have chosen a more efficient division of labour, and the question of whom this efficiency gain should be ascribed to cannot be answered on the basis of simple causal considerations. It is a matter of legal-political choice. However, if one sees it from the loss side, it could be argued that the (part-time) homemaker has not lost as much as the other spouse has gained, and that her compensation in any case should be limited to her loss. In my opinion, there may be good grounds to suggest an exception from equal division in cases in which one of the spouses builds up substantial assets during marriage. In such cases, it is unlikely that the homemaker would have earned the same amount of money had the roles been reversed. Neither need nor merit justifies an equal division of property in big money cases. This rationale differs from a broader 'partnership model' or 'joint family venture' where considerable fortunes could be divided evenly between the homemaker and the breadwinner.[21]

---

20 Another example: The Law Commission claims that buying groceries does not result in a retained benefit, where the respondent was able to pay the mortgage without that contribution being made, cf. Law Commission (n 14) para 4.45. Does this mean that coverage of consumer expenses does not constitute an indirect contribution to the acquisition of the house in cases where the respondent had inherited money that he, hypothetically, could have used to pay off the mortgage? If so, a financial loss is inherent in the comparative situation. A rationale of this type, in my opinion, is untenable. The purpose is not to find out what would most probably have happened in the alternative instance, but to trace the economic significance of the coverage of the household expenditure for the acquisition. In order to establish a causal connection sine qua non in these cases, the respondent's total financial assets must be kept constant in the comparative, hypothetical situation.
21 See for example the recent judgment in a cohabitation relationship from The Supreme Court of Canada, *Kerr v Baranow* [2011] SCC 10 [2011] 1 SCR 269, paras 137–42, paras 155–61.

Consumption: coverage of the family's expenses

An indirect contribution can also be in the form of covering the family's total consumption expenses. But the share of consumption expenses attributable to each spouse or cohabitant is open to debate. In the following, it is taken as a premise, that the spouses' factual amount of consumption is more or less the same. Two principles could guide the debiting of consumption expenses: either one can deduct *half* of the consumption expenses, or one can deduct expenses according to *ability*, that is, in proportion to the size of each of the spouses' respective work efforts.[22] The two methods lead to the same result if the spouses' total work efforts (paid and unpaid work) are equal.[23] But let us take an example where the spouses (or cohabitants) share domestic work equally and the one's income is markedly higher than the other's. In such cases, one has to choose between the two methods of calculating the indirect contribution.

In my view, the calculation according to ability better tracks the economic relationship between the spouses during marriage. The spouses must eat the same food, live in the same house, go on the same holidays, be responsible for their children's expenses, and so forth. In other words, they form a consumption unit and the one with the higher income will pull the total consumption expenses upward. Because they are forced to consume more or less the same, it seems unreasonable if half of the family's total consumption expenses are to be debited against the spouse who has the lower income. If the yearly investments are smaller than the yearly net income difference, she has not contributed to the acquisitions if she is debited half the expenses.

In 2011, the Norwegian Supreme Court rejected the ability principle in cohabiting relationships and held that a cohabitant had to pay more than half of the family's consumption expenses in order to have contributed to the surplus acquired during the relationship.[24] As the financial position of one cohabitant can hardly avoid the influence of the other's and this adaptation is the essence of living together in a unity, this way of reasoning is not in accordance with the logic of intimate relationships.

The court does not provide any explanation for its decision, apart from stating that no legal maintenance obligations exist between cohabitants. The actual, 'positive' explanation is apparently so obvious that it need not be said explicitly: The cohabitants have in fact consumed half the material goods each, and therefore they should 'pay' for just as much – in other words, the contractual principle that service should equal counter-service.

Division of assets acquired during marriage

As mentioned in the second section of the chapter above, only the assets acquired during marriage are subject to equal division in many Western countries. At first glance, this might

---

22 T Sverdrup, *Stiftelse av sameie i ekteskap og ugift samliv* (Co-ownership in Marriage and in Unmarried Cohabitation) (Universitetsforlaget 1997) 394–8 and 422–4.
23 The practices among cohabitants vary; some couples cover expenditure proportionally to overcome income disparities, cf. C Burgoyne and S Sonnenberg, 'Financial practices in cohabiting heterosexual couples', in J Miles and R Probert (eds) *Sharing Lives, Dividing Assets. An Inter-Disciplinary Study* (Oxford: Hart 2009) at 97–8.
24 Rt. 2011 at 1168. However, the Supreme Court seems to have excluded housing expenses (interest on the mortgage, maintenance, etc.) from the equal sharing of expenses, so in fact she was not debited half of the family's consumption expenses. Moreover, the Supreme Court kept the question open whether the ability principle would be applied in marriage.

seem to be a reasonable solution because premarital assets, gifts and inheritance are not part of the regular communion between spouses, and the other spouse is presumed not to have contributed to these acquisitions. However, the question is how far the interdependence between spouses actually goes. A fundamental economic adaptation between the parties lies solely in the fact that most spouses must be content with one dwelling; it is in the nature of family life that both parties live in a single family home. If only one of them owned the house before they started to cohabit, in most cases the other will not make future investments (savings) in a house. If one of the spouses brings a house into the relationship, the basic investments are already available to the family.

In this situation, it is natural for the spouses to apply most of their disposable income to current expenses during the union. The party without property will benefit from the other party's housing investment while they live together, but will sustain considerable losses if nothing is saved when the spouses part company after many years. In order to preclude the non-owning party's coming out of a dissolved union empty-handed, the said party must set aside part of his or her income during the relationship in the event of a possible breach. But how many people would do such a thing in practice? Court cases indicate that non-owning spouses do not make these provisions. Spouses (and cohabitants) live in a shared living relationship, one of the consequences of which is that they form a joint consumption unit. They adjust the level of consumption to each other and to the fact that basic investments such as a family home are already available. Owing to the fact that women generally have less income and property than men and tend to marry men who are older than themselves, this is primarily a problem for women.

In a market relationship, it would be unthinkable to claim compensation on the ground that one had been living in the owner's home, and therefore had been impeded from investing in a house oneself. In intimate relationships, however, the logic is quite different, among others, due to the fact that the parties constitute a joint consumption and investment unit as discussed above. As long as most couples must be content with one dwelling, the non-owning spouse should at least share in the price rise (and fall) in the real estate market, which is the case in Germany.[25] Unfortunately, this is not the case in the Franco-German optional matrimonial property regime; for instance, Article 9 (2) provides no distinctions between the family home and other items in that respect. In my opinion, the family home holds a unique position and cannot be compared with any other item of property. If the non-owning party cannot share in the rise in the housing market, he or she will be 'trapped', and be disproportionately equipped to acquire a new dwelling on the dissolution of marriage (and conversely, in the event of price fall). The appreciation of the family home should therefore be divided equally, whether or not the appreciation is related to any effort of the spouses.

Conclusion

In the preceding examples, the ALI, the Law Commission of England and Wales and the Supreme Court of Norway measure the parties' performances at market value, and this method of valuation is not questioned. In the second section (Examples A and B), domestic

---

25 However, this principle is not limited to the family home. Appreciation due to normal inflation according to the consumer price index, could be exempted from division, cf. N Dentloff, *Familienrecht* (Munich: Verlag C.H. Beck, 2012) 134 (§ 5 Rn109).

work is considered in the light of what it would cost to purchase an equivalent service in the market and in the third section, it is taken for granted that the cohabitant with the lowest income should cover her own consumption valued at the market price when assessing her indirect contribution. In all four examples, the legal reasoning seems to be based on a notion that spouses and cohabitants exchange services and counter-services as actors in a market. However, this is not true, as services are normally not conditioned upon a counter-service in couple relationships.

This issue is not problematised, neither by the legislators or the court. Part of the reason for this may be that private law thinking and terminology are based on corrective justice rather than distributive justice.[26] Reciprocity is the fundamental way of thinking in private law; not only contract law but also torts and unjust enrichment is based on reciprocation, i.e. the parties' performances are compared with an aim to achieve the highest possible correlation between performance and return – all measured at market value. The idea of corrective justice is marked by the fact that one transfer is the *reason* (or part of the reason) for the other transfer. This construction of equality highlights the interaction between the two parties, but overlooks the fact that they also form a collective unit. The mindset and usage of private law terminology may thus conceal reality. In a sense, the legal profession must view the couple relationships through the lenses of the market.

An interrelationship exists between the parties' services in marriages and domestic cohabitation, but it is not of a contractual nature but rather grounded in actual economic mechanisms. Both partners have an initial responsibility both to provide child care and financial support. If one undertakes either of these efforts, it proportionately affects the amount of effort the other has to undertake. The same applies to consumption, as the family's consumption level is based on both partners' level of income and they have to eat the same food and go on the same vacations. The spouses' (or cohabitants) investments are also interdependent; if one has invested in a home before the relationship starts, it is not necessary for the other to invest in housing. In other words, together, spouses and cohabitants form a work unit as well as a consumption and investment unit, and for that reason, the financial position of one party can hardly avoid being influenced by the other's. On the economic level, this adaptation is the essence of living together in a unit – it is the 'logic of marriage and cohabitation'. This phenomenon has no parallel in market relationships where service and counter-service (e.g. goods and money) normally have originated independently of each other. In this respect, the private law model based on corrective justice is structured in a way that is not suitable for couple relationships. The preceding examples indicate that the partners that are harmed the most by this legal reasoning are those who assume responsibility for child care and have the lowest income, i.e. primarily women.

Similarly, the legal reasoning concerning the conclusion of agreements seems to lose much of its validity when service and counter-service are not mutually conditioned, and no longer originate independently of each other. For example, the question as to whether the husband should understand that the wife would not have contributed if she had not attained co-ownership is difficult to answer in relationships where the parties' performances are not

---

26 For a distinction between these Aristotelian conceptions of justice, see for example EJ Weinrib, *The Idea of Private Law* (Cambridge, MA: Harvard University Press 1995) 56–114.

mutually conditioned.[27] Similarly, 'divining the parties' true intentions'[28] in English trust law, is often futile.[29] The search for the parties' intentions is like chasing a ghost.

As services are not mutually conditioned upon a counter-service during the relationship, concepts like 'equity', 'gift' and 'loan' lose some of their meaning. Because the parties' perceptions of ownership and entitlement are diffuse, there are no distinct demarcation lines between these legal categories during the relationship. Let us suppose that the female cohabitant entrusts an amount of inheritance money to the disposal of her male cohabitant, thus enabling him, by pooling the inheritance with his own funds, to purchase a boat. Often, it would be unnatural for her to state explicitly that her contribution was not meant as a gift or a loan, and to insist on a contract formalising co-ownership. An explicit agreement is not always in harmony with the basic rule of confidence that prevails both in marriage and cohabitation. In a family, it is often unacceptable or unnatural for one of the parties to formulate reciprocity explicitly and, for example, to say 'I will not look after the children unless I become co-owner of the house' or 'I will not be responsible for the debt unless I become co-owner of the car'. As mentioned above, in a number of cases, a contribution would lose its value if it were conditioned upon a counter-contribution. Just as importantly, even in situations where explicit reciprocity is acceptable and natural, the conditions are not usually clear. If asked whether the amount was intended as a gift or a loan, the female cohabitant in the example above could respond that this depends on the circumstances, and on what services are exchanged between the parties in the future.[30] If her partner paid for the children's education with his inheritance money, she would, for example, consider it a gift. The reluctance to freeze one item in such a delicate and fluid system of balance is understandable. Rational behaviour is often to keep such questions open. The concepts of private law were primarily developed with a view to market relationships, and fall short when applied to cohabitants and spouses.

Bibliography

American Law Institute, *Principles of the Law of Family Dissolution: Analysis and Recommendations* (Bender, Philadelphia, PA 2002).

Boele-Woelki K, Braat B and Curry-Sumner I (eds.), *European Family Law in Action. Volume IV – Property Relations between Spouses* (Intersentia, Cambridge 2009).

Burgoyne C and Sonnenberg S, 'Financial practices in cohabiting heterosexual couples', in J Miles and R Probert (eds) *Sharing Lives, Dividing Assets. An Inter-Disciplinary Study* (Hart Publishing, Oxford 2009) 97–8.

---

27 Cf. T Sverdrup, 'Nicht gekleidet, nicht nackend: Über das vertragsrechtliche Bewusstsein in Ehe und nichtehelicher Lebensgemeinschaft' in IA Büchler & M Müller-Chen (eds), *Private Law: National – Global – Comparative: Festschrift für Ingeborg Schwenzer zum 60. Geburtstag.* (Bern, Switzerland: Stämpfli Verlag 2011) 1675–97.

28 *Stack v Dowden* [2007] UKHL 17 [69] (Baroness Hale). Compare the statement by the Canadian Justice Cromwell: 'the notion of common intention may be highly artificial, particularly in domestic cases', *Kerr v Baranow*, 2011 SCC 10 [2011] 1 SCR 269, at para 26.

29 These difficulties are well illustrated in G Douglas, J Pearce and H Woodward, 'Money, property, cohabitation and separation', in J Miles and R Probert (n 23) 139, cf. Burgoyne and Sonnenberg (n 23) 104–5.

30 Compare the study where C Burgoyne and S Sonnenberg demonstrate that the cohabitant's perception of ownership 'concerning the treatment of money and property are not only difficult to ascertain at any particular point in time, they are also likely to change in the course of a relationship': see Burgoyne and Sonnenberg (n 23) 89, at 105.

Cretney SM, Masson JM and Bailey-Harris R, *Principles of Family Law* (7th edn, Sweet & Maxwell, London 2002).

Dentloff N, *Familienrecht* (Verlag C.H. Beck, Munich 2012).

Douglas G, Pearce J and Woodward H, 'Money, property, cohabitation and separation', in J Miles and R Probert (eds), *Sharing Lives, Dividing Assets. An Inter-Disciplinary Study* (Hart Publishing, Oxford 2009) Chapter 7.

Holland W, 'Legal status of cohabitants in Canada' in JM Scherpe/N Yassari (eds) *Die Rechtsstellung nichtehelicher Lebensgemeinschaften* (Mohr Siebeck, Tübingen 2005) 501.

Law Commission for England and Wales, Cohabitation: The Financial Consequences of Relationship Breakdown Law Com No 307 (Law Commission, London 2007).

Mee J, *The Property Rights of Cohabitees* (Hart Publishing, Oxford 1999).

Sverdrup T, *Stiftelse av sameie i ekteskap og ugift samliv* (*Co-ownership in Marriage and in Unmarried Cohabitation*) (Universitetsforlaget, Oslo 1997).

Sverdrup T, 'Maintenance as a separate issue – the relationship between maintenance and matrimonial property', in K Boele-Woelki (ed.), *Common Core and Better Law in European Family Law*, EFL Series, No. 10 (Intersentia, Cambridge 2005) 119–34.

Sverdrup T, 'Compensating gain and loss in marriage: a Scandinavian Comment on the ALI principles', in RF Wilson (ed.), *Reconceiving the Family. Critique on the American Law Institute's Principles of the Law of Family Dissolution* (Cambridge University Press, Cambridge 2006) part 9, 472.

Sverdrup T, 'An ill-fitting garment: why the logic of private law falls short between cohabitants', in B Verschraegen (ed.) *Family Finances* (Jan Sramek Verlag 2009) 355–68.

Sverdrup T, 'Nicht gekleidet, nicht nackend: über das vertragsrechtliche Bewusstsein in Ehe und nichtehelicher Lebensgemeinschaft' in IA Büchler and M Müller-Chen (eds), *Private Law: National – Global – Comparative: Festschrift für Ingeborg Schwenzer zum 60. Geburtstag.* (Stämpfli Verlag, Bern, Switzerland 2011) 1675–697.

Weinrib EJ, *The Idea of Private Law* (Harvard University Press, Cambridge, MA 1995).

Wong S, 'Shared commitment, interdependency and property relations: a socio-legal project for cohabitation' (2012) 24/1 *Child and Family Law Quarterly* 60–76.

7 Marriage and the data on same-sex couples

Robert Leckey

Introduction

This chapter's point of departure is the relative neglect of empirical research on same-sex couples in debates about their rightful legal treatment. Formal equality holds that the way to treat gay men and lesbians with dignity and equal respect is to give them access to marriage (or something almost identical under a different label). Calls for formally equal treatment for gay and lesbian couples have met with success. Meanwhile, on other fronts, claims for substantive equality – for respectfully different treatment based on past subordination or other relevant features – are meeting with failure.[1] The grant of formal equality to gay men and lesbians generates critique from conservative quarters and from feminist, queer, or other left viewpoints. Remarkably little scholarship, however, has studied how well the financial frameworks governing marriage and divorce might serve the catchment group of same-sex couples to whom they are henceforth available. Such inattention to evidence might not bother philosophers of marriage or legal scholars content to reason from the constitutional protection of abstract values or rights such as equality. But from a socio-legal perspective, it merits attention.

The question of fit should not be taken for granted. An obvious reason is that marriage traditionally bore women's economic dependency on men 'embedded deep within'.[2] Accordingly, reforms implementing gender neutrality may not have extirpated all gendered assumptions. Reflection on the ordering of same-sex couples' unwinding is increasingly important in jurisdictions such as the United Kingdom and Canada where, as time passes, the number of same-sex dissolutions is increasing. What regulatory approach would emerge from engagement with the empirical research on same-sex couples?

This chapter's aims are analytical and methodological: it raises the difficulties that undertaking such engagement might engender. Its first part calls for disaggregating the legal content of marriage for the purposes of analysis. By reference to the findings of social scientists, the second part sets out the evidentiary basis for challenging the assumption that access to marriage on the existing terms best remedies same-sex couples' long-time legal neglect. The third part flags crucial methodological difficulties with the enterprise of looking to research in order to assess the fitness of existing marriage law for same-sex couples. Pointing to the limits of social science research in the legal field, the fourth part draws out

---

1 RC Hunter (ed.), *Rethinking Equality Projects in Law: Feminist Challenges* (Oxford: Hart 2008).
2 A Barlow, 'Property and couple relationships: what does community of property have to offer English law?' in A Bottomley and S Wong (eds), *Changing Contours of Domestic Life, Family and Law: Caring and Sharing* (Oxford: Hart 2009) 32.

the role of justice claims in marriage law. It also highlights the differing identity politics associated with divorce for different-sex couples and the push for same-sex marriage. Overall the chapter highlights important considerations relevant not only to the question of same-sex couples, but also to that of cohabitation and to other boundary troubles raised by law's regulation of intimate life. It also speaks to the bluntness of general regulatory schemes, such as marriage, for same-sex or different-sex partners. Indeed, it may be understood less as critiquing the legal approach to same-sex relations than as aiming to open a space for asking questions about marriage generally.

Unbundling marriage law

The prevailing treatment of marriage takes it as a unitary contract and institution, as forest more than trees. Consequently, two important contrasts often pass unnoticed. One concerns the identity of the relevant actor or, in legal language, the debtor of the obligation correlative to a creditor's right. Much advocacy for formal recognition of same-sex couples has focused on the state benefits conferred on married, different-sex couples. As has been observed, the focus on benefits neglects the ways in which marriage operates as a state-imposed disciplining of sexuality.[3] Scholars have also of course referred to marriage's effects as between the spouses. It has been noted that 'the rights of marriage are not always "of the couple" but rather, often, lie *against* one spouse.'[4] But the distinction is often not tracked rigorously. For present purposes, the distinction lies between rules obligating third parties and ones reciprocally obligating the spouses. 'Third parties' in this sense includes governments and entities such as employers and insurance companies. Contrasting third parties with the spouses avoids the public/private dichotomy, which feminist and other critical scholars have challenged persuasively, for example on account of the state's role in defining and enforcing so-called private obligations.

The other contrast is temporal. Some rules operate only during the functioning of a formalised union such as marriage, civil union, or civil partnership. Others operate only on its breakdown. Ellickson contrasts the 'midgame' rules of a relationship with its 'endgame' rules (although the 'household relationships' of interest to him differ from the family and marital relationships relevant to this chapter).[5] Still other obligations, such as the spouses' duty to maintain one another, may operate while the relationship flourishes, but they typically require enforcement only once it has withered.

Juxtaposing the two contrasts brings into view four cells, which are filled for present purposes with content typical of Anglo-American family law.

It is critical to this chapter's exploration that the duties occupying those cells need not operate monolithically. That is, the duties in one or more of the cells might attach to a couple without triggering the duties in all four. To be sure, the duties of third parties and

---

3 M Murray, 'Marriage as punishment' (2012) 112 *Columbia Law Review* 1.
4 JE Halley, 'Recognition, rights, regulation, normalization: rhetorics of justification in the same-sex marriage debate' in R Wintemute and M Andenæs (eds), *Legal Recognition of Same-Sex Partnerships: A Study of National, European and International Law* (Oxford: Hart 2001) 109; on marriage as 'its own little social security system', see B Hale, 'Equality and autonomy in family law' (2011) 33 *Journal of Social Welfare and Family Law* 3, 4.
5 RC Ellickson, *The Household: Informal Order around the Hearth* (Princeton, NJ: Princeton University Press 2010) 92.

Table 7.1 Obligations or property rules entailed by marriage

Debtor (relevant actor)	Timing	
	During the relationship	On relationship end or afterwards
Third parties (governments, public bodies, employers, etc.)	Pensions; health care; insurance; employment benefits; welfare; restrictions on lender's security taken in the family home without consent of borrower's spouse.	Landlord's duty to transfer lease to non-lessee spouse.
Spouses one to another	Duty of maintenance; constraints on alienation without other's consent of family home; bar on unilateral gifting of acquest property; need to compensate for dissipation of family assets.	Duty of maintenance; sharing of gains in family property, whichever spouse held title; transfer of lease or use of family residence to other spouse.

of the spouses may be connected. State recognition for one purpose might be justified by reference to the spouses' having assumed reciprocal responsibility in relation to one another, although some observers would decry such justification as neoliberal and privatising. But whatever the politics, such connections have obvious limits. Unbundling occurs where spouses are permitted to modify their duties vis-à-vis one another by prenuptial agreement while leaving unaltered the duties of third parties towards the couple.[6] Thus conclusion of a prenuptial agreement altering the property rules applicable to spouses has no impact on the capacity for one to sponsor the other for immigration. Nor does it affect the entitlement to survivor's benefits under a public pension. Further evidence that the status of marriage is compatible with variation in the spouses' economic relations arises from the choice among two or more matrimonial regimes in civil-law jurisdictions.[7] The piecemeal treatment accorded by some jurisdictions to unmarried cohabitants – for example, recognised by third parties for many purposes, while owing one another nothing under family law – makes another reminder that no necessary unity binds the elements which register conjugality in law.

This sharpened analytical framework could prove useful for other matters, such as the cohabitation question.[8] Here it sets the groundwork for a brief review of the social science on same-sex couples and their households.

---

6 e.g. *Granatino v Radmacher* [2010] UKSC 42 [2011] 1 AC 534; *Hartshorne v Hartshorne* 2004 SCC 22 [2004] 1 SCR 550; Law Commission, *Marital Property Agreements*, Law Com CP198 (London: TSO, 2011); JM Scherpe (ed.), *Marital Agreements and Private Autonomy in Comparative Perspective* (Oxford: Hart 2012); A Sanders, 'Nuptial agreements, comparative law and the notion of contract' in A Popovici, L Smith and R Tremblay (eds), *Les intraduisibles en droit civil* (Montreal, QC: Thémis 2014).
7 J Pineau and M Pratte, *La famille* (Montreal, QC: Thémis 2006) 186, para 140; P Malaurie and L Aynès, *Les régimes matrimoniaux*, 3rd edn (Paris: Defrénois 2010) 75.
8 e.g. R Probert, 'Cohabitation: current legal solutions' (2009) 62 Current legal problems 316; on the difficulties of reform, see J Miles, F Wasoff and E Mordaunt, 'Reforming family law – the case of cohabitation: "things may not work out as you expect"' (2012) 34 *Journal of Social Welfare and Family Law* 167.

Distinctive traits of same-sex couples

It has been posited that the United Kingdom's Civil Partnership Act 2004 might rely on 'models of heterosexual behaviour (such as money sharing and mutual financial responsibility) that may not adequately reflect the lived experiences' of lesbian and gay couples.[9] One may say the same thing of the Marriage (Same Sex Couples) Act 2013. While varying findings and interpretations abound, social science research challenges the diktat of formal equality in which there is no difference between same-sex and different-sex couples potentially relevant to the regulation of their economic relations.

Shortly after the entry into force of Vermont's civil union, Balsam *et al.* studied three classes of couples: different-sex married couples and same-sex couples having and not having undertaken a civil union. The most noticeable differences emerged between same-sex couples as a group and heterosexual married couples. Whether in a civil union or not, same-sex couples showed a lesser likelihood of having children and a greater likelihood of sharing house work and finances.[10] Other researchers report that same-sex couples expect less financial entwinement than do different-sex couples. Most of Burns, Burgoyne, and Clarke's respondents would 'help a partner out' in the event of job loss or inability to work, but saw such help as ad hoc 'assistance' rather than as the obligational sharing of losses accruing to an integrated economic unit.[11]

Much research on same-sex domesticity points to a strong egalitarian ideal for division of labour, a reluctance for one spouse to be dependent on the other, and an emphasis on negotiation.[12] It is thought that bargaining power may be more evenly distributed within same-sex than different-sex couples, on account of their common gender and more closely matched preferences.[13] Beyond that ideal, research indicates that, while different-sex couples continue to divide tasks along traditional gendered lines, lesbian and gay male couples are indeed more egalitarian in division of housework and the respective allocations of time between home and labour market.[14] Same-sex couples may be likelier than different-sex

---

9 M Burns, C Burgoyne and V Clarke, 'Financial affairs? Money management in same-sex relationships' (2008) 37 *Journal of Socio-Economics* 481, 482.
10 KF Balsam, TP Beauchaine, ED Rothburn and S Solomon, 'Three-year follow-up of same-sex couples who had civil unions in Vermont, same-sex couples not in civil unions, and heterosexual married couples' (2008) 44 *Developmental Psychology* 102, 103.
11 Burns, Burgoyne and Clarke (n 9) 497.
12 LA Kurdek, 'The allocation of household labor by partners in gay and lesbian couples' (2007) 28 *Journal of Family Issues* 132; A Esmail, '"Negotiating fairness": a study on how lesbian family members evaluate, construct, and maintain "fairness" with the division of household labor' (2010) 57 *Journal of Homosexuality* 591; A Perlesz *et al.*, 'Organising work and home in same-sex parented families: findings from the work love play study' (2010) 31 *Australian & New Zealand Journal of Family Therapy* 374; D Julien and É Chartrand, 'La psychologie familiale des gais et des lesbiennes: perspective de la tradition scientifique nord-américaine' (1997) 29 *Sociologie et sociétés* 71.
13 M Klawitter, 'The effects of sexual orientation and marital status on how couples hold their money' (2008) 6 *Review of Economics of the Household* 423, 434.
14 e.g. Burns, Burgoyne and Clarke (n 9) 484; SE Solomon, ED Rothblum and KF Balsam, 'Money, housework, sex, and conflict: same-sex couples in civil unions, those not in civil unions, and heterosexual married siblings' (2005) 52 *Sex Roles* 561, 562; Kurdek (n 12); AE Goldberg, 'Doing and undoing gender: the meaning and division of housework in same-sex couples' (2013) 5 *Journal of Family Theory & Review* 85, 87; L Ross, 'Perinatal mental health in lesbian mothers: a review of potential risk and protective factors' (2005) 41 *Women and Health* 113, 122; L Giddings, JM Nunnely, A Schneebaum and J Zietz, 'Birth cohort and the specialization gap between same-sex and different-sex couples' (2014) 51 *Demography* 509, 530.

couples to keep their finances separate,[15] although younger heterosexual practices increasingly follow this practice.[16]

Other research, however, complicates these narratives. By contrast with the studies surveyed previously, these complicating strands of research call to mind the caution that sociological narratives regarding gay men and lesbians may be '(often unwittingly) driven by an overly affirmative agenda that often goes hand in hand with particular liberationist or emancipatory . . . agendas'.[17] Giddings reports that lesbian couples exhibit divisions of labour ranging from the purposefully egalitarian to distributions mirroring the most unequal heterosexual stereotypes.[18] The 'gender-empty' approach which views lesbian and gay domesticity as non-gendered and freely negotiated may be problematic.[19] Carrington reports a disjuncture between the 'public portrayals and presentations of egalitarianism' on the part of gay and lesbian families and their prevailing household realities.[20] Contrary to the accounts of negotiation and choice in which arise absent gender differences, partners in same-sex relationships who specialise in domestic labour may do so not out of inclination or choice, but on account of their paid work relative to that of other family members.[21] The partners' respective earning power, in turn, is affected by structural factors such as race and class.[22] Avowals of equality notwithstanding, on one assessment unequal incomes within a couple make it 'incredibly difficult to resist those patterns of dominance' that cohere around the role and status afforded the higher earner.[23]

The presence of children in a household likely intensifies the specialisation of labour addressed with such care by matrimonial law. What would follow then for same-sex couples?[24] Male couples with children are likelier than other parents to have a 'traditional' employment situation, with one partner out of the labour force.[25] Some studies indicate a distinct role for the biological mother vis-à-vis the social or step-mother, including greater

---

15 Burns, Burgoyne and Clarke (n 9) 484.
16 B Heaphy, 'Civil partnership and ordinary marriages' in N Barker and D Monk (eds), *From Civil Partnership to Same-Sex Marriage: Interdisciplinary Reflections* (Abingdon, UK: Routledge 2015) 128.
17 B Heaphy, 'The sociology of lesbian and gay reflexivity or reflexive sociology?' (2008) 13 *Sociological Research Online* para 3.4.
18 LA Giddings, 'Political economy and the construction of gender: the example of housework within same-sex households' (1998) 4 *Feminist Economics* 97, 97.
19 S Oerton, '"Queer housewives?" Some problems in theorizing the division of domestic labour in lesbian and gay households' (1997) 20 *Women's Studies International Forum* 421, 424.
20 C Carrington, *No Place Like Home: Relationships and Family Life among Lesbians and Gay Men* (Chicago, IL: University of Chicago Press 1999) 176.
21 Ibid. 193; on money and power, see B Heaphy, C Smart and A Einarsdottir, *Same Sex Marriages: New Generations, New Relationships* (New York: Palgrave Macmillan 2013) Ch. 5.
22 K Weston, *Render Me, Gender Me: Lesbians Talk Sex, Class, Color, Nation, Studmuffins* (New York: Columbia University Press 1996); S Taylor Sutphin, 'Social exchange theory and the division of household labor in same-sex couples' (2010) 46 *Marriage & Family Review* 191, 192.
23 Burns, Burgoyne and Clarke (n 9) 499.
24 This economic query is distinct from the argument, rightly rejected by Canadian courts, for denying same-sex couples the right to marry on the basis of marriage's supposedly intrinsic ties to child rearing *Hendricks v Québec (Procureur général)* [2002] RJQ 2506 [147] [149] (Sup Ct), varied *Ligue catholique pour les droits de l'homme c Hendricks* [2004] RJQ 851 (CA), *Halpern v Canada (Attorney General)* (2003) 65 OR (3d) 161 [94] (CA).
25 AH Prokos and J Reid Keene, 'Poverty among cohabiting gay and lesbian, and married and cohabiting heterosexual families' (2010) 31 *Journal of Family Issues* 934, 946.

responsibility running the household.[26] If one detects concern for child rearing in marriage law, it is germane that married same-sex couples are likelier than unmarried same-sex couples to be raising children. For example, the Canadian census of 2011 reported that over one-fifth (21.3 per cent) of female married couples had children versus 15.4 per cent of unmarried female couples; 5.9 per cent of married male couples had children versus 2.8 per cent of cohabiting male couples.[27] Still, if addressing the economic fallout of parenting is an aim of the regulation of marriage, the class of formalised same-sex couples is grossly over-inclusive.

It is true that some rules addressing the fallout of marriage incorporate flexibility by making provision for cases involving children. For example, the maintenance provisions in Canada's Divorce Act refer to 'the functions performed by each spouse during cohabitation' and the need to 'apportion between the spouses any financial consequences arising from the care of any child of the marriage'.[28] The presence of children has, however, no direct effect on the rules enacted by the legislatures of the provinces for dividing the value of property.[29] The application of property-sharing rules thus presumes some homogeneity regarding the economic partnerships subject to them.

There is a basis, then, for studying further whether the property rules made available to same-sex couples who formalise their union might not be a good fit. It would also be natural to wonder how well the rules associated with marriage accommodate the diversity of different-sex couples.[30] Still, the gay lobby for access to marriage as it stands justifies this chapter's focus on same-sex couples. In any case, as the next part of the chapter contends, significant obstacles bedevil any inquiry as to how 'ergonomically' the state shapes itself around the 'contours of [same-sex] relationships as they are lived'.[31]

Difficulties when looking to research

The sampling problems with the gay and lesbian population are well known. Studies repeatedly acknowledge that the samples accumulated by snowball sampling or other techniques result in groups that over-represent white, educated, and middle-class gay men and lesbians.[32] In addition, the recent availability of avenues for recognising same-sex relationships has implications for comparative research. It means that the groups of married

---

26 e.g. MR Moore, 'Gendered power relations among women: a study of household decision making in black, lesbian stepfamilies' (2008) 73 *American Sociological Review* 335; also MV Lee Badgett, *Money, Myths, and Change: The Economic Lives of Lesbians and Gay Men* (Chicago, IL: University of Chicago Press 2001) 159; but see Perlesz *et al.* (n 12) 386.

27 www.12.statcan.gc.ca/census-recensement/2011/dp-pd/tbt-tt/Rp-eng.cfm?LANG=E&APATH=3& DETAIL=0&DIM=0&FL=A&FREE=0&GC=0&GID=0&GK=0&GRP=1&PID=102659&PRID=0&PTYPE= 101955&S=0&SHOWALL=0&SUB=0&Temporal=2011&THEME=89&VID=0&VNAMEE=&VNAMEF=.

28 RSC 1985 c 3 (2nd Supp), ss 15.2(4)(b), 15.2(6)(b).

29 Compare Matrimonial Causes Act 1973 s 25(2)(f) ('contributions which each of the parties has made or is likely in the foreseeable future to make to the welfare of the family, including any contribution by looking after the home or caring for the family').

30 A Roy, 'Le régime juridique de l'union civile: entre symbolisme et anachronisme' in P-C Lafond and B Lefebvre (eds), *L'union civile: nouveaux modèles de conjugalité et de parentalité au 21e siècle: actes du colloque du Groupe de réflexion en droit privé* (Cowansville, QC, Yvon Blais 2003).

31 D Cooper, *Challenging Diversity: Rethinking Equality and the Value of Difference* (Cambridge: Cambridge University Press 2004) 185.

32 e.g. Balsam *et al.* (n 10) 114; E Schecter, AJ Tracy, KV Page and G Leuong, 'Shall we marry? Legal marriage as a commitment event in same-sex relationships' (2008) 54 *Journal of Homosexuality* 400, 419.

and unmarried same-sex couples may not be fairly comparable to the groups of married and unmarried different-sex couples, the latter having always had the option to marry.[33] Perhaps the preferences and conduct of same-sex couples are not independent, permanent variables to which law reform responds well or badly, but will change in response to that new law.[34]

Two further, generally unacknowledged difficulties emerge when the existing data are categorised according to the distinctions drawn above. These difficulties concern the uneven availability of empirical research. They point to methodological challenges with the aim of an empirically informed inquiry into the suitability of opening marriage to same-sex couples. Where marriage or civil partnership is made available to same-sex couples, the legal content of all four cells of Table 7.1, above, attaches to couples who so commit. As will be elaborated, although marriage law imposes duties on spouses and third parties, during the marriage and afterwards, the data on same-sex couples focus on recognition by third parties during the relationship. In short, the full obligational content of marriage has been made accessible, *en bloc*, to same-sex couples, but on the basis of data that speak more narrowly.

The first difficulty relates to the question of who bears the impact of marriage law: the spouses themselves or third parties? Recognition of the couple by third parties is observable as a prominent concern for researchers and those gay men and women who wish to marry. Indeed, much of the scholarly literature on same-sex couples focuses, for the purposes of third parties, on their moral worth and legibility as family. Affirmations are made that 'lesbian and gay people fit the bill'[35] as families in the economic sense and prove 'quite successful in creating stable long-term partnerships'.[36] Such emphasis on gay men's and lesbians' familial or conjugal commitment must be read in the light of the social and political hostility to same-sex relationships. It aims to combat the assumption that same-sex couples are uncommitted and unstable or qualitatively less committed than married different-sex couples.

Similarly, the focus of much activism has been the duties affecting governments and other third parties during the intact relationship. For example, the constitutional case in which the Supreme Court of Canada recognised sexual orientation as a suspect ground for governmental distinctions concerned the spousal allowance for intact couples under the Old Age Security Act.[37] In the UK, the regime of inheritance tax and the favourable treatment of spouses made the death of one partner another salient moment for governmental recognition. The concerns prominent in lobbying and debate did not include 'access to the courts for property redistribution purposes'.[38] Exceptionally, the Supreme Court of Canada has decided a discrimination claim concerning whether a maintenance obligation arose after two lesbians had ceased cohabiting.[39]

The reasons for marrying voiced by same-sex couples underscore the attention to third parties in the drive for marriage. While different-sex couples marry for many reasons, those

---

33 Balsam *et al.* (n 10) 114.
34 Klawitter (n 13) 441; on lesbian parenting practices, R Leckey, 'Law reform, lesbian parenting, and the reflective claim' (2011) 20 *Social & Legal Studies* 331, 338.
35 Badgett, *Money, Myths, and Change* (n 26) 164.
36 S Coltrane and M Adams, *Gender and Families* (2nd edn, Lanham, MD: Rowman & Littlefield 2008) 87.
37 *Egan v Canada* [1995] 2 SCR 513.
38 A Bottomley and S Wong, 'Shared households: a new paradigm for thinking about the reform of domestic property relations' in A Diduck and K O'Donovan (eds), *Feminist Perspectives on Family Law* (Routledge-Cavendish 2006) 44; N Barker, *Not the Marrying Kind: A Feminist Critique of Same-Sex Marriage* (New York: Palgrave Macmillan 2012) 99.
39 *M v H* [1999] 2 SCR 3.

identified by same-sex couples fasten on third parties. Schecter *et al.* provide rich narratives of couples' manifestations of commitment, including but not limited to same-sex marriage. Their respondents reported a political dimension: getting married in order to fight homophobia and claim greater acknowledgement of the couple by families and peers.[40] Authors of another study reported three main reasons for choosing a civil union: mutual love and commitment; a desire for legal status for their relationship; and to increase societal knowledge of gay and lesbian relationships.[41] Badgett's interviews included reasons directly regarding the couple.[42] But hers, too, flagged the wish to make a political statement about the equality of gay men and lesbians or a feminist statement related to the equality of men and women.[43]

Turning briefly from research to law, the reasoning at the core of the leading Canadian judgement on same-sex marriage as a constitutional right concerned the symbolism of marriage's restrictive definition. The government's failure to open marriage to same-sex couples telegraphed the message that same-sex couples were incapable 'of forming loving and lasting relationships' and that same-sex relationships were 'not worthy of the same respect and recognition as opposite-sex relationships'.[44] Such analysis focusses on the communicative significance of third parties' conduct towards gay and lesbian couples.[45]

The political thrust of gay or lesbian couples' decision to marry or contract a civil union may abate over time. Indeed, Auchmuty reports that, by contrast with older civil partners, the younger people she interviewed 'rarely spoke of making a public statement'.[46] But legislative drafters who purport to offer equality to gay men and lesbians should be aware of it. Such externally focused motives for marriage are not probative as to the degree of economic sharing intended by same-sex couples. Nor, more concretely, do they speak to the likelihood that legal title will result in a distribution of property that is unfair in the light of how such couples conducted their shared lives. By contrast with the focus in the literature on recognition by third parties, there is a notable shortage of data regarding the intraspousal obligations desired by same-sex couples. Specifically, much of the social practice demonstrates a wish to be recognised by third parties more than a will to be subjected to the regimes regulating spouses' economic relations during or after their union. To that end, data on spouses' household practices during the relationship are used to justify the attachment of obligations for third parties. But, it must be recalled, success at achieving recognition by third parties, combined with the unitary view of marriage, leads to potentially heavy effects for one spouse vis-à-vis the other after the relationship.

The second difficulty concerns the temporal focus, or the relationship stage, of social scientists' study of same-sex couples. Researchers have not studied the economic

---

40 Schecter *et al.* (n 32) 417; for further on recognition by family, see B Shipman and C Smart, '"It's made a huge difference": recognition rights and personal significance of civil partnership' (2007) 12 *Sociological Research Online* paras 4.8 to 4.10; see also R Auchmuty, 'Dissolution or disillusion: the unravelling of civil partnerships' in N Barker and D Monk (eds), *From Civil Partnerships to Same-Sex Marriage: Interdisciplinary Reflections* (Routledge 2015) 203.
41 Solomon, Rothblum and Balsam (above n 14); compare Heaphy, 'Civil partnership and ordinary marriages' (n 16).
42 MV Lee Badgett, *When Gay People Get Married: What Happens When Societies Legalize Same-Sex Marriage* (New York: New York University Press 2009) 89.
43 Ibid.
44 *Halpern* (n 24) [94].
45 On symbolic recognition, see further Barker (n 38) 103.
46 Auchmuty (n 40) 204.

Table 7.2 Economic and social practice regarding same-sex couples

Actor	During the relationship	On relationship end or afterwards
Third parties (governments, public bodies, employers, etc.)	Voluntary grant of employment benefits	
Spouses one to another	Organisation of households; sharing of domestic labour; sharing of expenses; joint accounts; raising of children.	Post-separation parenting

arrangements of same-sex couples as they wind up their relationships. Table 7.2 roughly fills in practices observable by social scientists minus legal recognition of same-sex couples.

By contrast with Table 7.1, which maps the economic rules entailed by marriage, Table 7.2's column for relationship end is mostly empty. Presumably, former same-sex partners form a population even more scattered and invisible than intact same-sex couples. In any event, there is little mention made of the dearth of knowledge regarding relationship termination and afterwards, even on the part of legal scholars who draw on social science. Relationship breakdown is addressed as it affects parenting, but not the partners' financial disentanglement. Given the intensity of the legal effects on and after relationship breakdown, however, querying the alignment between legal rules and prior expectations and practices seems crucial. For their part, gay and lesbian rights campaigns have kept silent 'about the possible meanings or application of the principle of equality in relation to separating lesbian and gay couples'.[47]

If one's view is that the legal recognition of same-sex relationships should aim to track them 'as they are lived', the evidentiary gap on the timing poses a significant problem. In other words, social science about intact same-sex couples has been deployed to justify providing for them a legal form that makes felt its effects for the spouses' relations vis-à-vis one another most keenly in other, unstudied circumstances.

Certainly concern about the absence of data on the post-breakdown practices of same-sex couples matters only if one thinks that discernible differences between same- and different-sex couples might justifiably affect their legal regulation. A contending view would dismiss differences in the economic organisation and incidence of children as a rational reaction to the exclusion from marriage's economic rules for inducing and rewarding specialisation of labour.[48] Badgett refers to a 'feedback loop' of legal inequality that supports the myth that gay people differ from heterosexual people in their attachment to family life and future generations.[49]

The focus by same-sex couples on securing recognition by third parties and the absence of data on how same-sex couples unwind their financial affairs as a matter of social practice might hint that it was unsuitable to make marriage, as it stood, available to same-sex couples.

---

47 D Monk, 'Commentary on *Re G (Children) (Residence: Same-Sex Partner)*' in RC Hunter, C McGlynn and E Rackley (eds), *Feminist Judgments: From Theory to Practice* (Oxford: Hart 2010) 98 [footnote omitted].
48 Badgett, *Money, Myths, and Change* (n 26) 160.
49 Ibid. 165.

At a minimum, it points to the challenges of assessing that suitability in an empirically grounded way. As the next part argues, however, key aspects of marriage law are not intended to fit the desires and practices of both spouses.

Identity politics and justice

The previous part's identification of gaps in the empirical data about same-sex couples' social practices may prompt the development of a clearer understanding of the group-based claims for formal equality in marriage. This part will aim to sharpen that understanding, by reference to the role of group-based justice claims in the crafting of legal rules for different-sex married couples.

Acknowledgement that marriage entails obligations not only for third parties but also for spouses underscores the delicacy of group-based claims for access to marriage. Successful claims have opposed the minority group of gays and lesbians – who may as a class experience 'pre-existing disadvantage and vulnerability'[50] – against the majority. The group-based paradigm 'suggests that lesbians and gay men have shared interests and needs, and that as a class equality means access to the benefits possessed by groups more privileged than they'.[51] In the American context, Badgett provides a textbook example of this framing:

> [S]ame-sex couples cannot marry, so providing any benefits to married couples by definition results in discrimination against gay people. If same-sex couples could marry, any benefits that go to married people would then be distributed without regard to sexual orientation.[52]

Note that benefits to married people might still discriminate on other bases, such as race and class.[53] Indeed, Brake contends that they might discriminate on the basis of 'amatonormativity', the undue favouring of relationships of romantic love.[54]

Concerning relationship recognition, it is important to emphasise the limited analytical purchase of focusing on claims advanced by a minority identity group defined by sexual orientation. Such a focus may capture the gist of what happens when the state or another third party withholds benefits from or delivers them to same-sex couples via their marital status. Think of pensions or the right to sponsor a spouse for immigration. Yet it is awkward for addressing the disadvantage that 'recognition' of their relationship may impose on some same-sex couples. For example, a newly aggregated household income may reduce entitlement to state benefits. Moreover, such effects may attach, disadvantageously, even to couples who have not formalised their relationship.[55]

The focus on the group is clumsier still for discussing the private law rules which allocate property and resources as between spouses. By contrast with the 'explicit homophobia in the old cases [which] positioned all lesbians and gays against the law', the economic rules

---

50 *M v H* (n 39) [69].
51 Cooper (n 31) 102.
52 Badgett, *Money, Myths, and Change* (n 26) 205.
53 e.g. R Conrad (ed.), *Against Equality: Queer Critiques of Gay Marriage* (Against Equality Publishing Collective 2010).
54 E Brake, *Minimizing Marriage: Marriage, Morality, and the Law* (Oxford: Oxford University Press 2012) 88.
55 R Harding, *Regulating Sexuality: Legal Consciousness in Lesbian and Gay Lives* (Routledge 2011) 121; also CFL Young and SB Boyd, 'Losing the feminist voice? Debates on the legal recognition of same sex partnerships in Canada' (2006) 14 *Feminist Legal Studies* 213.

which operate on dissolution of a *de jure* relationship create 'both winners and losers within the lesbian and gay community'.[56] As Monk puts it, 'When gays and lesbians are pitted against each other ... as opposed to against "homophobes", they [disputes] are more complex, they do not lend themselves to campaigns and taking sides is harder.'[57] Each order sharing the value of family property acquired during the marriage benefits one former same-sex partner at the other's expense. In other words, once it has achieved access to marriage and divorce law, a gay and lesbian equality movement allied with identity politics raises distributive questions that are 'identity-indifferent'.[58] One might want, then, to have a firmer grip on the corrective basis of divorce rules or a surer sense as to the justifications for the distributions they mandate.[59]

Here it is worth recalling the provenance of reforms to divorce law. Regimes for dissolution have their most obvious effects at a relationship's unwinding and afterwards, although exit rules may also of course condition parties' options and decisions during the relationship. Divorce law allocates property in ways other than the parties would do consensually. It addresses matters not of empirical evidence or of social practice, but of justice. Allocative measures on divorce have often not been justified on the basis that law was recognising or regularising the way that most divorcing couples would order their affairs absent enactment.[60] There is a clear contrast with some areas of private law, in which the default rules may roughly track custom and be intended to do so. Or they may fill in the rules that the parties might plausibly have agreed on had they thought about a matter. Instead, property division for separating partners imposes the distribution thought to be just by some external standard in the light of how spouses are expected to have acted during their union. For example, the law lords' application of the Matrimonial Causes Act 1973 matters because it resulted in a larger share of property for Mrs White than dictated, absent legal compulsion, by Mr White's sense of his wife's fair share.[61] Indeed, the sense that the relevant interests exceed those of the parties leads Herring to suggest provocatively that financial settlements on divorce should, from the spouses' perspective, be 'unfair'.[62] Similarly, it is from a perspective which is unabashedly normative, rather than sociologically descriptive, that one can characterise the state of affairs arising from unmarried cohabitants' prevailing practices on separation as unjust.[63]

Concretely, in many Western jurisdictions, reforms to family law undertaken in the 1970s and 1980s could be viewed as the upshot of a gender struggle (if not a war) between men

---

56 Monk (n 47) 98.
57 D Monk, 'Judging the Act: civil partnership disputes in the courtroom and the media' in N Barker and D Monk (eds), *From Civil Partnership to Same-Sex Marriage: Interdisciplinary Reflections* (Abingdon, UK: Routledge 2015) 193–4.
58 JE Halley, '"Like race" arguments' in J Butler, J Guillory and K Thomas (eds), *What's Left of Theory? New Work on the Politics of Literary Theory* (London: Routledge 2000) 55.
59 W Chan, 'Cohabitation, civil partnership, marriage and the equal sharing principle' (2013) 33 *Legal Studies* 46.
60 But see, for the suggestion of customary roots underlying a regime enacted in order to tackle economic inequality, N Kasirer, 'Testing the origins of the family patrimony in everyday law' (1995) 36 *Cahiers de Droit* 795.
61 *White v White* [2000] UKHL 54 [2001] 1 AC 596, 605; see also *Miller v Miller; McFarlane v Macfarlane* [2006] UKHL 24 [2006] 2 AC 618.
62 J Herring, 'Why financial orders on divorce should be unfair' (2005) 19 *International Journal of Law, Policy and the Family* 218.
63 e.g. G Douglas, J Pearce and H Woodward, 'Cohabitants, property and the law: a study of injustice' (2009) 72 *Modern Law Review* 24.

and women. The justifications for a presumption of equal sharing of gains, enacted in some jurisdictions, merit mention. How to make sense of such rules, given that they apply to the diversity of different-sex marriages? The question attaches, slightly attenuated, to the yardstick of equality that conditions the application of judicial discretion in the UK in the case of marriage and civil partnership.[64]

The starting point must be the pervasiveness of gendered divisions of labour and the systemic undervaluation of women's work. Economic analysis of marriage flags the problem of asymmetry: 'women, as a class, lose systematically far more than do men. Women are generally less highly valued in the marriage market following a divorce than they were prior to their first marriage'.[65] Some observers would see the systemic disadvantage experienced by women as appropriately conditioning the application of allocative rules on divorce,[66] or as justifying a place for distributive justice in divorce law.[67] Others, adopting a robust understanding of marriage as a partnership, might characterise rules of equal sharing, viewed in the light of systemic considerations, as straightforwardly corrective.[68] The point is that debates around the economic regulation of different-sex couples' dissolution, like those on the respective rights and duties of fathers and mothers post-separation, retain a connection to feminist identity politics and structural gender subordination.[69]

How are these observations to be squared with the question of same-sex couples, as illuminated by the data on their social practices? On the one hand, unevenness in the available data regarding same-sex couples might not matter, if the point of divorce law was never to mirror existing social practice. On the other hand, the prominence of a feminist politics around gender subordination in the development of allocative rules raises questions about those rules' unmediated application to same-sex couples. On dissolution of a same-sex marriage or civil union, who, to use Cohen's expression, gave whom the best years of his life? Might the gendered history and rationale of marriage's economic rules cast doubt on the project of formal marriage equality for same-sex couples?

Conclusion

What has proven politically powerful for the same-sex lobby is the claim that 'we are just like you' – based on the social practice of intact same-sex couples – and should thus be treated identically. Given its salience, it is understandable that lobbyists for gay and lesbian

---

64 For discussion of the proper approach to civil partnerships, *Lawrence v Gallagher* [2012] EWCA Civ 394 [2]; M Harper et al., *Same Sex Marriage and Civil Partnerships: The New Law* (Bristol, UK: Jordan Publishing 2014) 139–41; R George, '*Lawrence v Gallagher* [2012] EWCA Civ 394 – Playing a straight bat in civil partnership appeals?' (2012) 34 *Journal of Social Welfare and Family Law* 357; C Bendall, 'A break away from the (hetero)norm? *Lawrence v Gallagher* [2012] 1 FCR 557; [2012] EWCA Civ 394' (2013) 21 *Feminist Legal Studies* 303.
65 L Cohen, 'Marriage, divorce, and quasi rents; or, "I gave him the best years of my life"' (1987) 16 *Journal of Legal Studies* 267, 268.
66 *Moge v Moge* [1992] 3 SCR 813; A Diduck and H Orton, 'Equality and support for spouses' (1994) 57 *Modern Law Review* 681.
67 But for cautions about compensating for systemic social inequalities through the private obligations of family law, see L Ferguson, 'Family, social inequalities, and the persuasive force of interpersonal obligation' (2008) 22 *International Journal of Law, Policy and the Family* 61.
68 On a 'rich principle of contribution and compensation' responsive to gender-inflected sacrifice, see Chan (n 59) 60.
69 R Collier and S Sheldon (eds), *Fathers' Rights Activism and Law Reform in Comparative Perspective* (Oxford: Hart 2006).

rights should have used this argument. This chapter's starting point, however, was the relative neglect within socio-legal research of the ostensible similarity between same-sex and different-sex couples. Its first part laid out two distinctions: one between the obligations entailed by marriage for third parties and for the spouses themselves, the other between regulation during the marriage and afterwards. These distinctions combined to provide a tool for better understanding marriage as an institution of regulation. The four cells in Table 7.1 above are separable and this chapter's first part has analytical salience beyond the question of same-sex couples, notably for unmarried cohabitants and others in thick, interdependent relationships.[70]

The second part addressed differences between different-sex and same-sex couples signalled by the social science. Although alert to divergent findings, that part reported that same-sex couples demonstrate a more egalitarian division of labour than do different-sex couples, as well as substantially lower rates of child rearing. Given the claims of sameness advanced in efforts at law reform, those differences are relevant. Moreover, the distinctions in the first part bring into view difficulties germane to a turn to empirical research when assessing the fit between same-sex couples and marriage: the focus by couples and activists on third-party recognition of same-sex couples and the evidentiary gap concerning the unwinding of same-sex relationships absent a legal framework. For those endeavouring to develop evidence-based family policy, it would be helpful to have data about how same-sex couples disentangle their economic affairs absent a legal framework and to know more about the attitudes towards economic allocations of those in same-sex relationships. In particular, it would be helpful to know more about the intentions of same-sex couples who contract a marriage or civil partnership respecting the obtainment of third-party recognition versus the entry into an economic regime of reciprocal obligation.[71]

The fourth part of this chapter may provide a partial response to the evidentiary gaps insofar as it is a reminder that divorce law's economic allocations do not purport to be bottom-up. Instead they implement, top-down, some conception of justice. Yet the identity politics specific to different-sex marriage do not map onto same-sex couples as a class. One question, then, is whether the class or racial factors that may contribute to inequality as between same-sex partners can take on the justificatory weight pulled by gender in the case of different-sex marriage.

The policy conclusions emerging from this chapter are unclear. While the present study is primarily analytical and methodological, it would be possible to press more normatively against the rhetoric of formal-equality-as-sameness. An approach informed by the research might examine the possibility that the marriage rules applicable by default to same-sex couples should differ from those designed for different-sex couples. Separating the duties of third parties from the duties of the spouses themselves might provide a path forward, although a number of concerns and potential objections would need to be considered carefully.[72]

---

70 Law Commission of Canada, *Beyond Conjugality: Recognizing and Supporting Close Personal Adult Relationships* (Minister of Public Works and Government Services 2001).
71 For important but still relatively early empirical work, see Heaphy, Smart and Einarsdottir (n 21); Auchmuty (n 40).
72 R Leckey, 'Must equal mean identical? Same-sex couples and marriage' (2014) 10 *International Journal of Law in Context* 5; see also R Leckey, 'Introduction: after legal equality' in R Leckey (ed.), *After Legal Equality: Family, Sex, Kinship* (London: Routledge 2015).

It is nevertheless possible to tailor preliminary remarks for the UK's ongoing consideration of matrimonial property and needs, in the context of divorce and dissolution of civil partnership, and of the general situation of unmarried cohabitants. In the case of marriage, the reduction of legal aid is boosting the case for rules over judicial discretion with regard to ancillary relief.[73] This chapter might support a call for any eventual rules to target factors likely to produce economic dependence, such as the raising of children, rather than relying solely on relationship status. Still, liberal considerations might justify identical treatment regarding the symbolically weighted law of marriage and civil partnership, given that empirical research has recorded a desire for formal legal equality on the part of many gay men and lesbians (Harding 2011). Cohabitation, though, might call for a different approach. For unmarried cohabitants, this chapter's disaggregation of the duties entailed by marriage might sharpen analysis by pressing reformers to locate the perceived problems with the status quo. The focus on recognition by third parties that underlies the arguments for same-sex marriage or civil partnership does not apply to unmarried cohabitants, who have not together sought recognition as a couple. That factor, combined with the lesser inequality within many same-sex relationships, might lead to hesitancy about assuming that any regime eventually developed for unmarried cohabitants should apply identically to same- and different-sex couples. Same-sex couples may be equal in moral worth and dignity to different-sex ones, but evidence of difference should be relevant where the justification for rules is one class of relationships' ostensibly functional equivalence to another.

In the meantime, the prevailing discourse of formal equality merges moral equality and the ostensibly identical functioning of same-sex and different-sex couples without empirically grounded scrutiny. Further research and debate on these issues might yield rich insights, not only into the legal institutions of marriage or civil partnership as they stand in an increasing number of Western states – for same-sex or different-sex partners – but also into the complex relationship between social practice and visions of justice.

Bibliography

Auchmuty R, 'Dissolution or disillusion: The unravelling of civil partnerships' in Barker N and Monk D (eds), *From Civil Partnerships to Same-Sex Marriage: Interdisciplinary Reflections* (London: Routledge 2015).

Balsam KF et al., 'Three-year follow-up of same-sex couples who had civil unions in Vermont, same-sex couples not in civil unions, and heterosexual married couples' (2008) 44 *Developmental Psychology* 102.

Barker N, *Not the Marrying Kind: A Feminist Critique of Same-Sex Marriage* (New York: Palgrave Macmillan 2012).

Barlow A, 'Property and couple relationships: What does community of property have to offer English law?' in Bottomley A and Wong S (eds), *Changing Contours of Domestic Life, Family and Law: Caring and Sharing* (Oxford: Hart 2009).

Bendall C, 'A break away from the (hetero)norm? *Lawrence v Gallagher* [2012] 1 FCR 557; [2012] EWCA Civ 394' (2013) 21 *Feminist Legal Studies* 303.

——, 'Some are more "equal" than others: Heteronormativity in the post-White era of financial remedies' (2014) 36 *Journal of Social Welfare and Family Law* 260.

---

73 Law Commission, *Matrimonial Property, Needs and Agreements*, Law Com CP208 (London: TSO, 2012) paras 4.89, 4.90.

Bottomley A and Wong S, 'Shared households: A new paradigm for thinking about the reform of domestic property relations' in Diduck A and O'Donovan K (eds), *Feminist Perspectives on Family Law* (Abingdon, UK: Routledge-Cavendish 2006).

Brake E, *Minimizing Marriage: Marriage, Morality, and the Law* (Oxford Oxford University Press 2012).

Burns M, Burgoyne C and Clarke V, 'Financial affairs? Money management in same-sex relationships' (2008) 37 *Journal of Socio-Economics* 481.

Carrington C, *No Place Like Home: Relationships and Family Life Among Lesbians and Gay Men* (Chicago, IL: University of Chicago Press 1999).

Chan W, 'Cohabitation, civil partnership, marriage and the equal sharing principle' (2013) 33 *Legal Studies* 46.

Cohen L, 'Marriage, divorce, and quasi rents; or, " I gave him the best years of my life"' (1987) 16 *Journal of Legal Studies* 267.

Collier R and Sheldon S (eds), *Fathers' Rights Activism and Law Reform in Comparative Perspective* (Oxford: Hart 2006).

Coltrane S and Adams M, *Gender and Families* (2nd edn, Lanham, MD: Rowman & Littlefield 2008).

Conrad R (ed.) *Against Equality: Queer Critiques of Gay Marriage* (Lewiston, ME: Against Equality Publishing Collective 2010).

Cooper D, *Challenging Diversity: Rethinking Equality and the Value of Difference* (Cambridge: Cambridge University Press 2004).

Diduck A and Orton H, 'Equality and support for spouses' (1994) 57 *Modern Law Review* 681.

Douglas G, Pearce J and Woodward H, 'Cohabitants, property and the law: a study of injustice' (2009) 72 *Modern Law Review* 24.

Ellickson RC, *The Household: Informal Order Around the Hearth* (Princeton, NJ: Princeton University Press 2010).

Esmail A, '"Negotiating fairness": a study on how lesbian family members evaluate, construct, and maintain "fairness" with the division of household labor' (2010) 57 *Journal of Homosexuality* 591.

Ferguson L, 'Family, social inequalities, and the persuasive force of interpersonal obligation' (2008) 22 *International Journal of Law, Policy and the Family* 61.

George R, '*Lawrence v Gallagher* [2012] EWCA Civ 394 – playing a straight bat in civil partnership appeals?' (2012) 34 *Journal of Social Welfare and Family Law* 357.

Giddings L *et al.*, 'Birth cohort and the specialization gap between same-sex and different-sex couples' (2014) 51 *Demography* 509.

Giddings LA, 'Political economy and the construction of gender: the example of housework within same-sex households' (1998) 4 *Feminist Economics* 97.

Goldberg AE, 'Doing and undoing gender: the meaning and division of housework in same-sex couples' (2013) 5 *Journal of Family Theory & Review* 85.

Hale B, 'Equality and autonomy in family law' (2011) 33 *Journal of Social Welfare and Family Law* 3.

Halley JE, '"Like race" arguments' in Butler J, Guillory J and Thomas K (eds), *What's Left of Theory? New Work on the Politics of Literary Theory* (London: Routledge 2000).

——, 'Recognition, rights, regulation, normalization: rhetorics of justification in the same-sex marriage debate' in Wintemute R and Andenæs MT (eds), *Legal Recognition of Same-Sex Partnerships: A Study of National, European and International Law* (Oxford: Hart 2001).

Harding R, *Regulating Sexuality: Legal Consciousness in Lesbian and Gay Lives* (London: Routledge 2011).

Harper M *et al.*, *Same Sex Marriage and Civil Partnerships: The New Law* (Bristol, UK: Jordan Publishing 2014).

Heaphy B, 'The sociology of lesbian and gay reflexivity or reflexive sociology?' (2008). 13 *Sociological Research Online*. www.socresonline.org.uk/13/1/9.html doi:10.5153/sro.1675.

——, 'Civil partnership and ordinary marriages' in Barker N and Monk D (eds), *From Civil Partnership to Same-Sex Marriage: Interdisciplinary Reflections* (London: Routledge 2015).

Heaphy B, Smart C and Einarsdottir A, *Same Sex Marriages: New Generations, New Relationships* (New York: Palgrave Macmillan 2013).

Herring J, 'Why financial orders on divorce should be unfair' (2005) 19 *International Journal of Law, Policy and the Family* 218.

Hunter RC (ed.), *Rethinking Equality Projects in Law: Feminist Challenges* (Oxford: Hart 2008).

Julien D and Chartrand É, 'La psychologie familiale des gais et des lesbiennes: perspective de la tradition scientifique nord-américaine' (1997) 29 *Sociologie et sociétés* 71.

Kasirer N, 'Testing the origins of the family patrimony in everyday law' (1995) 36 *Cahiers de Droit* 795.

Klawitter M, 'The effects of sexual orientation and marital status on how couples hold their money' (2008) 6 *Review of Economics of the Household* 423.

Kurdek LA, 'The allocation of household labor by partners in gay and lesbian couples' (2007) 28 *Journal of Family Issues* 132.

Law Commission, *Marital Property Agreements* (London: TSO, 2011).

——, *Matrimonial Property, Needs and Agreements* (London: TSO, 2012).

Law Commission of Canada, *Beyond Conjugality: Recognizing and Supporting Close Personal Adult Relationships* (Minister of Public Works and Government Services 2001).

Leckey R, 'Law reform, lesbian parenting, and the reflective claim' (2011) 20 *Social & Legal Studies* 331.

——, 'Must equal mean identical? Same-sex couples and marriage' (2014) 10 *International Journal of Law in Context* 5.

——, 'Introduction: after legal equality' in Leckey R (ed.), *After Legal Equality: Family, Sex, Kinship* (London: Routledge 2015).

Lee Badgett MV, *Money, Myths, and Change: The Economic Lives of Lesbians and Gay Men* (Chicago, IL: University of Chicago Press 2001).

——, *When Gay People Get Married: What Happens When Societies Legalize Same-Sex Marriage* (New York: New York University Press 2009).

Malaurie P and Aynès L, *Les régimes matrimoniaux* (3rd edn, Défrenois 2010).

Miles J, Wasoff F and Mordaunt E, 'Reforming family law – the case of cohabitation: 'things may not work out as you expect'' (2012) 34 *Journal of Social Welfare and Family Law* 167.

Monk D, 'Commentary on Re G (children) (residence: same-sex partner)' in Hunter RC, McGlynn C and Rackley E (eds), *Feminist Judgments: From Theory to Practice* (Oxford: Hart 2010).

Monk D, 'Judging the act: civil partnership disputes in the courtroom and the media' in Barker N and Monk D (eds), *From Civil Partnership to Same-Sex Marriage: Interdisciplinary Reflections* (Abingdon, UK: Routledge 2015).

Moore MR, 'Gendered power relations among women: a study of household decision making in black, lesbian stepfamilies' (2008) 73 *American Sociological Review* 335.

Murray M, 'Marriage as punishment' (2012) 112 *Columbia Law Review* 1.

Oerton S, '"Queer housewives?" Some problems in theorizing the division of domestic labour in lesbian and gay households' (1997) 20 *Women's Studies International Forum* 421.

Perlesz A *et al.*, 'Organising work and home in same-sex parented families: findings from the work, love, play study' (2010) 31 *Australian & New Zealand Journal of Family Therapy* 374.

Pineau J and Pratte M, *La famille* (Montreal, QC: Les éditions Thémis 2006).

Probert R, 'Cohabitation: current legal solutions' (2009) 62 *Current Legal Problems* 316.

Prokos AH and Keene JR, 'Poverty among cohabiting gay and lesbian, and married and cohabiting heterosexual families' (2010) 31 *Journal of Family Issues* 934.

Ross L, 'Perinatal mental health in lesbian mothers: a review of potential risk and protective factors' (2005) 41 *Women and Health* 113.

Roy A, 'Le régime juridique de l'union civile: entre symbolisme et anachronisme' in Lafond P-C and Lefebvre B (eds), *L'union civile: nouveaux modèles de conjugalité et de parentalité au 21e siècle: actes du colloque du Groupe de réflexion en droit privé* (Cowansville, QC: Yvon Blais 2003).

Sanders A, 'Nuptial agreements, comparative law and the notion of contract' in Popovici A, Smith L and Tremblay R (eds), *Les intraduisibles en droit civil* (Montreal, QC: Les éditions Thémis 2014).

Schecter E *et al.*, 'Shall we marry? Legal marriage as a commitment event in same-sex relationships' (2008) 54 *Journal of Homosexuality* 400.

Scherpe JM (ed.) *Marital Agreements and Private Autonomy in Comparative Perspective* (Oxford: Hart 2012).

Shipman B and Smart C, '"It's made a huge difference": Recognition rights and personal significance of civil partnership' (2007) 12 *Sociological Research Online*.

Solomon SE, Rothblum ED and Balsam KF, 'Money, housework, sex, and conflict: same-sex couples in civil unions, those not in civil unions, and heterosexual married siblings' (2005) 52 *Sex Roles* 561.

Sutphin ST, 'Social exchange theory and the division of household labor in same-sex couples' (2010) 46 *Marriage & Family Review* 191.

Weston K, *Render Me, Gender Me: Lesbians Talk Sex, Class, Color, Nation, Studmuffins* (New York: Columbia University Press 1996).

Young CFL and Boyd SB, 'Losing the feminist voice? Debates on the legal recognition of same sex partnerships in Canada' (2006) 14 *Feminist Legal Studies* 213.

8 Value in personal relationships and the reallocation of property on divorce

Craig Lind

> *He discovered the cruel paradox by which we always deceive ourselves twice about the people we love – first to their advantage, then to their disadvantage.*[1]

Introduction

Analysis of the distribution of property and income on divorce is often framed by discussion of the problems of gender equality[2] and the public/private divide that requires that there be law in the sphere of the state and the market, but profoundly limits the involvement of law in the sphere of the family and the individual.[3] In these analyses, the persistence of gender roles and gender differentiation in both family life and in employment beyond the family home are given as the unyielding characteristics that result in the injustices that are perpetrated by systems of property distribution on divorce (which itself, has proliferated in Western democracies in the last fifty years). In this chapter, I wish to suggest an alternative frame of reference for an analysis of the seemingly intractable problems that beset those engaged in thinking about the redistribution of property on divorce.[4] In doing so, I do not wish to detract from the importance of analyses, which highlight the inequities caused by the persistence of the division between 'public' and 'private' spheres of life, and the way in which the law's engagement in the latter is deficient. Nor do I wish to undermine the fundamental importance of analyses that focus on the way in which persistent gendered differences in marriage and in child (and other) care are ignored in the pursuit of formal equality. But I do wish to suggest that an analysis that deliberately avoids focusing on those

---

1 A Camus, *A Happy Death* (trans by R Howard, New York: Alfred A Knopf 1972).
2 For a summary of research, see, e.g. J Herring, *Family Law* (6th edn, London: Pearson 2013) 211. For similar America perspectives, see, e.g. P Laufer-Ukeles, 'Selective recognition of gender difference in the law: revaluing the caretaker Role' (2007–2008) 31(1) *Harvard Journal of Law and Gender* 1 and J Carbone, 'Feminism, gender, and the consequences of divorce' in M Freeman (ed.), *Divorce: Where Next?* (Dartmouth, MA: Dartmouth 1996).
3 For a summary of the history of this phenomenon, see A Diduck and F Kaganas, *Family Law, Gender and the State* (2nd edn, Oxford: Hart 2006) 13. See too, e.g. A Bottomley and S Wong, 'Shared households: a new paradigm for thinking about the reform of domestic property relations' in A Diduck and K O'Donovan (eds), *Feminist Perspectives on Family Law* (Abingdon, UK: Routledge-Cavendish 2006).
4 See Laufer-Ukeles (n 3) especially at 2, for the variety of American responses to this perennial problem.

issues will cast a new light on familiar issues and provide a solution to property distribution dilemmas that focuses not on what one spouse should be allowed to claim from the estate of the other, but on what she deserves from him, and what he owes her because it is hers by right (a claim based on entitlement and not some redistributive discretion). What is imperative in the analysis I offer, though, is that the entitlement is not simply to half of the communal estate (as is the case in many United States of America and continental European jurisdictions). The analysis I offer suggests that spouses are owed valuable assets and incomes by their ex-spouses because of the value that they have brought to their relationships. And it is necessary for us to see the value they bring to their relationships and its consequences on their entitlement to property so that we can, finally, resolve the problems of the distribution of property that appear to be as intractable now[5] as they have ever been.[6]

To this end, in this chapter, I wish to argue, in the first instance, that we should reflect upon the absence of an appropriate mechanism for settling value in personal relationships. We should remind ourselves that we have no method to determine, nor do we have a currency to represent, the value that people in personal relationship have for one another. Nor do we have a method to determine, or currency to represent, the value that they and their relationships (even if those relationships are not life-long, and do not result in the rearing of children) bring to society. Our thoughts (and our analysis) should, I will argue, in the second instance, turn to a recognition of the fact that the things to be distributed on divorce are acquired or possessed under a system of value that has no bearing upon personal relationships (I will demonstrate that the method for settling value – the market mechanism for settling 'price' – is crude and less than adequate to the task of assisting in the distribution of property on divorce). I will suggest that our problems are exacerbated by the existence of a market mechanism for settling the value or price of activities that are, in the context of paid work, understood to be the work that is at the heart of relationships (that is, caring and home-making work). The market mechanism, in this instance, has a tendency to allocate a (gender-constructed) low numerical value to this work which, I will argue, is an inappropriate value for use in the context of property distribution on divorce.

It will be clear that gender concerns and the private/public divide will never be far from the analysis I propose here. But I will try, in this chapter, to steer clear of an analysis that simply relies on gender and on the private/public boundary. And, in the latter stages of this essay I will problematise my own analysis because of the (probable) gendered problems that it will create and the possible relegation that it might suggest of matters relating to property distribution to the 'private' sphere. I will, of course, try to offer a way around the problems I anticipate to arise in the context of my own analysis.

---

5 See, e.g. S Cretney, 'Community of property imposed by judicial decision' (2003) 119(3) *Law Quarterly Review* 349, J Eekelaar, '*Miller v Miller*, the descent into chaos' [2005] 35(11) *Fam Law* 870, A Diduck, 'Ancillary relief: complicating the search for principle' (2011) 38(2) *Journal of Law and Society* 272, E Cooke, A Barlow and T Callus, *Community of Property: A Regime for England and Wales?* (London: The Nuffield Foundation 2006), Law Commission *Marital Property Agreements* (Consultation Paper no. 198, 2011), Law Commission *Matrimonial Property, Needs and Agreements* (Consultation Paper no. 208, 2012), and J Scherpe (ed.), *Marital Agreements and Private Autonomy in Comparative Perspective* (Oxford: Hart 2012).
6 See S Cretney, *Family law in the Twentieth Century: A History* (Oxford: OUP 2003) Ch 10.

Distributing property on divorce[7]

In England and Wales, property is separately and individually owned and acquired during marriage by each spouse.[8] The property they bring into the marriage remains, individually, theirs. But at the end of the marriage '[t]he Matrimonial Causes Act 1973 confers wide discretionary powers on the courts over all the property of the husband and the wife.'[9] Judges may (re)distribute any of the property (both assets and (future) income) of one party to the other.[10] In the exercise of their discretion, judges are given two statutory guiding principles. In the first instance, they must consider the welfare of children; although this is not their 'paramount' concern – as it is under the Children Act 1989[11] and the Adoption and Children Act 2002[12] – section 25(1) of the Matrimonial Causes Act 1973 (MCA 1973) makes it their first consideration in the context of property redistribution. In the second instance, judges must consider making orders that will achieve a clean break in the financial interdependence of divorcing spouses.[13] The clean break principle attempts to make divorce real in terms of both status and the material consequences of formal relationships. Before its embodiment in statute, Lord Scarman had expressed the sentiment of the principle in the following terms: 'An object of the modern law is to encourage each to put the past behind them and to begin a new life which is not overshadowed by the relationship which has broken down.'[14]

However, the court in *Clutton v Clutton*[15] warned against imposing the clean break principle too readily (and too thoughtlessly).

> But there is perhaps a danger in referring to [the clean break principle] as a 'principle', since it might lead courts to strive for a clean break, regardless of all other considerations. This is not what s 25A requires. It requires the court to consider the appropriateness of a clean break.[16]

The statutory 'principles', then, are guidelines. They do not compel any particular distribution but impose requirements only of 'consideration'.

The Act goes on to provide a checklist of additional factors that judges must consider when deciding how to exercise their power to distribute the property and income of the

---

7 Although I will talk about marriage and divorce, I am, for the most part, also talking about civil partnerships and their dissolution. Although gendered problems lie at the heart of many of the difficulties I am discussing, my ambition is to elucidate a view that resolution of the gender problems may not be enough to resolve the problems that preoccupy courts charged with property redistribution at the end of relationships. Alternatively, it will become evident that I believe the gendered problems at the heart of the problems of property distribution (or, at least, many of them) are not necessarily avoided in same sex relationships. I will also deal with unmarried relationships in this analysis (where I take the view that the problems discussed are, if not exactly the same, so closely aligned that they should not be treated in law as different). See too Bottomley and Wong (n 4).
8 See Law Commission, *Family Law-Report on Financial Provision in Matrimonial Proceedings* (Law Com No 25, 1969). See too Cooke, Barlow and Callus (n 6) and Cretney (n 7).
9 *White v White* [2001] 1 AC 596, 596 (Lord Nicholls).
10 For the extent of the power, see ss 23–24D of the Matrimonial Causes Act 1973.
11 S 1(1), in the context of raising children.
12 S 1(2), in the context of adopting children.
13 MCA 1973, s 25A.
14 *Minton v Minton* [1979] AC 593, 608.
15 [1991] 1 All ER 340.
16 Ibid. 343 (Lloyd LJ).

Value in personal relationships 121

parties to ancillary relief proceedings. These range across things like their income, earning capacity and other resources,[17] their financial needs, obligations and responsibilities,[18] their standard of living when their relationship ended,[19] their ages and the duration of their marriage,[20] and their broad contributions (both past and future) to the family.[21] Because neither the checklist nor the statutory principles dictate an overarching ambition which should frame the exercise of this wide judicial discretion, the appeal courts have, from time to time, enunciated the overarching aspiration that should guide courts making ancillary relief decisions.

In 1973, when the Act was passed, Lord Denning in *Wachtel v Wachtel*[22] held that the ambitions of the Act were to allocate a 'fair share' of the property to divorced wives and that, at a rough estimation, a fair share would probably be a third of the property in most cases. A little later, in *Browne (formerly Pritchard) v Pritchard*[23] and again in *O'D v O'D*,[24] Ormrod LJ found this to be too generous and held that discretion should be used to provide for the needs of the parties (and that distribution should take place where the needs of one spouse demanded distribution of property or finance to meet (usually her) needs). The rest of the property and income would be left where it was owned.[25]

In more recent years a new trend has been introduced. In *White v White*[26] 'fairness' was launched as the new overarching principle guiding courts, which distribute property on divorce. While the judges acknowledged the difficulties of fairness, one of the objects of this version of 'fairness' was to subvert the gender discrimination that lies at the heart of a system of family life in which women do unpaid work at home and accumulate very little material value, while men work away from home and continue to amass valuable estates. The principle of fairness was refined in *Miller v Miller;* and *McFarlane McFarlane*.[27] In those cases, the court maintained that fairness required, first, that the parties' *needs* be met,[28] second, if there were funds or property for distribution once needs were catered for, that there be compensation for any 'relationship generated disadvantage',[29] and third that a marriage as a partnership required the equal sharing of any property or finance that remained after needs had been met and compensation recovered.[30] In this way the 'fairness' spoken of in *White*, framed by the 'yardstick' of equality, could be achieved. In the words of Baroness

---

17 MCA 1973, s. 25(2)(a).
18 MCA 1973, s. 25(2)(b).
19 MCA 1973, s. 25(2)(c).
20 MCA 1973, s. 25(2)(d).
21 MCA 1973, s. 25(2)(f).
22 [1973] Fam 72.
23 [1975] 1 WLR 1366.
24 [1976] Fam 83.
25 See too *Page v Page* (1981) 2 FLR 198; *Preston v Preston* [1982] Fam 17, and more recently, *Dart v Dart* [1996] 2 FLR 286, CA, and even *Conran v Conran* [1997] 2 FLR 617 (in which the court seemed to be becoming more generous in its recognition of the value that a wife might bring to her husband's business enterprise, which led to his accumulation of wealth, but was still not prepared to make more than a token of his wealth over to her on that account). For a contemporary analysis of the exercise of the discretion, see S Cretney, 'Trusting the judges: money after divorce' (1999) 52(1) *Current Legal Problems* 286.
26 *White* (n 10).
27 [2006] UKHL 24.
28 Ibid. [138] (Baroness Hale).
29 Ibid. [140] (Baroness Hale).
30 Ibid. [141] (Baroness Hale).

Hale of Richmond, '[t]he ultimate objective is to give each party an equal start on the road to independent living.'[31]

Gender, fairness and equality and the distribution of property

What is most evident from the advent of the most recent enunciation of overarching principle is that an ambition to achieve a contemporary (public) vision of gender justice lies at the heart of what courts must do in redistributing property on divorce (finally, the 'equal pay' ideal is brought into the family and family law). In the words of Lord Nicholls of Birkenhead:

> Traditionally, the husband earned the money, and the wife looked after the home and the children. This traditional division of labour is no longer the order of the day. Frequently both parents work. Sometimes it is the wife who is the money-earner, and the husband runs the home and cares for the children during the day. But whatever the division of labour chosen by the husband and wife, or forced upon them by circumstances, fairness requires that this should not prejudice or advantage either party . . .[32]

However, as many commentators have noted, it is almost impossible for any scholarly analysis to make sense of the principles enunciated in the courts so as to produce clear results in disputed cases; the principles at play – fairness, gender justice, need, duration of marriage, contribution, equality, sharing, children's welfare – are all infinitely malleable.[33] As Rebecca Bailey-Harris has said:

> For both practitioner and academic, the pattern of the law's development fails to please. It is impossible to predict when an articulated statutory principle will be seized upon in a judgment, or when a new sub-principle will be invented, or when the search for principle will simply be disclaimed. Moreover, as every practitioner in the county court knows, judicial pronouncements of appellate courts which are intended to be read within the confines of a specific factual matrix are frequently taken out of context by district

---

31 Ibid. [144] (Baroness Hale).
32 *White* (n 10) 605.
33 See, e.g. E Hitchings, 'The impact of recent ancillary relief jurisprudence in the "everyday" ancillary relief case' (2010) 22(1) *Child and Family Law Quarterly* 93, R Bailey-Harris, 'Case comment: fairness in financial settlements on divorce'(2001) 117(2) *Law Quarterly Review* 199, J Eekelaar, 'Back to basics and forward into the unknown' (2001) 31(1) *Fam Law* 30, J Eekelaar, 'Asset distribution on divorce – the durational element' (2001) 117(4) *Law Quarterly Review* 552, J Eekelaar, 'Asset distribution on divorce – time and Property' (2003) 33(11) *Fam Law* 828, J Eekelaar, 'Shared income after divorce: a step too Far' (2005) 121(1) *Law Quarterly Review* 1, J Eekelaar, '*Miller v Miller*: the descent into chaos' (2005) 35(11) *Fam Law* 870, J Miles, 'Principle or pragmatism in ancillary relief: the virtues of flirting with academic theories and other jurisdictions' (2005) 19(2) *International Journal of Law, Policy and the Family* 242, A Meehan, '*Miller and McFarlane*: an opportunity missed? (2006) 36(7) *Fam Law* 566, J Miles, '*Charman v Charman (No 4)* – making sense of need, compensation and equal sharing after *Miller; McFarlane*' (2008) 20(3) *CFLQ* 378, P Moor and V Le Grice, 'Periodical payments orders following *Miller* and *McFarlane*: a series of unfortunate events' (2006) 36(8) *Fam Law* 655, E Hess, 'Assessing the quantum of periodical payments after McFarlane' (2006) 36(9)*Fam Law* 780. But see P Duckworth and D Hodson, '*White v White* – bringing section 25 back to the people' (2001) 31(1) *Fam Law* 24.

judges and thus influence outcomes in situations where fairness should demand otherwise.[34]

Thus, while a base line ambition to eliminate discrimination along gender lines in property adjustment at divorce is clearly at the heart of what courts must do, how that is to be achieved remains a mystery. Do husbands, for example, have to pay their wives because the (public) wage market discriminates against women and in favour of men?[35] Are men paying their wives for their (private) caring and home-making services?[36] If so, why at a rate that is unrelated to the market price for work of that kind?[37] Given that it is not the market rate, how is that rate to be set? What should they be 'paid' and exactly what is it for? Finally, if men are paying women for socially endemic gender discrimination – the gendering of types of work (where well paid work is gendered male and badly paid work is gendered female),[38] wage differentials in the economy (even where work is not gendered by type),[39] the undervaluing of domestic work,[40] etc. – then men's payments to address those problems exacerbate society's gender problems. Rather than end the disadvantageous gendering of society and family roles, do property transfers and regular income payments magnify women's dependence on men? According to Michael Selmi:

> Emphasizing the importance of care work, and the need for women to have different relations to the workplace than men . . . is likely to reinforce existing gender stereotypes and seems unlikely to bring about greater equality for women. Is this not another way to perpetuate gender inequality?[41]

The overarching question, then, is why an ambition to address the issue of gender discrimination – which seems to go to the heart of gendered power relations in society at large, and gendered social construction – should be met or even addressed at the time of the distribution of property at divorce. Given the scale of the gendered problems in our

---

34 R Bailey-Harris, 'The paradoxes of principle and pragmatism: ancillary relief in England and Wales' (2005) 19(2) *International Journal of Law, Policy and the Family* 229. This view persists after the decision in *Miller* and *McFarlane* (n 28): see, for example, Meehan (n 33).
35 J Herring, 'Why financial orders on divorce should be unfair' (2005) 19(2) *International Journal of Law Policy and the Family* 218.
36 See SM Bianchi *et al.*, 'Housework: who did, does or will do it, and how much does it matter?' (2012) 91(1) *Social Forces* 55; M Lachance-Grzela and G Bouchard, 'Why do women do the lion's share of housework? A decade of research' (2010) 63(11) *Sex Roles* 767; BA Shelton and D John, 'Does marital status make a difference? Housework among married and cohabiting men and women' (1993) 14(3) *Journal of Family Issues* 401.
37 Why is paying for services rendered in the relationship recast as payment for needs generated by the relationships, or relationship generated disadvantage? See *Miller* (n 28) [138] – [140] (Baroness Hale).
38 See, e.g. C Hill, C Corbett, and A St. Rose, *Why So Few? Women in Science, Technology, Engineering, and Mathematics* (AAUW 2010) and L McDowell, 'Sexuality, desire and embodied performances in the workplace' in B Brookes-Gordon *et al.* (eds), *Sexuality Repositioned* (Oxford: Hart 2004).
39 AT Lo Sasso *et al.*, 'The $16,819 pay gap for newly trained physicians: the unexplained trend of men earning more than women' (2011) 30(2) *Health Affairs* 2193, G Hundley, 'Why women earn less than men in self-employment' (2001) 22(4) *Journal of Labor Research* 817. See too M Pollmann-Schult, 'Marriage and earnings: why do married men earn more than single men?' (2011) 27(2) *European Sociological Review* 147.
40 See Herring (n 35) and J Carbone 'A feminist perspective on divorce' (1994) 4(1) *The Future of Children* 183.
41 M Selmi 'Care, work, and the road to equality: a commentary on Fineman and Williams' (2000–2001) 76(3) *Chicago-Kent Law Review* 1557.

society, it is evident – and all too often acknowledged – that those problems will not be resolved by property adjustments at the time of divorce.[42]

In that context, the question then remains: what should be the object of a court called upon to distribute property on divorce? And even if it were accepted that courts should attempt to equalise the material benefits and detriments of the relationship as between the parties (free from gender prejudice), it must be made clearer how that should be done.

Justice and the distribution of property at the end of relationships

I want to suggest that framing the problem and its analysis in slightly different terms might help us to see clearer answers to these difficult questions than we have been able to see before. If redistribution decisions did not focus on repairing gender inequality or resolving the tensions at the heart of the law's ambivalent, continuing embrace of some version of the public/private divide, a clearer mechanism might emerge for achieving those objectives in a principled way. In the rest of this chapter, I want to suggest a focus on something much more mundane and pragmatic: the processes or mechanisms of valuing *both* the property and income to be distributed from the relationship *and* the more ethereal contents of the relationship in relation to which the distribution is to take place.

I want to further suggest that, when a marriage ends, although only the *material* value is available for redistribution (the insubstantial value in the relationship having come to an end), the mechanism for settling the redistributive allocations of that material property must take proper account of *all* the value that was to be found in the relationship during its subsistence (and not just the *material* value that has been produced by the parties to it and that lingers in its aftermath). In making this suggestion, I want to try to outline an ethical argument for a distribution that allows people – and women, in particular – to take material property from their ending relationships because they deserve it or are owed it, despite the fact that the value they have brought to the relationship was principally 'immaterial' and may have expired. My argument will be for the recognition of a kind of 'immaterial property' in relationships – in economic or accounting terms, 'goodwill' – and for a way of valuing and accounting for that property that will, in the material property distribution, do justice between the parties.

The ambition of this chapter is to argue that people should take from their ending relationships something different from the quantity of property (and income) that is, in the law of property, theirs in title.[43] But they should not, it will be further argued, simply take a strictly equal share of the property that either or both have accumulated.[44] I will argue that people should take from their relationships that have ended an allocation of property and income that accords with a Rawlsian conception of justice;[45] property rights should be adjusted so as to give due weight to the position of the more disadvantaged of the parties (and to provide appropriate compensation to her).[46] But, at the same time, I will try to set out an adjustment which will reflect value and deservedness so that those who think that,

---

42 See, e.g. Carbone (n 3) and (n 40), Herring (n 3) and (n 35), and Diduck (n 6).
43 As would be the case in England and Wales were it not for MCA 1973, s. 23. See Cretney (n 7).
44 As would happen in a community of property regime like those that operate in most continental European legal systems and in many US states; see Cooke, Barlow and Callus (n 6).
45 J Rawls, *A Theory of Justice* (Cambridge, MA: Harvard University Press 1971; revised edn 1999).
46 Ibid. 13.

in justice, work ought to be rewarded by allowing people to benefit from the proceeds of their labour are not left dissatisfied by the mechanism for property redistribution.[47]

In order to make this argument, I will, in the first instance, outline my view of the kinds of value that people bring to their relationships. I will then go on to discuss the way in which the value they bring to their relationships might be used to account for what each party to a relationship should take from it (to discuss, in other words, why I think parties to a relationship 'deserve' an allocation of property and income that does not accord with strict equality of resources, or with a strict idea of the legal ownership of tangible property).

Value in relationships: the valuable and the invaluable

What is valuable in relationships, I would like to suggest (uncontroversially, I think), takes two forms. In the first instance there is material which is *calculably valuable*. The past acquisition of property (assets) and the continuing abilities of the parties to acquire it after divorce (income earning capacity) are, it is submitted, relatively easily capable of economic valuation; we can give each a numerical, money value because we can, relatively easily, know what those values are in a world of markets in which those values are settled.[48]

In the second instance, there is what I would like to call the *invaluable value* that is brought to, engaged in, and born out of personal relationships. Here, I am talking about two kinds of value that, it is submitted, must be brought into account when property is being distributed at the end of relationships.

First, relationships (while they last) are personally invaluable to the parties to them. There is an overtly intangible value to relationships that arise in the euphoria, passion, fondness, ease, comfort, contentment, and companionship – in short, love – that people in them bring to one another (what the Romans must have had in mind when they coined the term 'consortium omnis vitae' in the context of marriage).[49] The extent to which this value is real – and frequently more valuable than lucrative economic (calculably valuable) value – is borne out by the frequency with which people (and, again, women in particular)[50] make what appear to be economically irrational decisions because of it.

---

47 Such a 'labour theory of value' is often attributed to John Locke: see, for example, KI Vaughn, 'John Locke and the Labor Theory of Value' (1978) 2(4) *Journal of Libertarian Studies* 311. But the theory comes into its own in the 19th century: see PC Dooley, *The Labour Theory of Value* (Routledge 2005). It continues to have an intuitive appeal to, at least, some judges (see, e.g. *Cowan v Cowan* [2001] EWCA (Civ) 679, *Sorrell v Sorrell* [2005] EWHC (Fam) 1717, and *Charman v Charman* [2006] EWHC (Fam) 1879) and some commentators (see, for example, F Gibb, 'Legal process in dock as judges rule ex-wife is worth record £48 million payout' *The Times*, 25 May 2007 – discussing *Charman*).
48 Of course, there will always be disputes about the effectiveness of markets to value property and labour appropriately: see, e.g. C Laux and C Leuz, 'The crisis of fair-value accounting: making sense of the recent debate' (2009) 34(6–7) *Accounting, Organizations and Society* 826.
49 Defined as '[a] community for the whole life' which is 'a basic element of the Roman Marriage mentioned by Modestinus (D23.2.1)': A Berger, *Encyclopedic Dictionary of Roman Law*, Vol 43 (The American Philosophical Society 1980) 409. For a detailed consideration of 'consortium' and its appropriateness as a basis for tort actions against third parties, see, e.g. *Best v Samuel Fox Co. Ltd.* (1952) 2 All ER 394.
50 Although, for a contrasting gender dimension, see the South African case of *Kritzinger v Kritzinger* [1989] 1 All SA 325 (A) (in which the career sacrifice was made by the husband and not the wife). *Radmacher (formerly Granatino) v Granatino* [2010] UKSC 42 is another case in which a man makes what might be considered an irrational economic decision (for himself) in changing his career when he marries and, because of his marriage, in signing the ante-nuptial agreement which on its face restricts the legal claims he would more clearly have been able to make without it.

When, for example, people decide, as Mrs McFarlane[51] did, to forgo a lucrative career which is at least as good as their husbands', in favour of raising children and bolstering their families, they are clearly making an economically irrational decision; they lose their incomes and their career prospects entirely on the gamble that they will be able to rely on their husbands for support for the rest of their lives. But even people like Mrs Miller[52] make economically irrational decisions when they choose to forgo lucrative careers to move to cities in which their husbands have much more lucrative careers; while they may be economically better off with their husbands, they too lose their earnings and reduce their earning capacity on the gamble that their (now dependent) relationships will last. That gamble is made more dangerous because they sacrifice their careers, and the social and economic capital that they would accumulate if they were to keep them. If we think about their economic decisions as decisions focused solely on their probable long-term individual well-being, taking account of divorce statistics, the gamble is, it is submitted, economically irrational. Clearly, in cases like Mrs Miller's, the decision to give up a career would prove to be economically irrational were it not for the intervention of a court to redistribute the wealth of the husband to make good a wife's economic sacrifice.

Of course, the gendering of these decisions should not be regarded as simply one sided. For people like Mr McFarlane,[53] the decision that results in their wives forgoing lucrative careers casts on them alone the burden of supporting their families financially. To participate in such decisions is also economically irrational for them; they accept a smaller family income and greater family costs for reasons that are not economically informed. But in men's eyes too, we must assume, that the economic 'sacrifice' is valuable. So valuable, indeed, that it is worth a considerable loss of income, and at a time when there will often be an increase in family cost (a growing family costs more to maintain). But its value is clearly incalculable in market economic terms.

Before I leave the 'personally invaluable' of relationships, it is worth noting that this category of value might also include the enhanced value of things acquired (things that are calculably valuable) because they are acquired in personal relationships. Although tea pots, or items of clothing, or pieces of art, or rings, or necklaces, or compact discs all have market values, those values can alter when they are brought into a relationship because of the circumstances and the conditions which surround their acquisition. This is often referred to as 'sentimental value' and is also, clearly, incalculable and personal to the parties to a relationship.[54]

The second kind of invaluable value that is to be found in relationships is the kind that extends to us all. We are frequently told[55] (especially by policy makers)[56] that marriage has socially beneficial consequences. In his reflections on the importance of marriage the former British Prime Minister, David Cameron, said:

---

51 *Miller; MacFarlane* (n 28).
52 Ibid.
53 Ibid.
54 See J Goode, 'Whose collection is it anyway? An autoethnographic account of 'dividing the spoils' upon divorce' (2007) 1(3) *Cultural Sociology* 365.
55 See, e.g. DC Ribar, *What Do Social Scientists Know About the Benefits of Marriage? A Review of Quantitative Methodologies* Discussion Paper no. 998 (Bonn, Germany: Institute for the Study of Labor 2004).
56 D Cameron, 'Marriage is good for Britain - and that's why I'm backing it with a tax break, says David Cameron' *The Daily Mail*, 27 September 2013. See too T Parker-Pope, 'Is marriage good for your health?' *New York Times*, 14 April 2010.

Alongside the birth of my children, my wedding was the happiest day of my life. Since then, Samantha and I have been a team. Nothing I've done since – becoming a Member of Parliament, leader of my party or Prime Minister – would have been possible without her.[57]

And David Ribar, starts his (more critical) reflections on the social science on marriage benefit by saying:

> Marriage is positively associated with a large number of outcomes including improved cognitive, emotional and physical well-being for children, better mental and physical health for adults, and greater earnings and consumption for family members. These associations have been documented in hundreds of quantitative studies covering different time periods and different countries.[58]

The personal claim made by Cameron and the professional assessments reflected in Ribar's opening statement seem to make it clear beyond doubt that marriage is valuable in public policy terms; it is a social good. So valuable in the eyes of the Prime Minister, indeed, that he would not have been Prime Minister without it. And yet this extraordinary value cannot be given in money. It is invaluable. The individual contributions to this value are, likewise, incapable of easy valuation. The value remains economically indeterminate.

Adjusting value when relationships end: what do people deserve?

The question, then, is how the calculably valuable and the invaluable should be used in an exercise of property redistribution when relationships end. Because the object of the redistribution exercise is to reallocate (in the way of ownership or a similar kind of entitlement) the *material* property of the parties to a marriage (i.e. that which is calculably valuable), it has always seemed easy to start with the idea of ownership of those economically valuable things; we start with the identifiable assets and income.[59] And because the adjustment of title in these things must be done in an economically valued way (currency value assets and currency value income transfers are made over from one person to the other),[60] it has always seemed necessary either to convert the 'invaluable' activities of marriage into something calculably valuable or simply to ignore them and find some other basis for the exercise of a discretion to distribute property.

---

57 Cameron (n 56).
58 (n 55) 1.
59 It is worth noting that the starting position – separate ownership of property and income in marriage – is open to challenge, if only because, even in the West, the system of separate ownership of property in marriage is not universally adopted (see Cooke, Barlow and Callus (n 6) for a discussion of the varieties of community of property regimes operating in Europe and the US and which might provide lessons for the UK). However, wherever one starts, I suggest that a redistributive discretion is necessary because ownership of tangible property does not adequately reflect value in relationships. See JG Sherman, 'Prenuptial agreements: a new reason to revive an old rule' (2006) 53(3) *Cleveland State Law Review* 359 (for an overview of how differently different US states deal with prenuptial agreements and property adjustment and for an argument to revive the judicial refusal to accede to those agreements).
60 MCA 1973, s 23. See too the Family Procedure Rules, Part 9 and Practice Direction 9A for the regulations governing a court's access to the accounting information relating to the value of assets and income that will enable it to make financial orders on divorce.

Where the invaluable (or at least part of it) could be linked directly to the acquisition of wealth – as in *Conran*,[61] in which Mrs Conran had 'contributed' to her husband's business success by being the kind of supportive spouse that encouraged (with advice and other assistance) the growth of his business – the courts could account for it in the ordinary way; they could work out its calculable value and distribute that part of the property owned by one spouse but derived through the efforts of the other back to her. However, where such a calculation could not be made, where the comfort and society of a spouse did not directly influence the other's acquisition of wealth, the invaluable of the relationship was simply ignored.[62] Instead the courts have used other mechanisms – needs, generously interpreted before *White*,[63] and then fairness after *White* – to allocate the property of one spouse to the other without having to contend with a forensic analysis of what each spouse deserves. It is interesting that it has always seemed intuitive that the conversion from 'invaluable' to 'calculable value' could not be done simply by using a market valuing mechanism; the invaluable value of wives and husbands in family relationships has never been reduced to the money value their activities (their 'work' in the relationship) would attract in a market for the kinds of work that are represented by them.

But this has meant that our legal system has never come to terms with the problem of value that lies, it is submitted, at the very heart of any property redistribution enterprise. In allowing people to make claims against one another on the basis of needs (as we once did and still, to a lesser extent, do) or on the grounds of gender neutral fairness (as we now do) we have circumvented the important central questions: what is the moral basis for taking the property of one person and giving it to another in a culture that values property rights? Why is it that 'need' or 'fairness' can undermine property rights in the context of a personal, intimate relationship of a particular sort, but not in the myriad other relationships that people form? Why are business partners' disputes not similarly premised on 'need' and 'fairness'? And why are our judgements about the extent of 'need' and the quality of 'fairness' so very different in the context of relationships which are ending than they are in any other property redistributive context (as, for example, when the state allocates social welfare benefits)?

In the rest of this chapter, I want to outline some of the tentative answers I wish to propose to these questions. I want to suggest that our intuitions about redistribution are often less random than they might appear to be and that all that is required for them to work better is for a more principled justification for them to be made more explicit. If that were done, I will argue, we will uncover the ideas required for a better accounting for property redistribution at the end of relationships. And, most importantly, our ideas and justifications will finally inform a redistributive discretion that focuses on what people deserve to take from their relationships because of the value they have brought to them.

I will start by making a bland statement about calculable value: it is, by its very nature, relative; in markets, value is determined by 'sellers' and 'buyers'. If these people were different people, the value of things for sale in markets would be different. Even though a 'general' market value may be ascertained for any particular product, we know that different personalities will negotiate a different value for it in different circumstances. In effect, my argument is that the 'demand' side of supply and demand is malleable because of the people and the personalities involved. I want to suggest that invaluable value is, if anything, even

---

61 (n 25).
62 See, for example, *Dart* (n 25).
63 (n 10).

more relative than calculable value. What one spouse gets from another is, in the very nature of the relationship, dependent upon the other; it is impossible for anyone else to grasp fully the value that each brings to the relationship. This relativity of value is, it is submitted, born out of the reasons people have for giving value to anything or anyone. A person values things and other people for what they bring to her. And what they give her is not uniform across a population of individuals. What she values is not what another person, even very similarly situated, would value. In the words of Andrew Youpa:

> A desire–satisfaction theory [of value] says that what has value is the satisfaction of one's desires and whatever leads to the satisfaction of one's desires. So, for example, what has value for a greedy person is the satisfaction of her desire for an abundance of wealth and whatever leads to the satisfaction of her desire for wealth. What has value for an ambitious person is the satisfaction of his desire for fame and whatever brings him fame. Something has value because it is desired. It is not the case that something is ever desired because it is valuable.[64]

Once we understand that value is relative, we can begin to understand how the invaluable in a relationship can be valued very differently in different relationships. We can see how our intuitions that 'need' and 'fairness' might produce different outcomes in different relationships may be right. But we should still try to be more explicit about exactly what differences are justifiable. To this end, we should try to understand how the invaluable in relationships might come to be useful in relation to calculably valuable property when distribution is in question. A single observation about what I have said so far might lead us to an appropriate conclusion: if we accept that both calculable value and invaluable value are relative, in relationships the value of one must be reflected in the other. The gift of an expensive piece of jewellery must be 'worth' the 'insubstantial' return that the giver obtains in his relationship. Thus we can say that, what a spouse brings to her relationship, even when she brings no assets, is related to or reflected in (for the purpose of redistributive valuation) what her spouse brings to that same relationship. They value each other. And because we are in the habit of maintaining that in Western marriage, at least, the value they have for one another is 'equal' we must assume the quantification of value to be equal. Her affection is 'worth' his money and his affection.

The conclusion I have just reached might be taken to suggest that property should be distributed equally at the end of a relationship, that my analysis produces an argument for the adoption of a community of property regime. However, I want to argue that that is not the inevitable outcome of what I have said so far. To begin that argument, I want to think of the invaluable value of relationships as something like goodwill in business relationships. Goodwill represents, in accounting, the additional value that a business is worth because of incalculable things like its reputation:

> Goodwill is measured and recorded as the amount paid to acquire a business in excess of the fair value of its net identifiable assets. While this measurement approach is intended to capture the excess value created by a going concern, it is possible that the amount of goodwill recorded may also reflect an overpayment for the acquired firm.[65]

---

64 A Youpa, 'Spinoza's theories of value' (2010) 18(2) *British Journal for the History of Philosophy* 209, 209.
65 NT Churyk, 'Reporting goodwill: are the new accounting standards consistent with market valuations?' (2005) 58(10) *Journal of Business Research* 1353, 1353.

Although goodwill is difficult to value and may be 'incorrectly' valued, it is undeniably valuable. And in the circumstances of a business sale, a currency value will be established for it. But like the value of the invaluable in personal relationships, goodwill is premised on some quality of a mutual personal relationship that cannot easily be reduced to a money value:

> My title [Goodwill and the Spirit of Market Capitalism] refers to goodwill rather than benevolence because benevolence . . . is something shown in relations between unequals, by superior to inferior, the reciprocal of which is usually called loyalty. Goodwill is more status-neutral, more an expression of Hobhouse's 'principle of mutuality'. And it is that broader meaning which I intend. A formal definition of my subject might be: the sentiments of friendship and the sense of diffuse personal obligation which accrue between individuals engaged in recurring contractual economic exchange.[66]

It is this aspect of the roots of goodwill that suggests a link with personal relationships. The invaluable and personal of an economic relationship grows into something that acquires economic value and requires a system of valuation and financial accounting. While spouses are not engaged in 'recurring contractual economic exchange' their well-being is, in the broadest possible sense, mutually dependent and interdependent. They are, in a much more fundamental and pervasive way, an economic unit (although an economically irrational unit). Certainly, as I have argued above, the state regards them as such and depends upon them for that reason (part of their 'invaluable value' is our perception of their contribution to a better society). It should, therefore, be relatively easy to understand the way in which goodwill accounting might be useful to us in our attempts to find a mechanism for valuing the invaluable in the redistributive exercise when relationships end.

It is important to note that I am not suggesting that valuing the invaluable in personal relationships is exactly like valuing goodwill. There are clearly some significant differences between the two which would counsel against a wholesale adoption of goodwill accounting practices into the divorce property redistributive exercise. In particular, we are instantly aware that, whereas goodwill valuations only occur when there is goodwill to value (goodwill serves as an imperfect predictor of calculable value into the future), the valuation of the invaluable in personal relationships only occurs at a time when it no longer exists. However, the determination of what proportion of the wealth of a relationship should be allocated to each party to it must, it is submitted, take account of all value that was brought into the relationship and not just that value which remains at its termination. That requires a kind of goodwill accounting across the duration of the relationship.

One final word of caution is necessary before I conclude. Because I have used the metaphor of goodwill in the closing stages of this discussion, and because goodwill is a feature of business accounting and business practice, it might be tempting to suggest that people should be able to set the value of the invaluable in their relationships by contract (that a prenuptial agreement could settle the value that the parties agree should accrue to each other as a result of their relationship). However, in this respect too I would argue that goodwill accounting differs from valuing the invaluable in personal relationships.

I have three bases for this argument. In the first instance, whereas goodwill is valued in a contract negotiated at arm's length between relative strangers and with a view to

---

66 R Dore, 'Goodwill and the spirit of market capitalism' (1983) 34(4) *The British Journal of Sociology* 459, 460.

future profitability, valuing the invaluable in relationships is neither at arm's length nor about profitability. A contract that settled the invaluable in personal relationships would be one produced in a setting of intimacy in which people behave economically irrationally (as I have argued above). Furthermore, it is the kind of economic irrationality that, because it is frequently selfless, we consider it to be honourable and even noble. To hold parties to bargains of that sort when their relationships fail would be to reward the party who was economically rational (and arguably less honourable) and punish the one who was economically irrational and selfless. It is submitted, therefore, that to reward with recognition and legal enforcement what might be regarded as a cynical ploy to avoid an appropriate valuation of the invaluable would be to introduce an imbalance to the relationship that it should not be required to bear.

Second, there is the additional consideration that the invaluable of a relationship extends beyond the parties themselves (to the benefits that society derives from the existence of relationships); the parties cannot, therefore, be responsible for (and capable of) valuing it by agreement between themselves alone.

Third, a prenuptial agreement to value the invaluable of a relationship would, by its nature, be valuing something it cannot begin to grasp. The 'thing' being valued has no present existence and is, as I have argued throughout this chapter, almost impossibly difficult to value once we come to know what it was. It would be like suggesting to a person that they should value the goodwill of a business before the business begins and without any idea of when the business will be sold. To make that suggestion in an economic setting should be enough to demonstrate the unsustainability of such a suggestion. It would be difficult even to suggest an early valuation of calculable value to business people along these lines. That people are even prepared to enter prenuptial agreements at all, therefore, seems to me to be another measure of their economic irrationality in relationships and the profound unreliability of agreements of this sort to settle the terms of property adjustment at divorce.

Conclusion

In this chapter, I argued that the bases upon which property distribution takes place in England and Wales are unclear and less than satisfactory. I have suggested that the reason for the sense of unease that preoccupies almost all commentators might be addressed by shifting the centre of consideration to the question of value in personal relationships. I have suggested that a proper consideration of value, and then a reformed mechanism of accounting for value, might bring us closer to certainty and predictability in the settlement of disputes about the distribution of property on divorce. I have not tried to provide details of the mechanism which I have begun to outline here; that will require further work and another (longer) analysis which is not possible here.

However, I hope that, in setting out the thoughts that have brought me to this position, others will be encouraged to reflect with renewed vigour on what have seemed to be intractable problems relating to property distribution on divorce. My hope is that we will emerge with a framework for distributing property on divorce that has a clearer understanding of what value people bring to each other in relationships and, therefore, what they deserve to take from those relationships when they end. It is submitted that a closer analysis and understanding of value and, in particular, of the interrelatedness of calculable value and the invaluable is essential if we are to come to a properly principled understanding of the way in which property ought to be distributed at the end of relationships.

Bibliography

Bailey-Harris R, 'Case comment: fairness in financial settlements on divorce' (2001) 117:2 *Law Quarterly Review* 199–203.

Bailey-Harris R, 'The paradoxes of principle and pragmatism: ancillary relief in England and Wales' (2005) 19:2 *International Journal of Law, Policy and the Family* 229–41.

Berger A, *Encyclopedic Dictionary of Roman Law*, Vol 43, Part 2 (The American Philosophical Society 1980) 409.

Bianchi SM et al., 'Housework: who did, does or will do it, and how much does it matter?' (2012) 91:1 *Social Forces* 55–63.

Bottomley A and Wong S, 'Shared households: a new paradigm for thinking about the reform of domestic property relations' in A Diduck and K O'Donovan (eds), *Feminist Perspectives on Family Law* (Abingdon, UK, Routledge-Cavendish 2006), pp. 39–57.

Cameron D, 'Marriage is good for Britain – and that's why I'm backing it with a tax break, says David Cameron' *The Daily Mail*, 27 September 2013.

Camus A, *A Happy Death* (New York, Alfred A Knopf, 1972).

Carbone J, 'A feminist perspective on divorce' (1994) 4:1 *The Future of Children* 183–209.

Carbone J, 'Feminism, gender, and the consequences of divorce' in M Freeman (ed.), *Divorce: Where Next?* (Aldershot, UK, Dartmouth 1996), pp. 181–227.

Churyk NT, 'Reporting goodwill: are the new accounting standards consistent with market valuations?' (2005) 58:10 *Journal of Business Research* 1353–61.

Cooke E, Barlow A and Callus T, *Community of Property: A Regime for England and Wales?* (London, The Nuffield Foundation 2006).

Cretney S, 'Trusting the judges: money after divorce' (1999) 52:1 *Current Legal Problems* 286–312.

Cretney S, 'Community of property imposed by judicial decision' (2003) 119:3 *Law Quarterly Review* 349–52.

Cretney S, *Family Law in the Twentieth Century: A History* (Oxford, OUP 2003).

Diduck A and Kaganas F, *Family Law, Gender and the State*, 2nd edn (Oxford, Hart 2006).

Diduck A, 'Ancillary relief: complicating the search for principle' (2011) 38:2 *Journal of Law and Society* 272–300.

Dooley PC, *The Labour Theory of Value* (London, Routledge 2005).

Dore R, 'Goodwill and the spirit of market capitalism' (1983) 34:4 *The British Journal of Sociology* 459–82.

Duckworth P and Hodson D, '*White v White* – bringing section 25 back to the people' (2001) 31:1 *Fam Law* 24–9.

Eekelaar J, 'Asset distribution on divorce – the durational element' (2001) 117:4 *Law Quarterly Review* 552–60.

Eekelaar J, 'Back to basics and forward into the unknown' (2001) 31:1 *Fam Law* 30–2.

Eekelaar J, 'Asset distribution on divorce – time and property' (2003) 33:11 *Fam Law* 828–32.

Eekelaar J, '*Miller v Miller*: the descent into chaos' (2005) 35:11 *Fam Law* 870–72.

Eekelaar J, 'Shared income after divorce: a step too far' (2005) 121:1 *Law Quarterly Review* 1–4.

Gibb F, 'Legal process in dock as judges rule ex-wife is worth record £48 million payout' *The Times*, 25 May 2007.

Goode J, 'Whose collection is it anyway? An autoethnographic account of "dividing the spoils" upon divorce' (2007) 1:3 *Cultural Sociology* 365–83.

Herring J, 'Why financial orders on divorce should be unfair' (2005) 19:2 *International Journal of Law Policy and the Family* 218–28.

Herring J, *Family Law*, 6th edn (London, Pearson 2013).

Hess E, 'Assessing the quantum of periodical payments after McFarlane' (2006) 36:9 *Fam Law* 780–94.

Hill C, Corbett C, and St. Rose A, *Why So Few? Women in Science, Technology, Engineering, and Mathematics* (Washington, DC, AAUW 2010).

Hitchings E, 'The impact of recent ancillary relief jurisprudence in the 'everyday' ancillary relief case' (2010) 22:1 *Child and Family Law Quarterly* 93–114.

Hundley G, 'Why women earn less than men in self-employment' (2001) 22:4 *Journal of Labor Research* 817–29.

Lachance-Grzela M and Bouchard G, 'Why do women do the lion's share of housework? A decade of research' (2010) 63:11 *Sex Roles* 767–80.

Laufer-Ukeles P, 'Selective recognition of gender difference in the law: revaluing the caretaker role' (2008) 31:1 *Harvard Journal of Law and Gender* 1–66.

Laux C and Leuz C, 'The crisis of fair-value accounting: making sense of the recent debate' (2009) 34:6–7 *Accounting, Organizations and Society* 826–34.

Law Commission, *Family Law-Report on Financial Provision in Matrimonial Proceedings* (Law Com No 25, London, 1969).

Law Commission *Marital Property Agreements* (Consultation Paper no. 198, London, 2011).

Law Commission *Matrimonial Property, Needs and Agreements* (Consultation Paper no. 208, London 2012).

Lo Sasso AT, Richards MR, Chou CF and Gerber, S 'The $16,819 pay gap for newly trained physicians: the unexplained trend of men earning more than women' (2011) 30:2 *Health Affairs* 193–201.

McDowell L, 'Sexuality, desire and embodied performances in the workplace' in B Brookes-Gordon, L Gelsthorpe, and A Bainham (eds), *Sexuality Repositioned* (Oxford, Hart 2004), pp. 85–107.

Meehan A, '*Miller and McFarlane*: an opportunity missed?' (2006) 36:7 *Fam Law* 566–74.

Miles J, 'Principle or pragmatism in ancillary relief: the virtues of flirting with academic theories and other jurisdictions' (2005) 19:2 *International Journal of Law, Policy and the Family* 242–56.

Miles J, '*Charman v Charman (No 4)* – Making sense of need, compensation and equal sharing after *Miller; McFarlane*' (2008) 20:3 *CFLQ* 378–94.

Moor P and Le Grice V, 'Periodical payments orders following *Miller* and *McFarlane*: a series of unfortunate events' (2006) 36:8 *Fam Law* 655–58.

Parker-Pope T, 'Is marriage good for your health?' *New York Times*, 14 April 2010.

Pollmann-Schult M, 'Marriage and earnings: why do married men earn more than single men?' (2011) 27:2 *European Sociological Review* 147–63.

Rawls J, *A Theory of Justice* (Cambridge, MA, Harvard University Press 1971; revised edn 1999).

Ribar DC, *What Do Social Scientists Know About the Benefits of Marriage? A Review of Quantitative Methodologies* Discussion Paper no. 998 (Bonn, Germany, Institute for the Study of Labor 2004).

Scherpe J (ed), *Marital Agreements and Private Autonomy in Comparative Perspective* (Oxford, Hart 2012).

Selmi M, 'Care, work, and the road to equality: a commentary on Fineman and Williams' (2000–2001) 76:3 *Chicago-Kent Law Review* 1557–68.

Shelton BA and John D, 'Does marital status make a difference? Housework among married and cohabiting men and women' (1993) 14:3 *Journal of Family Issues* 401–20.

Sherman JG, 'Prenuptial agreements: a new reason to revive an old rule' (2006) 53:3 *Cleveland State Law Review* 359–98.

Vaughn KI, 'John Locke and the labor theory of value' (1978) 2:4 *Journal of Libertarian Studies* 311–26.

Youpa A, 'Spinoza's theories of value' (2010) 18:2 *British Journal for the History of Philosophy* 209–29.

9 Intestate succession and the property of unmarried cohabitants in England and Wales

Simone Wong

Introduction

The significant increase in cohabitation rates in England and Wales since the 1970s[1] has raised the question of whether legal recognition should be given to cohabitation in order for cohabitants to be better protected when their relationships terminate, whether by separation or the death of a partner. Cohabitants are currently provided little protection in relation to their financial and property matters and resort must be made to other areas of law such as contract, trusts and estoppel. The Law Commission subsequently reviewed the law and made recommendations in the Cohabitation Report published in 2007[2] to permit qualifying cohabitants to apply for financial remedies upon termination of their relationships.[3] Certain amendments were further proposed with regards to family provision claims on death.[4]

The intestacy rules apply when the deceased fails to either make a will or dispose of the whole estate in the will. They are intended to provide a fair and reasonable distribution of the intestate estate, based on certain presumptions about the deceased's wishes regarding such distribution. While the succession rights of spouses and other relatives have been previously subject to review,[5] the rights of cohabitants have received less attention until recently.[6] A review of the law of intestacy and family provision claims was subsequently

---

1 For more information about the data, see Law Commission, *Cohabitation: The Financial Consequences of Relationship Breakdown* (Law Com No 307, 2007) paras 1.8–1.13 and Law Commission, *Intestacy and Family Provision Claims on Death* (Law Com Consultation Paper no. 191, 2009) para 4.2.
2 Law Commission, *Cohabitation* (n 1).
3 Ibid. Pts 3 to 5.
4 Ibid. Pt 6. These include removing the two-year minimum duration requirement for cohabiting parents and amending 'reasonable financial provision' to a cohabitant by removing the current limitation to reasonable maintenance.
5 See Law Commission, *Family Law: Distribution on Intestacy* (Law Com No 187, 1989). The Law Commission back then had recommended a 14-days survivorship requirement and that the surviving spouse should be entitled to the whole estate. The latter was rejected amidst concerns that it might prejudice the deceased's children, especially where the surviving spouse was a step-parent and might not be relied upon to pass on the estate to the children after his or her death. The survivorship requirement was implemented but was raised to 28 days: Administration of Estates Act 1925(AEA), s 46(2A). See also R Kerridge, 'Distribution on intestacy, the Law Commission's Report (1989)' (1990) *Conv* 358; S Cretney, 'Reform of intestacy: the best we can do?' (1995) 111 *LQR* 77.
6 One change affecting cohabitants was implemented after the Law Commission's review in 1989. The Inheritance (Provision for Family and Dependants) Act 1975 (IHA) was amended to allow cohabitants who meet certain criteria to apply for family provision as a separate category: IHA, ss 1(1)(ba), 1(1A) and 1(1B).

undertaken by the Law Commission, which led to the publication of the Intestacy Report in 2011.[7]

The Administration of Estates Act 1925 (AEA), as amended by the Inheritance and Trustees' Powers Act 2014 (ITPA), has since given effect to the Law Commission's recommendations in relation to the entitlement of surviving spouses, issue and other family members under the intestacy rules.[8] The position of cohabitants, however, remains unchanged and there is little evidence of any political will by the government to give effect to any of the recommendations made by the Law Commission.

A cohabitant's death may have devastating consequences for the surviving partner, especially where property is not jointly owned and/or the deceased dies intestate, since s/he is not entitled to any part of the deceased's estate under the intestacy rules. A surviving partner may thus be left financially vulnerable. Women may be more susceptible because of existing economic inequalities between men and women.[9] Second, as the life expectancy of women (82.5 years) in England and Wales is higher than men's (78.5 years), they are more likely to survive their partners.[10]

A claim to a share in the deceased partner's estate may be made by either arguing a common intention constructive trust or applying for family provision under the Inheritance (Provision for Family and Dependants) Act 1975 (IHA). However, resort to constructive trusts may be highly problematic.[11] A family provision application may be equally unattractive as a cohabitant may find herself competing with other beneficiaries of the deceased's estate, for example, a surviving or former spouse and children of the deceased, including children that she has had with the deceased.

For the purposes of this chapter, the discussion is in relation to the intestacy rules as they stood at the time of the review by the Law Commission. Thus, all subsequent references to the provisions of the AEA are to those prior to amendment by the ITPA 2014. The chapter considers the Law Commission's recommendations for the reform of the law of intestacy for cohabitants. While the Marriage (same sex couples) Act 2013 extends marriage to same sex couples in England and Wales this chapter focuses on opposite-sex spouses and cohabitants mainly for the reason that the normative issues discussed may not be equally relevant to same-sex couples. The chapter seeks to argue that, while seemingly progressive in terms of extending (more) rights to cohabitants, the intestacy proposals in fact reinforce a traditional family form and provide only fairly modest protection against financial hardship in the event of intestacy. There are, in particular, three issues with which the chapter is concerned. The first is the normative reasons for extending rights to qualifying cohabitants. Notwithstanding an acknowledgement of the importance of promoting and affording protection to committed and stable couple relationships, whether married or unmarried, the law still draws a distinction, especially in its conceptualisation of commitment. Consequently, this serves to restrict the

---

7 Law Commission, *Intestacy and Family Provision Claims on Death* (Law Com No 331, 2011).
8 See s 46(1) of AEA as amended. The amendments to the AEA 1925 came into effect on 14 May 2014.
9 See S Dema Moreno and C Díaz Martínez, Chapter 3 and D Price, D Bisdee and T Daly, Chapter 4 in this collection.
10 Office of National Statistics, *Life expectancy at birth and at age 65 by local areas in the United Kingdom, 2004–06 to 2008–10* (2011), 4, Table 1. The chapter will thus refer to the female cohabitant.
11 See, e.g. S Gardner, 'Rethinking family property' (1993) 109 *LQR* 263; N Glover and P Todd, 'The myth of common intention' (1996) 16 *LS* 323; S Wong, 'Would you "care" to share your home?' (2007) 58 *NILQ* 268; G Douglas, J Pearce and H Woodward, 'Cohabitants, property and the law: a study of injustice' (2009) 72 *MLR* 24.

rights afforded to cohabitants. To qualify, cohabitants must demonstrate that their relationships and, relatedly, their 'commitment' can (and must) be analogised with marriage.

The second is that the intestacy reform proposals retain a spouse-focused approach, thereby adding another group that has priority over other beneficiaries, such as the deceased's children. This leads to protection being afforded to cohabitants at the expense of other financially vulnerable stakeholders (e.g. minor or disabled children) in the event of intestacy. Lastly, there is the issue of the inheritance tax liability of cohabitants, a matter which received little attention in the Intestacy Report.

Intestacy, the law and property claims by cohabitants

The distribution of an intestate estate depends on whether the deceased is survived by a spouse, his issue and other relatives, such as parents and siblings. Where the deceased has issue, the surviving spouse would be entitled to the deceased's personal chattels, a statutory legacy of £250,000 and a life interest in half of the remaining estate. The issue would be entitled to the other half and the capital upon termination of the spouse's life interest. If there are no issue, the spouse would take a larger statutory legacy of £450,000 and a half share in the remaining estate. The other half would pass to the deceased's parents or, if they predecease the deceased, to his full siblings. Where there are no surviving parents or siblings, the surviving spouse would inherit the whole estate.[12] If the deceased is survived only by his issue, they would take the whole estate.[13] The intestacy rules thus take a spouse-focused approach where a large proportion, if not the whole, of the estate will pass to the surviving spouse in most cases.

With no entitlement under the intestacy rules, a cohabitant may only inherit a share of the estate by making a family provision claim under the IHA as an eligible cohabitant or, where the criteria are not met, a dependant. A claim is based on the deceased's failure to make reasonable financial provision for her. These claims supplement succession rights as the applicant may challenge the distribution of the estate where the distribution rules do not seem to operate appropriately. The lack of financial provision *per se* does not mean that reasonable provision has not been made. The aim of the IHA is to make reasonable financial provision to the applicant rather than to effect a fair (re)distribution of the estate. The issue, therefore, is whether the provision, or lack thereof, to the applicant is unreasonable.

To be eligible, the cohabitant must have lived with the deceased as his spouse for two years immediately before his death,[14] whereas a dependant must establish that she was maintained, either wholly or partly, by the deceased immediately before his death.[15] However, financial provision to a cohabitant under either category is less generous than to a spouse. A spouse may apply for provision that would be reasonable in the circumstances for her to receive and is not limited to reasonable maintenance.[16] A cohabitant, on the other hand, is limited to reasonable maintenance.[17] The test therefore is not whether the cohabitant

---

12 AEA, s 46(1)(i).
13 AEA, s 46(1)(ii). Where the deceased leaves neither spouse nor issue, the estate is distributed among his relatives in accordance with s 46(1)(iii) – (v).
14 IHA, s 1(1)(ba) in conjunction with either s 1(1A) or s 1(1B).
15 IHA, s 1(1)(e).
16 IHA, ss 1(2)(a) and 1(2)(aa).
17 IHA, s 1(2)(b).

is in need of maintenance but rather, looking objectively at the circumstances, it is unreasonable that no provision from the estate has been made for her.[18]

'Reasonable maintenance' has, nevertheless, been generously interpreted by the courts. Goff LJ in *Re Coventry* states, for instance, that reasonable maintenance should be neither defined too narrowly nor limited to provision at subsistence level.[19] Browne-Wilkinson J in *Re Dennis* similarly states that it 'connotes only payments which, directly or indirectly, enable the applicant in the future to discharge the cost of his daily living at whatever standard of living is appropriate to him'.[20] Consequently, awards have been made to maintain the lifestyle that the applicant was accustomed to while living with the deceased. A case in point is *Negus v Bahouse* where Mummery LJ stated that the assessment of maintenance is not a wholly objective exercise and is dependent on the specific context of the relationship, that is, the nature and quality of the lifestyle which the applicant and the deceased previously enjoyed.[21]

The courts have powers to make a wide range of orders that include periodical and lump sum payments, transfer of property and provision from the estate to enable the applicant to acquire property.[22] In determining what orders to make, the courts must consider matters, such as the financial resources and needs of the applicant and any other beneficiaries of the estate, any physical or mental disabilities that the applicant may have and the size and nature of the net estate.[23] Where the applicant is a cohabitant, the court must further consider her age, the length of cohabitation and any contributions (including caregiving) made by her towards the welfare of the deceased's family.[24] The courts' wide powers, coupled with the generous interpretation of the meaning of 'reasonable maintenance', have led to awards such as provision from the estate to enable the applicant to purchase a house or flat to live in[25] and even allowing her to stay in the deceased's property during her lifetime.[26]

The Law Commission's law reform proposals

One of the striking things about the recent review of intestacy law is the Law Commission's preference for relying on empirical data, such as public opinion surveys,[27] to help inform the formulation of the reform proposals. According to research, the rate of making wills is generally low in England and Wales, and even lower among cohabitants.[28] The low rate

---

18 *Re Coventry* [1980] Ch 480, 488 (Goff LJ).
19 [1980] Ch 461, 485.
20 [1981] 2 All ER 140, 145; *Piglowska v Piglowska* [1999] 1 WLR 1360.
21 [2008] EWCA Civ 1002 [12] and [24].
22 IHA, s 2.
23 IHA, s 3(1)(a)-(g).
24 IHA, s 3(2A).
25 See, e.g. *Graham v Murphy* [1997] 1 FLR 860; *Re Watson* [1999] 1 FLR 878.
26 *Re Baker* [2008] 2 FLR 767.
27 G Morrell, M Barnard and R Legard, *The Law of Intestate Succession: Exploring Attitudes Among Non-Traditional Families – Final Report* (National Centre for Social Research 2009) www.lawcom.gov.uk/wp-content/uploads/2015/06/law_of_intestate_succession_research.pdf [accessed 23 February 2012] and A Humphrey et al., *Inheritance and the family: attitudes to will-making and intestacy* (National Centre for Social Research 2010) www.natcen.ac.uk/media/23979/inheritance-family-attitudes-will-making.pdf [accessed 23 February 2012].
28 Humphrey et al., *Inheritance and the family* (n 27) 27. Their study found that only 37 per cent of respondents have made a will and 20 per cent of cohabitants have made a will. See also S Brooker, 'Finding the will: a report on will-writing behaviour in England and Wales' (2007) www.convenient-wills.co.uk/Consumer%20council%20NCC174rr_finding_the_will.pdf [accessed 23 February 2012]. Brooker found that only 36 per cent of adults in England and Wales have made a will and 17 per cent of cohabitants have done so.

of making wills among cohabitants may be unsurprising as Barlow and others found a high level of inertia among cohabitants, even those who are legally aware, with regards to making arrangements about their financial and property matters.[29] Home ownership[30] and cohabitation[31] rates in England and Wales have also increased over the years. Haskey, however, found that spouses (43 per cent) are more likely than cohabitants (33 per cent) to own property jointly.[32] The rise in cohabitation and its social acceptance as an alternative form of partnering and child-bearing has prompted the broader question of whether greater legal recognition, including under the intestacy rules, should be given to cohabitation. Given the lower rates of joint home ownership and making wills among cohabitants, there is greater potential for intestacy rules to be applicable unless more cohabitants are encouraged to make wills sooner rather than later in their lives.

The Law Commission found that, in 2011, excluding jointly owned property which passes automatically to the survivor under the rule of survivorship, 90 per cent of intestate estates were valued at less than £250,000, while 98 per cent were valued at less than £450,000. The median value was £56,000.[33] Thus, a spouse would take the whole estate in most cases since its value is likely to fall within the lower, if not the higher, statutory legacy.[34] This makes the argument for amending the intestacy rules to allow the spouse to inherit the whole estate more compelling as that seems to be the case in practice. The public opinion surveys indeed indicate that there is generally strong public support for giving all or priority to the spouse.[35]

However, given the unenthusiastic response to previous recommendations for an 'all to spouse' system, the Law Commission refrained from reviving that recommendation. It opted instead for the abolition of the spouse's life interest where the deceased is survived by a spouse and issue and replacing that with an outright half share in the remaining estate. Where there are no issue but other surviving relatives, such as parents, the spouse should take the whole estate.[36] The key thrust of the Law Commission's proposals is simplicity and administrative efficiency: the proposed rules would simplify the operation of the intestacy rules and, arguably, avoid the costs and complexities of holding part of the estate under a trust.

---

29 A Barlow et al., 'Cohabitation and the law: myths, money and the media' in A Park et al. (eds), *British Social Attitudes: The 24th Report* (London: SAGE 2008) 29. Such inertia may be partly due to the vast majority of cohabiting couples (about 59 per cent) believing erroneously in the common law marriage myth. See A Barlow et al., *Cohabitation, Marriage and the Law: Social Change and Legal Reform in the 21st Century* (Oxford: Hart 2005).
30 Office of National Statistics, *Social Trends No 41 - Housing* (2011) 1 and 6. The number of dwellings in Britain rose to 26.2 million in 2008, with 69.9 per cent of these being owned either outright or with the help of a mortgage.
31 There are around 5.9 million people cohabiting in the UK in 2012, which is twice the number in 1996. See Office for National Statistics (ONS), *Short Report: Cohabitation in the UK in 2012* (2012), Figure 1, p. 1.
32 J Haskey, 'Cohabitating Couples in Great Britain, Accommodation Sharing, Tenure and Property Ownership' (2001) 103 *Population Trends* 26. NatCen's study on separated cohabitants produced similar findings: 42 per cent of the study's couples lived in owner-occupied properties but only 46 per cent of these were jointly held: see S Arthur et al., *Settling Up: Making Financial Arrangements after Separation* (National Centre for Social Research 2002) 13.
33 The Law Commission preferred the median to the mean value of intestate estates because the latter might be distorted by some very small and very large ones; cf the median value of testate estates is £160,000.
34 Law Commission, *Intestacy* (n 1) para 3.11.
35 See Humphrey et al., *Inheritance and the family* (n 27) ch 4. Nearly four-fifths of respondents favoured giving the spouse either all or priority over other beneficiaries, such as the deceased's parents and issue.
36 Law Commission, *Intestacy* (n 7) paras 2.25 and 2.62.

The Law Commission found significant public support for a cohabitant inheriting something from the deceased's estate under the intestacy rules. The level of support depended upon factors such as the length of cohabitation and the presence of children.[37] Consequently, it recommended that a cohabitant should be entitled to inherit under certain conditions.[38] First, the deceased must not be married or in a civil partnership immediately before his death.[39] Second, the cohabitant and the deceased must have lived together in a spousal-like relationship before his death for a minimum period of two years for parenting cohabitants and five years for non-parenting ones.[40] The child(ren) must further have lived in the same household before the deceased's death.[41] A qualifying cohabitant will then have the same entitlement as a spouse under the intestacy rules. With regards to family provision claims, the Law Commission's main recommendation was the abolition of the minimum two-year requirement for parenting cohabitants in order for the IHA to be more accessible.[42]

Are cohabitants better off?

A key reason for reforming the intestacy rules is to alleviate the financial hardship that a cohabitant may face when her partner dies intestate. This section will examine the extent to which the reform proposals are likely to achieve this as well as their impact on other stakeholders, such as the deceased's children and parents. The section focuses on three issues: the way in which commitment is being conceptualised in order to provide access to rights; the scope of protection provided to the financially vulnerable; and lastly, the inadequate consideration of the fiscal consequences of inheritance which negatively impact cohabitants more than spouses.

Commitment

While cohabitations are increasing in length, they tend to be less durable than marriages.[43] This has led to the perception of cohabitants being less committed. The Law Commission's choice of definition of qualifying cohabitants unsurprisingly emphasises stability and commitment as the cornerstones for recognition. This is echoed in judicial observations

---

37 Humphrey et al., *Inheritance and the family* (n 27) ch 4. 49 per cent of respondents were in favour of giving all or priority to the cohabitant from a two year relationship, 64 per cent from a five year relationship and 74 per cent from a ten year relationship.
38 Law Commission, *Intestacy* (n 7) para 8.42. These recommendations are further subject to the recommendations of the Cohabitation Report being implemented.
39 Ibid. para 8.68.
40 Ibid. para 8.87.
41 Ibid. para 8.102. The shorter period for cohabiting parents may be partly influenced by functional arguments. Barlow and James, for instance, observe the functional similarity of cohabitation with marriage especially in terms of parenting: see A Barlow and G James, 'Regulating Marriage and Cohabitation in 21st Century Britain' (2004) 67 *MLR* 143; cf R Probert, 'Cohabitation: Current Legal Solutions' (2009) 62 *CLP* 316. Probert cautions against a functional approach on the grounds that the functional similarity between marriage and cohabitation needs more thorough investigation.
42 Law Commission, *Intestacy* (n 7) para 8.153.
43 Barlow et al., 'Cohabitation and the law' (n 29) 33. The average length of cohabiting relationships has increased from 6.5 years in 2000 to 6.9 years (median is five years) in 2006; the average length of parenting cohabiting relationships in 2006 is even longer at 8.5 years (median is seven years). The median length of a marriage has not changed significantly since 2005 and was 11.4 years in 2010: see *Divorces in England and Wales* (ONS, 2011), 6 www.ons.gov.uk/ons/dcp171778_246403.pdf [accessed 9 March 2012].

that cohabitants 'share their lives and make their home together';[44] where the 'essential quality of the relationship, its *marriage-like* intimacy, stability, and social and financial interdependence' (emphasis added) are important to them and they want 'stability and permanence which go with sharing a home and a life together, with or without … children'.[45] However, no uniform definition of cohabitation has been adopted in the law. As marriage remains the golden standard, the notion of marital commitment is valorised. That has led to qualifying cohabitations being defined in many statutes by the marriage analogy, that is, two persons who live together as husband and wife.[46] Yet, others define them differently as, for example, partners living in an enduring family relationship.[47]

The definition adopted by the Law Commission in the Intestacy report results in fewer cohabitations being included. The Law Commission justifies the detention of the marriage-like definition on the grounds that it is well established and familiar to judges and lawyers. By contrast, the definition used in the Cohabitation Report is couple-based (living together as a couple). This was in response to arguments against the use of the marriage analogy to cohabitation which was seen as reinforcing conjugality as the basis for recognition. The enquiry then focuses on the parties' sexual intimacy which some argue as being irrelevant.[48] Others further argue that the marriage analogy reproduces 'patterns of semblance' in order to assimilate cohabitation with marriage;[49] that the 'marriage-like' notion forms a means of stabilising and disciplining informal relationships such as cohabitation.[50] The continued use of the marriage analogy might also partly be responsible for perpetuating the large-scale belief in the common-law marriage myth.[51]

In retaining the marriage-like definition, the existence of a spousal-like relationship, coupled with parenthood, remain not only evidentially but also ideologically important in establishing cohabitants' requisite commitment under the intestacy reform proposals. The appropriateness of the marriage analogy to cohabitation is, however, open to question. As Lewis observes, spouses and cohabitants exhibit similar dimensions of cognition of commitment, namely: commitment to relationship (and, relatedly, to children); commitment to partner; and feelings of entrapment.[52] Notwithstanding that, Lewis further observes that there are differences in their interpretation and expression of commitment. Spouses express

---

44 *Ghaidan v Mendoza* [2004] 3 All ER 411 [17] (Lord Nicholls).
45 Ibid. [139] (Lady Hale).
46 eg IHA, s 1(1A); Family Law Act 1996, s 62(1)(a); Fatal Accidents Act 1976, s 1(3).
47 eg Adoption and Children Act 2002, s 144(4)(b).
48 See, e.g. N Bala and R Jaremko Bromwich, 'Context and inclusivity in Canada's evolving definition of the family' (2002) 16 *IJLPF* 145; S Cretney, 'Comment – Sex is Important' (2004) 34 *Fam Law* 777; B Sloan, 'The concept of coupledom in succession law' (2011) 7 *CLJ* 623.
49 A Bottomley and S Wong, 'Shared households: a new paradigm for thinking about the reform of domestic property relationships' in A Diduck and K O'Donovan (eds), *Feminist Perspectives on Family Law* (Abingdon, UK: Routledge-Cavendish 2006).
50 A Diduck and K O'Donovan, 'Feminism and families: *plus ça change*?' in A Diduck and K O'Donovan (eds), *Feminist Perspectives on Family Law* (Abingdon, UK: Routledge-Cavendish 2006) 14; B Cossman and B Ryder, 'What is marriage-like? The irrelevance of conjugality' (2001) 18 *Canadian J Fam Law* 269.
51 R Probert, 'Common-law marriage: myths and misunderstandings' (2008) 20 *CFLQ* 1.
52 J Lewis, *The End of Marriage?* (Cheltenham, UK: Edward Elgar Publishing 2001), 140. The three dimensions of commitment referred to by Lewis is based on social psychological research findings: see, e.g. J Adams and W Jones, 'The conceptualization of marital commitment: an integrative analysis' (1997) 72 *J Pers Soc Psychol* 1177; SM Drigotas, CE Rusbult and J Verette, 'Level of commitment, mutuality of commitment, and couple well-being' (1999) 6 *Pers Relationships* 389.

their commitment through public acknowledgement in the marriage ceremony and particularly among wider family and friends. Cohabitants, on the other hand, tend to dislike such public expression of their commitment, seeing it much more as a personal private matter.[53]

Consequently, the law does not question the presence, or even the quality, of spouses' commitment as marriage *per se* presupposes the existence of such commitment regardless of the length of the marriage. However, the situation is quite different for cohabitants given the lack of formality in entering cohabitation and their preference for a more private expression of commitment. The imposition of a marriage-like definition means that the law expects cohabitants to express their commitment in a more public, albeit non-formalised, manner which is at odds with their general preference for privacy. Certain assumptions are thus made about the way that committed couples, married and cohabiting, should act and the homogeneous manifestation of that commitment. Cohabitants should therefore be more like spouses through mimicry. Lewis, however, observes that, for most couples, it is the existence of commitment that is important rather than how that commitment manifests itself by way of relationship type.[54]

Furthermore, cohabitation must, through satisfying a minimum duration requirement, demonstrate sufficient durability as evidence of commitment. While there may arguably be a link between commitment and a relationship's durability, the nature of commitment is more complex and multi-dimensional.[55] The choice of the five-year and two-year periods is clearly influenced by public opinion surveys which indicated a correlation between the level of public support and the length of cohabitation. While the length of cohabitation might possibly be an indicator of stability and commitment, it may be harder to agree on a particular length of time, thus reinforcing concerns about the choice of a minimum duration being arbitrary.[56]

The length of cohabitation may paint only a partial picture and be a blunt assessment of commitment. While it may provide *prima facie* evidence of a relationship's durability, it does not necessarily shed light on a couple's own (internal) substantive cognition of commitment and its effect on their interdependence.[57] Moreover, the five-year requirement imposed on non-parenting cohabitants is out of line with the two-year one that is imposed on cohabitants, parenting and non-parenting, in other statutes. The different criteria for determining eligibility may cause further confusion among cohabitants as to when legal rights might accrue to them.

Given cohabitants' preference for a more private mode of expression of commitment, it may be harder for them to establish a spousal-like relationship and to satisfy the minimum duration requirements set. According to Hayward and Brandon, the need to meet a

---

53 Ibid. 142.
54 Ibid. 145.
55 C Smart and P Stevens, *Cohabitation Breakdown, Family and Parenthood Policy and Practice* (London and York, UK: Family Policy Studies Centre 2006). Smart and Stevens observe two types of commitment among cohabitants – mutual and contingent – which are not mutually exclusive but rather at two ends of a continuum. It would seem that the type of commitment required by the proposals is mutual commitment.
56 This view was expressed by some participants in the survey by Humphrey and others, who felt that a minimum duration requirement was an arbitrary way to determine commitment: see A Humphrey, L Mills, G Morrell, G Douglas and H Woodward, *Inheritance and the Family* (n 27) 46.
57 S Wong, 'Shared commitment, interdependence and property relations: A socio-legal project for cohabitation' (2012) 24 *CFLQ* 60.

minimum duration of at least two years, let alone five years, will mean that only a relatively small proportion of cohabitants are likely to qualify.[58] A larger proportion will need to look to state benefits to meet their economic needs, adding greater cost to taxpayers.[59] The only recourse for a cohabitant will be to apply for family provision. However, a successful claim is not guaranteed and provision remains limited to reasonable maintenance.

Fair and reasonable distribution to whom?

Another issue raised by the proposals is that a qualifying cohabitant has the same intestacy entitlement as a spouse. The underlying policy is to provide for a 'fair and reasonable' distribution of the estate. However, the preference increasingly has been to further enhance the 'fair and reasonable' provision to spouses and (spouse-like) partners by taking a partner-focused approach. Consequently, the surviving spouse or partner is given preference over other stakeholders who may be equally economically vulnerable, such as the intestate's children who are minors or disabled and ageing parents. A further motivation is the Law Commission's desire for simplicity and administrative efficiency. Given that, in practice, the spouse takes all in most cases except high value ones, the Law Commission suggests that the replacement of the spouse's life interest with an outright half share will make the system simpler and avoid unnecessary time and costs of administering a trust.

The Law Commission justifies the proposals by relying on public opinion surveys which broadly indicate support for giving priority or all to spouses/cohabitants. Yet, placing too much weight (or not) on such surveys may be problematic. Burns, for instance, notes the Law Commission's selective process of relying on certain data while ignoring others.[60] She cites by way of example public responses giving less support to a spouse taking the whole estate where there are surviving children from previous relationships.[61] Burns alludes to other problems with relying on surveys to shape reform proposals, for example: respondents may not be sufficiently legally informed when responding to survey questions; responses may be insufficiently measured and considered; respondents may not understand, or at least be aware of, the ramifications of their responses in relation to possible reform of the law; and the possibility of the survey questions skewing responses.[62]

Concerns over the lack of provision to children, especially those who may be economically vulnerable because of their dependencies, for example, being minors or disabled, are arguably based on the 'conduit' theory. That theory postulates that the surviving spouse/cohabitant may be an unreliable conduit for passing on the deceased's estate to his children, particularly those from previous or other relationships.[63] While it may be reasonably

---

58 J Hayward and G Brandon, *Cohabitation in the 21st century* (Birmingham, UK: Jubilee Centre 2011), 1 www.jubilee-centre.org/cohabitation-21st-century-john-hayward-guy-brandon/ [accessed 9 March 2012]. According to Hayward and Brandon, only about 18 per cent of all cohabitations lasted more than five years in 2006 and 50 per cent of cohabitants separated within five years of the birth of a child. Their analysis further indicates that only 34 per cent of cohabitations reported in the British Household Panel Survey were still ongoing, with 40 per cent ending in marriage and 26 per cent in separation. The mean length of those cohabitations that ended in separation is 35 months (median is 23 months).
59 Ibid. 6.
60 F Burns, 'Surviving spouses, surviving children and the reform of total intestacy law in England and Scotland: past, present and future' (2013) 33 *LS* 85.
61 Law Commission, *Intestacy* (n 7) paras 2.37-2.38.
62 Burns, 'Surviving spouses, surviving children' (n 60) 25.
63 Kerridge, 'Distribution on intestacy' (n 5) 364–5.

assumed that she may pass on the estate after her death to any children she has had with the deceased, the same might not be said in relation to step-children. The only alternative then is for the deceased's children to make a family provision claim but a successful claim is not guaranteed. Moreover, step-children are unable to make a family provision claim against the step-parent in such cases since s 1(1)(d) of the IHA refers only to 'children of the family' in relation to a marriage or civil partnership, thus excluding cohabitations. Their only option is to apply as a dependant, which may be problematic if they are adults or had not been 'maintained' by the step-parent. The addition of cohabitants under the proposals will lead to the deceased's children, especially those from previous and other relationships, being further removed from entitlement.

The proposals will also further remove the entitlement of the deceased's parents to a share in the estate. The UK is facing the problem of an ageing population and the issue of care for an ageing population is a growing concern.[64] Thus, the need for care by the elderly will lead to ageing parents placing greater reliance on their adult children for financial and care support. The removal of this group of stakeholders means that they will need to either make a family provision claim as dependants or rely on state welfare to fund the cost of their care. Again, the former cannot be guaranteed to be successful in all cases as the requisite dependence on the deceased for maintenance needs to be demonstrated.[65] The latter will increase the burden on taxpayers.

Overall, the proposals aim to enable the surviving spouse to take the whole estate in practice, if not in law, since she will take the whole estate in most cases except high value ones. This is tempered with the aim that the system should be simple and efficient. The addition of cohabitants means that, after spouses, this group will take in preference to the deceased's children and other possible beneficiaries. This may in some ways go towards addressing the financial hardship that cohabitants face upon the death of a partner. However, the proposals arguably provide fair and reasonable distribution only to the spouse/cohabitant but not other stakeholders.

The difficulty faced in attempting to reform the intestacy rules is balancing between the desire for simplicity in terms of the application of the rules and the estate size and relationship dynamics between various stakeholders especially within modern families. For children, their entitlement would be reduced to a half share where the estate is large enough but in most cases, this is unlikely to happen. This reduced entitlement is likely to hit hardest the deceased's surviving children from previous or other relationships who may be economically vulnerable. The greatest losers are the deceased's parents since, under the proposals, they stand to lose their existing right to entitlement.

Inheritance Tax

A further limitation on the level of the protection afforded to cohabitants is inheritance tax. Under the Inheritance Tax Act 1984 (IHTA), inheritance tax is payable on chargeable

---

64 As at 2010, there are 10 million people in the UK aged over 65. This is projected to rise by 5.5 million over the next 20 years and for the number to double to 19 million by 2050. See R Cracknell, 'The Ageing Population' in *Key Issues for the New Parliament 2010* www.parliament.uk/documents/commons/lib/research/key_issues/Key-Issues-The-ageing-population2007.pdf [accessed 7 September 2012].

65 IHA, s 1(1)(d).

transfers of value made either during the deceased's lifetime or on his death.[66] Tax is chargeable retrospectively on a lifetime transfer if the deceased dies within seven years of the transfer.[67] Inheritance tax is charged on transfers on death at the rate of 40 per cent but the first £325,000 (the nil-rate band) is exempt. A family provision order under the IHA is treated as having devolved on the deceased's death.[68] This may therefore affect the tax liability of the intestate estate as an amount that was originally payable by the estate may no longer be payable, or may be less as a result of a family provision order. Revision of tax calculations may thus be needed. Consequently, the Law Commission recommends that courts be given the power to treat the net estate as having included a repayment of inheritance tax or the payment of any other amount which would be payable as a result of the order.[69]

Apart from that, there was little discussion of the inheritance tax consequences of the intestacy reform proposals for cohabitants. English law currently exempts all inter-spouse transfers of value from inheritance tax.[70] Spouses are further permitted to transfer any unused nil-rate band to the surviving spouse.[71] These provisions are particularly important for tax planning among spouses. However, no such largesse is given to cohabitants. A cohabitant's share in the estate would be subject to inheritance tax as the transfer would be a chargeable transfer of value. Given the relatively lower values of intestate estates, the estates would, in many cases, fall within the nil-rate band and liability for inheritance tax might be a non-issue.[72] That, however, misses the point regarding the difference in tax treatment between spouses and cohabitants and, particularly, whether that differential treatment remains justifiable from a human rights' perspective if the intestacy rules were to be reformed.

Payment of inheritance tax has been held to fall within the scope of Article 1 Protocol 1 of the European Convention on Human Rights (ECHR), which deals with the right to peaceful enjoyment of possessions.[73] Consequently, Article 14, which prohibits discrimination in the enjoyment of the ECHR rights, will be applicable. There have been a few human rights challenges to the imposition of inheritance tax by parties in close personal relationships, such as cohabitants and siblings. However, none to date have been successful. For instance, in *Holland v IRC*, a surviving cohabitant claimed a violation of Article 14 read together with Article 8[74] and/or Article 1 of Protocol 1. The Special Commissioners held that, even if the Human Rights Act 1998 (HRA) were to be applicable in that particular case, there was no violation for three main reasons.[75]

First, the Special Commissioners held that the exemption provided by s 18 of the IHTA relates only to inter-spouse transfers. 'Spouse' for the purposes of the section is based on

---

66 IHTA, s 1. A 'chargeable transfer' and a 'transfer of value' are defined in s 2(1) and s 3(1) respectively.
67 A further distinction is drawn between lifetime transfers that are defined by s 3A as potentially exempt transfers (PETs) and those that are not. A PET does not immediately attract tax; it is exempted if the transferor lives for more than seven years after the transfer. The rate of tax on non-PET lifetime transfers is 20 per cent.
68 IHTA, s 146.
69 Law Commission, *Intestacy* (n 7) para 7.130.
70 IHTA, s 18.
71 IHTA, s 8A.
72 A chargeable transfer will include the deceased's share in any jointly held property that passes to the cohabitant under the survivorship rule which might then raise the value above the nil-rate band.
73 See *Burden v UK* (2007) 44 EHRR 51; (2008) 47 EHRR 38 (Grand Chamber).
74 Article 8 covers the right to respect for private and family life.
75 [2003] STC (SCD) 43. The HRA was not applicable in that case because the deceased died before the Act came into force.

the understanding of the ordinary man using that word which, in contemporary British society, still means a man and a woman who are legally married. As the provision makes no reference to persons 'living together as husband and wife' (so as to include cohabitants), it was not possible to give the word 'spouse' a broader interpretation for the purposes of s 3(1) of the HRA. The second, and more crucial, reason is that the chosen comparator in these cases will (usually) be spouses but a cohabitant is generally not seen to be analogously situated to a spouse. This view has been reaffirmed by the European Court of Human Rights (ECtHR), which has noted that '[m]arriage continues to be characterised by a corpus of rights and obligations which differentiate it markedly from the situation of a man and woman who cohabit'.[76] Lastly, it was held that the tax exemption provided to spouses pursues a legitimate aim, that is, the promotion of marriage. States are given a fairly wide margin of appreciation to justify a difference in treatment of spouses and cohabitants in certain matters, for example, taxes: the differential treatment will be permissible provided that it is reasonable and objectively justifiable, and the means used are proportionate to the legitimate aim sought.[77]

The view that cohabitants and spouses are not analogously situated is partly due to spouses being perceived as being more committed to a life together as a result of the marriage contract; a similar commitment may be lacking, or at least cannot be assumed, with cohabitants. Freedom of choice and autonomy arguments may further serve to reinforce the differential treatment of these two groups.[78] However, if the law were to be reformed to provide rights to certain cohabitants, a continuation of the differential tax treatment of spouses and qualifying cohabitants might be subject to greater scrutiny. Arguments justifying differential treatment that are couched in terms of the promotion of marriage and/or the protection of the traditional family become harder to sustain unless there are very 'weighty' reasons. The inheritance tax liability of cohabitants may therefore potentially raise human rights issues that have yet to be resolved.

Conclusion

The Law Commission's recommendations for reforming the law of intestacy and family provision are part of an ongoing initiative to provide some legal recognition to cohabitants in England and Wales even though there is, at present, little political will by the government to do so. While financial hardship is a key concern, it is commitment that, normatively speaking, is central to defining whether a cohabiting relationship is eligible and should thus be afforded some legal protection. Commitment is the nexus between formation of an intimate relationship of emotional and financial interdependence and any resulting financial hardship. Yet, the notion of commitment has not actually been subject to rigorous interrogation within the law. The law instead continues to use the marriage analogy to

---

76 *Lindsay v UK* (1987) 9 EHRR CD555, 560. *Shackell v UK* (App No 45851/99) (27 April 2000, unreported). The ECtHR has further viewed Article 8 as not imposing any positive obligation to recognise the status of cohabitation: see *Johnston v Ireland* (App No 9697/82) (18 December 1986); *Serife Yigit v Turkey* (2011) 53 EHRR 25.
77 In *Burden* (n 73), a claim of an infringement of Article 14 in conjunction with Article 8 and/or Article 1 of Protocol 1 by two elderly sisters was unsuccessful for the same reasons.
78 See, e.g. Simone Wong, 'The Human Rights Act 1998 and the shared home: issues for cohabitants' (2005) 27 *JSWFL* 265; S Sanz Caballero, 'Unmarried cohabiting couples before the European Court of Human Rights: parity with marriage?' (2005) 11 *Colum J Eur L* 151.

perform the task of defining eligible committed cohabiting relationships, thereby requiring cohabitants to demonstrate that their relationships mimic marriage and bear the (assumed) hallmarks of marriage, that is, conjugality, procreation and financial interdependence such as shared financial arrangements.

The Law Commission's choice of definition as well as the minimum duration requirements set for parenting and non-parenting cohabitants respectively follow in that tradition and are thus quite conservative. Given the diverse nature of marriages and cohabitation and the multi-dimensionality of the notion of commitment, commitment has myriad meanings and the idea of a universal notion of commitment, even a marital one, is debatable. Thus, the proposed minimum duration requirements may be no more than a blunt measure of a couple's commitment. More importantly, those requirements will effectively limit the number of qualifying cohabitants, leaving many to either make family provisions claims against the deceased's estate for reasonable maintenance or look to the public purse for help.

The Law Commission's proposals will further negatively impact other beneficiaries, namely, the deceased's children and parents. These stakeholders will see their rights diminished and abolished respectively. While simplicity and administrative efficiency are meritorious aims, especially given the average sizes of intestate estates, those aims have to be balanced against ensuring that the reform of the intestacy rules will provide a 'fair and reasonable' distribution to those with a vested interest in the estate, and not just one particular beneficiary, that is, the surviving spouse or cohabitant.

A fuller consideration of the fiscal implications of the Law Commission's proposals is also needed. The differential tax treatment of spouses and cohabitants has been generally accepted by the ECtHR as being within a state's margin of appreciation and reasonable and objectively justifiable in pursuit of a legitimate aim. However, if the law of cohabitation were to be reformed and qualifying cohabitants were to acquire rights under the intestacy rules, the difference in inheritance tax treatment might be vulnerable to challenge. This is especially so if the definition of a qualifying cohabiting relationship is based on the marriage model which presupposes that, in order to qualify, the characteristics of the former must mirror the latter. As cohabitation is analogised with marriage, there may no longer be good reasons for spouses and cohabitants to be subject to differential inheritance tax treatment. In that case, notwithstanding that s 18 of the IHTA refers only to spouses, there may possibly be scope to argue that qualifying cohabitants, having demonstrated the spousal-like nature of their relationship, are analogously situated to spouses and that their exclusion from the inter-spouse exemption is discriminatory on the grounds of marital status.

Bibliography

Adams J and Jones W, 'The conceptualization of marital commitment: an integrative analysis' (1997) 72 *J Pers Soc Psychol* 1177.

Arthur S, Lewis J, Maclean M, Finch S and Fitzgerald R, *Settling Up: Making Financial Arrangements after Separation* (London: National Centre for Social Research 2002).

Bala N and Bromwich RJ, 'Context and inclusivity in Canada's evolving definition of the family' (2002) 16 *IJLPF* 145.

Burns F, 'Surviving spouses, surviving children and the reform of total intestacy law in England and Scotland: past, present and future' (2013) 33 *LS* 85.

Bottomley A and Wong S, 'Shared households: a new paradigm for thinking about the reform of domestic property relationships' in A Diduck and K O'Donovan (eds), *Feminist Perspectives on Family Law* (Abingdon, UK: Routledge-Cavendish 2006).

Barlow A, Burgoyne C, Clery E and Smithson J, 'Cohabitation and the law: myths, money and the media' in Park A, Curtice J, Thomson K, Phillips M, Johnson M and Clery E (eds), *British Social Attitudes: The 24th Report* (London: SAGE 2008).

Barlow A, Duncan S, James G and Park A, *Cohabitation, Marriage and the Law: Social Change and Legal Reform in the 21st Century* (Oxford: Hart 2005).

Barlow A and James G, 'Regulating marriage and cohabitation in 21st century Britain' (2004) 67 *MLR* 143.

Brooker S, *Finding the Will: A Report on Will-Writing Behaviour in England and Wales* (2007).

Cossman B and Ryder B, 'What is marriage-like? The irrelevance of conjugality' (2001) 18 *Canadian J Fam Law* 269.

Cretney S, 'Reform of intestacy: the best we can do?' (1995) *LQR* 77.

——, 'Comment – Sex is important' (2004) 34 *Fam Law* 777.

Diduck A and O'Donovan K, 'Feminism and families: *plus ça change*?' in A Diduck and K O'Donovan (eds), *Feminist Perspectives on Family Law* (Abingdon, UK: Routledge-Cavendish 2006).

Douglas G, Pearce J and Woodward H, 'Cohabitants, property and the law: a study of injustice' (2008) 72 *MLR* 24.

Drigotas SM, Rusbult CE and Verette J, 'Level of commitment, mutuality of commitment, and couple well-being' (1999) 6 *Pers Relationships* 389.

Gardner S, 'Rethinking family property' (1993) 109 *LQR* 263.

Glover N and Todd P, 'The myth of common intention' (1996) 16 *LS* 323.

Hayward J and Brandon G, *Cohabitation in the 21st Century* (Birmingham, UK: Jubilee Centre 2011).

Humphrey A, Mills L, Morrell G, Douglas G and Woodward H, *Inheritance and the Family: Attitudes to Will-Making and Intestacy* (National Centre for Social Research 2010).

Kerridge R, 'Distribution on intestacy, the Law Commission's Report (1989)' (1990) *Conv* 358.

Law Commission, *Family Law: Distribution on Intestacy* (Law Com No 187, 1989).

——, *Cohabitation: The Financial Consequences of Relationship Breakdown* (Law Com no. 307, 2007).

——, *Intestacy and Family Provision Claims on Death* (Law Com Consultation Paper no. 191, 2009).

——, *Intestacy and Family Provision Claims on Death* (Law Com No 331, 2011).

Lewis J, *The End of Marriage?* (Cheltenham, UK: Edward Elgar Publishing 2001).

Morrell G, Barnard M and Legard R, *The Law of Intestate Succession: Exploring Attitudes Among Non-Traditional Families – Final Report* (National Centre for Social Research 2009).

Probert R, 'Common-law marriage: myths and misunderstandings' (2008) 20 *CFLQ* 1.

——, 'Cohabitation: current legal solutions' (2009) 62 *CLP* 316.

Rusbult CE and van Lange PAM, 'Interdependence, interaction, and relationships' (2003) 54 *Annu Rev Psychol* 351.

Sanz Caballero S, 'Unmarried cohabiting couples before the European Court of Human Rights: parity with marriage?' (2005) 11 *Colum J Eur L* 151.

Sloan B, 'The concept of coupledom in succession law' (2011) 7 *CLJ* 623.

Smart C and Stevens P, *Cohabitation Breakdown, Family and Parenthood: Policy and Practice* (London and York, UK: Family Policy Studies Centre 2006).

Wong S, 'The Human Rights Act 1998 and the shared home: issues for cohabitants' (2005) 27 *JSWFL* 265.

——, 'Would you "care" to share your home?' (2007) 58 *NILQ* 268.

——, 'Shared commitment, interdependence and property relations: a socio-legal project for cohabitation' (2012) 24 *CFLQ* 60.

10 The role of child support in tackling child poverty

Heather Keating

Introduction

The history of child support legislation in England and Wales may still be relatively short – 25 years – but it has proved to be profoundly controversial, involving as it does issues of moral, legal, familial and the state's obligations to financially support children with whom one parent does not live. This chapter considers some of the key twists and turns the legislation has taken within the context of 'responsibilisation' and reprivatisation and commitments to eradicate or at least reduce child poverty. In particular, it considers the role which child support can play in raising children out of poverty, a phenomenon which grew in the latter part of the twentieth century to become a blight upon the life chances of almost one in three children.

In order to assess the effectiveness of child support as one of the tools available to the state in securing its aim, the chapter draws a distinction between the different types of families which may need to resort to the child support system. The chapter then considers whether the new emphasis upon private agreement is compatible with the drive to eradicate child poverty. It concludes that, although privately agreed 'family-based' agreements can secure support for some children, the direction child support policy has now taken threatens to undermine any hard won consensus that parents should support their children where they are able to do so and has the potential to hamper initiatives to reduce child poverty.

Background to the Child Support Acts

Prior to the enactment of the Child Support Act 1991, child maintenance following parental separation largely fell within the jurisdiction of the courts (although the social security 'liable relative' scheme did exist alongside). It was thus self-initiated, adversarial and discretionary.[1] The White Paper, *Children Come First* which preceded the legislation condemned the court-based system of child maintenance as 'slow, fragmented, uncertain and ineffective'.[2] Levels of maintenance were very low (£18 per week seeming to be the going rate for a child at a time when the National Foster Care Association figures were £35 per child under five years per week)[3] with only a quarter of children receiving any maintenance at all. In disputes following marital separation issues of child maintenance were frequently subordinate to the

---

1   P Legler, 'The impact of welfare reforms on the child support legislation' in JT Oldham and MS Melli (eds), *Child Support: The Next Frontier* (Ann Arbor, MI: University of Michigan Press 2000) 55.
2   Department of Social Security, *Children Come First* (White Paper, Cm 1264, 1990), i.
3   Ibid. para 1.5.

perceived desirability of achieving a 'clean break' between the adults and trying to resolve the question of housing, with courts frequently taking into account the parent's need to support a subsequently formed second family and explicitly acknowledging the role which could be played by the benefit system in supporting the first family.[4]

As a consequence, much of the burden of supporting separated families fell upon the state – and the number of such families increased very significantly in the decade prior to the legislation: in 1961, 6 per cent of families were headed by a single parent. This figure had risen to 14 per cent by 1987 (and to 25 per cent by 2001[5]) – although not all, of course, resulted from separation. In 1980, for example, the numbers in receipt of Supplementary Benefit stood at 300,000 – by 1989, the numbers had risen to 770,000 [6] and in the year 1988–1989, the 'cost in real terms to the taxpayer of income related benefits for lone parents and their children' was £3.2 billion.[7] By 1990, two-thirds of lone parent families were dependent on welfare.[8] At the same time, as will be discussed later, the latter part of the twentieth century witnessed a very significant increase in child poverty. Prefacing the government's proposed response to these developments, the White Paper stated:

> The government seeks to establish a system ... that will ensure that parents honour their legal and moral responsibility to maintain their children whenever they can afford to do so. It is right that other taxpayers should help maintain children when the children's own parents, despite their best efforts, do not have enough resources to do so themselves. ... But it is not right that taxpayers, who include other families, should shoulder that responsibility instead of parents who are able to do so themselves.[9]

According to Mavis Maclean (who at the time of the reforms was working as a consultant to the Interdepartmental Child Maintenance Group), the reforms were 'strongly influenced by the personal commitment of Prime Minister Thatcher to make men take responsibility for their children'[10] and there is no doubt as to the strength of the Prime Minister's views: 'legislation cannot make irresponsible parents responsible. But it can and must ensure that absent parents pay maintenance for their children.'[11] It is true that the resulting Child Support Act 1991 does attempt to do this and thus, the legislation can be seen as an instrument of social policy, trying to effect a sea-change in attitudes whereby maintenance ceased to be regarded as optional[12] or as Carbone has stated (in the context of similar reforms in the United States), it was an attempt to create a new ethic of parenthood.[13] But even if the

---

4 *Delaney v Delaney* [1990] 2 FLR 457 (Fam Div).
5 L Duckworth, 'Single parents now head a quarter of all British families' *The Independent* (27 September 2002).
6 *Children Come First* (n 2) vol II, i.
7 Ibid. para 1.5.
8 J Bradshaw and J Millar, *Lone Parent Families in the UK* (London: Department of Social Security 1990).
9 *Children Come First* (n 2) para 1.5.
10 M Maclean and B Fehlberg, 'Child support policy in Australia and the United Kingdom: changing priorities but a similar tough deal for children?' (2009) 23 *IJLPF* 1.
11 The First National Children's Home George Thomas Society Annual lecture, 17 January 1990). In her memoirs, Margaret Thatcher wrote that she had been 'appalled by the way in which men fathered a child and then absconded, leaving the single mother – and the tax payer – to foot the bill for their irresponsibility and condemning the child to a lower standard of living', *The Downing Street Years* (New York: Harper Collins 1995) 630.
12 H Keating, 'Children come first?' (1995) 1 *Contemp Issues L* 29.
13 J Carbone, 'Child support comes of age: an introduction to the laws of child support' in JT Oldham and MS Melli (eds), *Child Support: The Next Frontier* (Ann Arbor, MI: University of Michigan Press 2000) 11.

Prime Minister had this as her primary aim (as Maclean asserts), the White Paper and legislation most certainly had another: that of reducing the expenditure of the Treasury upon lone parent families. In other words, the legislation was also an instrument of fiscal policy. This was articulated very strongly by Lord Houghton of Sowerby during the passage of the Bill: 'This Bill is not a Child Support Bill, it is a taxing Bill. . . . In short, this tax is PAYT – pay as you are told. . . . The Bill is more concerned with support to the Treasury than support to children.' [14]

So it appears as if there were two objectives: to try to raise the standard of living of single parent families by making parents meet their responsibilities and, second, to reduce the size of the social security bill. In light of these conflicting and ambitious aims, it is not surprising that success has proved to be elusive (indeed, Stephen Cretney has commented that the White Paper was 'astonishingly naïve in its assumptions'[15]) and that at least one commentator has concluded that 'in reality *children's* (my emphasis) needs and interests came some way down the list of interested parties'.[16] Most of this chapter will focus upon the difficulties which have dogged efforts to achieve the first objective.

The Child Support Act 1991

The Child Support 1991 (which came into force in 1993 and was influenced by similar legislation in Australia) rested on the assumption that responsibility rested with the birth family wherever it could to support children; as such, June Carbone has commented that child support laws are part of a larger trend, 'from the husband-wife relationship to parent-child ties as the defining element of family obligation'.[17] Section 1 provided for a general duty to maintain: 'each parent is responsible for maintaining' his or her children. The state would only step in if parents could not do so. The 'person with care' fulfilled this responsibility by the day to day care of the 'qualifying child' (a child born to the parents, or adopted or born as a result of assisted reproduction).[18] The 'absent parent' (so-called in the original legislation, later somewhat less offensively renamed 'non-resident parent' and now simply as the 'paying parent') fulfilled this responsibility by paying child support. To achieve this goal, the Act created a system by which maintenance was assessed by way of formula (the precise nature of which changed during subsequent years in response to criticism) and enforced against natural parents. Child Support Officers (as part of the Child Support Agency (CSA)) took over from the courts the assessment, collection and enforcement of maintenance payments (under the overall control of the Department of Social Security (DSS) until the Child Maintenance and Enforcement Commission (C-MEC) took control between 2008 and July 2012, whereupon the Agency came under the control of the Department for Work and Pensions (DWP).

---

14 HL Deb 25 February 1991, vol 526, cols 811–14.
15 S Cretney, *Principles of Family Law* (7th edn, London: Sweet & Maxwell 2002) 543.
16 T Ridge, 'Supporting children? The impact of child support policies on children's wellbeing in the UK and Australia' (2005) 34 *JSP* 122. Some fifteen years after Act was passed, Henshaw concluded that 'the current system was originally designed primarily to reclaim money for the taxpayer when parents with care are on benefits. This may be difficult to achieve in a cost-effective way alongside tackling child poverty'. See also Sir David Henshaw's Report to the Secretary of State for Work and Pensions, *Recovering Child Support: Routes to Responsibility* (Cm 6894, 2006) 16.
17 Carbone (n 13) 3.
18 Child Support Act 1991, s 3.

It is worth noting that, unlike other areas of child law, the welfare of the child was not (nor is) the first or paramount consideration (section 2 merely states that those administering the system ought to have *regard to* the welfare of *any* child likely to be affected by his decision – and there were few instances where there was any discretion to which this section could apply). Further, subsequent case law has made it clear that child support is neither a right of the child[19] nor the right of the parent with care.

Under the original scheme parents with care who were not in receipt of state benefit could enter into voluntary, private, agreements (which were not binding upon the CSA if the parent subsequently claimed benefits)[20] or they could apply to the CSA for an assessment. However, a person with care in receipt of state benefit was held, by dint of receiving the benefit, to have made an application to the CSA to secure child support from the absent parent and was under duty to cooperate with the CSA by giving details of the parent.[21] Failure to cooperate might lead to a reduction in benefits (a 'reduced benefit declaration'[22]). Originally the reduction was 20 per cent for 26 weeks and 10 per cent for the following 52 weeks. In 1996 the reduction was raised to 40 per cent for up to three years. There was, however, a discretion (insisted upon by the House of Lords during the passage of the Bill) not to take action to recover child maintenance from the absent parent where there was a risk of harm or undue distress to the mother or child.[23] It was not until the 2008 Act that sections 6 and 46 were abolished as part of the reshaping of the policy objectives of the child support legislation, with, as we shall see, a much sharper (arguably short-lived) focus upon child poverty reduction.[24]

'Deadbeat dads', 'feckless fathers' and responsibility

The Act was conceived and passed into law on a tide of rhetoric concerning 'deadbeat dads' or 'Jack-the-Lads fathering away on the council estates'.[25] It was sold as legislation for the lower classes: such absent fathers had to be made to take responsibility for their children. This was against a backdrop of increasing concern about 'a range of social ills – the criminality of male youth, family breakdown and urban disorder – . . . all laid at the door of the single parent family and linked to the detrimental consequences of father absence'.[26] Thus, the legislation can be seen as part of the wider strategy, which David Garland has referred to as 'responsibilisation',[27] most acutely seen in relation to policy and legislative developments concerning youth offending.[28]

However, the reality behind the rhetoric is, as would be expected, more complex in a number of significant respects. First, the original legislation took an extremely narrow view

---

19 *R v Sec of State for Work and Pensions ex parte Kehoe* [2006] 1 AC 42 (HL), Baroness Hale dissenting; *Kehoe v UK* [2008] 2 FLR 1014 (ECHR).
20 Child Support Act 1991, s 9.
21 Ibid. s 6.
22 Ibid. s 46.
23 Ibid. s 6(2).
24 Child Maintenance and other Payments Act 2008, s 15.
25 P Toynbee, *The Guardian* (2 February 1994).
26 R Collier, 'The campaign against the Child Support Act: "errant fathers" and family men' (July 1994) *Family L* 384.
27 D Garland, *The Culture of Control* (Oxford: Oxford University Press 2001).
28 A James, 'Responsibility, children and childhood' in J Bridgeman, H Keating and C Lind (eds), *Responsibility, Law and the Family* (Farnham, UK: Ashgate Publishing 2008) 150–3.

of what being a 'responsible' father entailed – it meant paying.[29] The Act had nothing to do with attempting to 're-engage' fathers in their children's lives in any richer sense;[30] indeed, claims that the higher payments, which resulted from the formula prevented them from doing so (and, for example, travel costs to see children were not taken into account in the formula), were ignored. In this way, it was a social policy initiative which reinforced rather than challenged gender roles in relation to parenting.[31]

Second, while the passage of the legislation may have proceeded on the basis of crude assumptions about irresponsible sexual procreation, in fact, the Act had as much, if not more, impact upon middle-class fathers who were perceived to be 'soft targets' by the Agency.[32] Indeed, the first head of the CSA stated that the Act had always been intended to make such fathers 'responsible'.[33] At least some of these fathers had given up their share of equity in the former matrimonial home so as to provide their children with a home and felt deeply aggrieved at then being required to 'pay twice' (as they saw it) when their former spouses fell within the benefit system, triggering a child support assessment.[34] The resulting demonstrations and campaign against the Act and the CSA have been well documented.[35] It is worth noting that parents with care were much less successful than fathers' groups in making their grievances with the legislation and the CSA known.

From the point of view of this chapter, the key question is whether this move towards making fathers (of whatever socio-economic position) 'responsible' had any impact upon the standard of living of their children.

Raising children out of poverty?

As noted above, by 1996, over 60 per cent of children in lone parent families were in poverty. Quite what constitutes poverty and how it should be measured has never been fully resolved and has become more controversial. Although as the Child Poverty Action Group notes, there has been some degree of consensus that 'poverty is relative and must be understood in relation to typical living standards in society'[36] this is by no means universally accepted. For many years governments' headline measure of poverty[37] has been one of relative poverty: where the household income is below 60 per cent of the median household income (both before and after housing costs have been paid). At the start of the 1970s, approximately 15 per cent of children were regarded as living in poverty – by 1990, it had risen to over

---

29 Keating (n 12) 31.
30 For discussion of how policy has attempted to do so subsequently, see S Sheldon, 'From "absent objects of blame" to "fathers who want to take responsibility": reforming birth registration law 13' (2009) 31 *JSWFL* 373–89; R Collier, 'Engaging fathers? Responsibility, law and the "problem of fatherhood" in *Responsibility, Law and the Family* (Farnham, UK: Ashgate Publishing 2008).
31 Keating (n 12) 43.
32 Child Poverty Action Group, *Putting the Treasury First: The Truth About Child Support* (CPAG 1994) 70–1.
33 Collier (n 26) 385; citing Mears, *The Sunday Telegraph* (27 March 1994).
34 See *Crozier v Crozier* [1994] Fam 114 (Fam Div).
35 See Collier (n 26).
36 Child Poverty Action Group, 'Child poverty facts and figures' (2013) www.cpag.org.uk/povertyfacts.htm [accessed 5 January 2103].
37 Although other measurements are also used, and see www.poverty.ac.uk/content/consensualmethod.htm for a 'consensual' or 'perceived deprivation model based on enforced lack of necessities as determined by public opinion.

30 per cent of children.[38] Clearly, not all these children are in lone parent families; similarly, by no means are even a majority of children in families where the adults are unemployed.[39]

Poverty is a blight on the life chances of children: child poverty is known to be associated with low birth weight (on average 200 grams lower in social classes IV and V) which is associated with higher rates of infant death and chronic disease in later life,[40] slower rates of development: by the age of three poorer children may lag by up to nine months behind their richer peers;[41] by 14-years-old, children from poorer families may be as much as two years' behind in their development,[42] poor educational attainment with higher rates of school exclusion, poor employment prospects, poor mental and physical health and drug abuse.[43] Poverty also shortens lives:[44] the life expectancy of someone living in Glasgow's Calton area is 28 years less than someone living just eight miles away in Lenzie.[45]

The extent to which commentators regard child support legislation as a valuable tool in lifting children out of poverty varies considerably. Some regard it as having the 'potential to play a vital role'.[46] Others are much more cautious: June Carbone, for example, comments (when writing about child support legislation in the United States), that 'we cannot substantially reduce children's poverty through child support alone' although she does go on to comment that 'we can, however, increase the level of support awarded and paid'.[47]

It is against the backdrop of these differing views that consideration must be given to the effectiveness of the United Kingdom child support legislation. Considering fully whether the Act raised children out of poverty would require a discussion not only of whether absent fathers had the means to pay, but also the steps taken by some fathers to avoid payment, the enforcement methods used against those who were reluctant to pay and the impact it had upon the standard of living of second families. This chapter can only give an indication of some of the difficulties with these issues. Some fathers were prepared to go to great lengths to avoid paying child support: this included disputing paternity (in circumstances well beyond those where it might be thought reasonable to challenge) or arranging their

---

38 Child Poverty Action Group (n 36).
39 See C Belfield et al., *Living Standards, Poverty and Inequality in the UK: 2015* (London: Institute for Fiscal Studies/Joseph Rowntree Foundation, 2015) which reports that the proportion of children living in a working family rose from 54% in 2009–2010 to 63% in 2013–2014. Despite this, and in the face of considerable opposition, including the House of Lords, as will be discussed later, the conservative government abolished the definitions of child poverty contained in the Child Poverty Act 2010 (renamed the Life Chances Act 2010) and introduced a new measure of child poverty, in part based on workless households; Welfare Reform and Work Act 2016, s 7.
40 N Spencer, *Health Consequences of Poverty for Children* (London: End Child Poverty 2008) 4.
41 Institute for Longitudinal Studies, *User's Guide to the Second Millennium Cohort Study* (London: UCL Institute for Education 2007).
42 Department for Education and Skills, *Social Mobility: Narrowing Social Class Educational Attainment Gaps* (London: TSO 2006).
43 See Fabian Commission on Life chances and child poverty, *Narrowing the Gap* (London: Fabian Society 2006).
44 End Child Poverty, 'Why end child poverty' www.endchildpoverty.org.uk/why-end-child-poverty/the-effects [accessed 24 October 2103]. It also leads to poorer health in adulthood: see N Spencer, *Childhood Poverty and Adult Health* (London: End Child Poverty 2008).
45 United Kingdom Office for National Statistics, *Inequalities in Life Expectancy at 65 in UK* (2007).
46 P Parkinson, 'Re-engineering the Child Support Scheme: An Australian perspective on the British Government's proposals' (2007) 70 *Modern L Rev* 812; citing J Bartfield, 'Child support and the post divorce economic well-being of mothers, fathers, and children' (2000) 37 *Demography* 203; J Bradshaw, 'Child support and child poverty' (2006) 14 *Benefits* 199; D Meyer and M Hu, 'A note on the antipoverty effectiveness of child support among mother-only families' (1999) 34 *J Hum Resources* 225.
47 Carbone (n 13) 32.

financial affairs so that they had a nil income (the formula dealt with income only and not capital). A self-employed non-resident parent running a company might, for example, arrange to be paid by dividends rather than by salary.[48] The original formula was extremely complex – delays in providing the required information could ensure that assessment dragged on and on. Even if an assessment was completed accurately (and by 2000, 90 per cent of the CSA's work was on assessment), it became clear that the original Act was 'a toothless dragon'[49] when it came to enforcing the assessment against an unwilling 'absent' parent (this was addressed by subsequent legislation in 2000 and 2008 when draconian measures such as removal of passports and driving licences were introduced[50]).

The result of either the non-resident parent's inability to pay (or so reordering their affairs) was that, in 1997, for example, 40 per cent of those who were assessed had a 'nil' liability because of their level of income; a further 15 per cent were paying a nominal amount. The average award in the same year was £39 per week for all children of the family (and £23 per week for families where the non-resident parent was self-employed).[51] Further, in 1997, 250,000 accounts were in arrears – at this point in time £1.1 billion was owed in arrears (by 2011 the figure was £3.9 billion).[52]

Differing types of families

Although these issues were hugely problematic, an even more fundamental barrier to raising standards of living was created under the original scheme. To explain this requires drawing a distinction between differing types of families as Garrison has done (when writing about the child support laws in the United States).[53] She distinguishes between, on the one hand, children living in middle-class divorcing families for whom, she argues, the debate concerns living standards, equity between the parents and the best ways in which to minimise the potentially harmful effects of separation and, on the other hand, children living in poor families for whom the really important issues are benefits, child care and employment opportunities for both parents. While child support measures may play a role in insulating the former families from the full decline in living standards which accompanies divorce, in the case of the latter families 'if parents lack the resources to avoid poverty when together child support alone cannot remedy the problem'.[54] By dealing with both sets of families in the same way 'child support policy will offer the most help to the least needy: it cannot be expected to achieve a major reduction in children's poverty'.[55]

Garrison's distinction can be drawn in broadly similar terms on this side of the Atlantic: under the 1991 Act, there were two types of applicant to the CSA – the voluntary cases and the section 6 benefit cases. In the case of voluntary applicants for whom the CSA succeeded in obtaining child support, the money went to the family and could thus be said

---

48 See *Phillips v Pearce* [1996] 2 *FLR* 230 (Fam Div).
49 N Wikeley, G Davis and R Young, *Child Support in Action* (Oxford: Hart 1998) 97–8.
50 See Child Maintenance and Other Payments Act 2008, ss27–30.
51 DSS, *Social Security Statistics* (London: TSO 1997).
52 C-MEC 2011, 'Maria Miller targets CSA debt mountain' www.childmaintenance.org/en/news/article30.html [accessed 16 March 2012].
53 M Garrison, 'The goals and limits of child support policy' in JT Oldham and MS Melli (eds), *Child Support: The Next Frontier* (Ann Arbor, MI: University of Michigan Press 2000).
54 Ibid. 22.
55 Ibid. 25.

to improve their standard of living – even if the sums obtained were modest. However, by 1996, only 8 per cent of applicants were voluntary.[56] The controversy surrounding the Act and the CSA led those parents who did not have to use it to avoid it if at all possible, relying instead upon private agreements. The difficulty with such agreements is, of course, that they are legally unenforceable and, as will be discussed later, expose the family, at the very least, to uncertainty.

Section 6 benefit cases did not have the option of private agreements; as explained above, receipt of benefits deemed the parent with care to have made an application to the CSA. However, any child support obtained from an absent parent in such cases did not go to the family but to the Treasury to offset against the benefit paid to the family. It gave neither parent with care nor absent parent any incentive to cooperate with the Agency. This is where the reality of the Child Support scheme as fiscal policy bites hard. Under the original Act, such families' standard of living did not improve at all and was a non-starter as an anti-poverty measure. As Wikeley, Davis and Young have commented, the failure to prioritise the role of child support as part of a wider strategy to tackle child poverty [proved] highly damaging to public perceptions of the new scheme.[57]

Changing strategies: the move towards the 'eradication of poverty'

Since its implementation, the child support legislation has been amended repeatedly, some of the changes being cosmetic and others more far-reaching. This chapter does not consider in detail the rather dismal history of governments' attempts to mitigate perceived unfairness and increase collection (which include two further Acts of Parliament), but fast forwards to 2006–2007. At this time, only one in three eligible children was receiving any support and the mean liability was £24 per week for children under the revised formula introduced by legislation in 2000 (although not implemented until 2003).[58] The CSA was condemned as 'a failing organisation . . . in crisis'[59] and 'not fit for purpose' by the Work and Pensions Secretary, John Hutton.[60] He commissioned Sir David Henshaw to write a report on the Act and the Agency.[61] Following his recommendations, the government decided to introduce a new, tougher, streamlined system based upon four 'new' principles, the first two of which are key here: to help tackle child poverty and to promote parental responsibility 'by encouraging parents to make their own maintenance arrangements wherever possible, but by taking firm action – through a tough and effective system of enforcement – to enforce payment if this is necessary'.[62] This led to the passing of the Child Maintenance and Other Payments Act 2008, which established an independent Child Maintenance Enforcement Commission (C-MEC) to take on the role of both providing information and support to parents as well as overseeing the work of the CSA staff.[63]

---

56 Child Support Agency, *Quarterly Summary of Statistics*, February 1997 (London: TSO 1997).
57 (n 49) 122.
58 Department for Work and Pensions, Child Support Agency, *Summary of Statistics* (London: TSO 2006).
59 House of Commons, Work and Pensions Committee (2005).
60 A Grice, 'CSA faces major reform after being branded "not fit"' *The Independent* (9 February 2006).
61 Henshaw Report (n 16).
62 Department for Work and Pensions, *A New System of Child Maintenance* (White Paper) (London: TSO 2006) para 15.
63 See N Wikeley, 'Child support reform – throwing the baby out with the bathwater' (2007) 19 *Child Family LQ* 434. C-MEC was in place between 2008 and 2012, when it was abolished in the bonfire of the quangos and its work taken on by the DWP.

At the same time as the child support legislation was being reshaped with renewed (or real, depending on how one judges the original Act's aims[64]) emphasis upon tackling poverty, the Child Poverty Unit was established (in 2007) with the stated government policy and of halving child poverty by 2010 and 'eradicating' child poverty by 2020. At this point, a key target for the 'eradication' of child poverty was that less than 10 per cent of children should be living in relative income poverty.[65]

So how has the commitment to reducing and eventually eradicating child poverty played out in relation to the reformed child support (now described as maintenance) legislation? What has happened has been a radical shift in the relationship between child support and benefit payments, having been heralded by the introduction of the child maintenance premium (CMP). As discussed above, originally lone parents on benefits received none of the money collected by the CSA from the non-resident parent. From 2000 onwards (as a result of changes made by the Child Support, Pensions, and Social Security Act 2000 Act), a £10 CMP was introduced. The first £10 per week of child support was disregarded in assessing the parent with care's entitlement to income support although, regrettably, this only applied to applications under the revised scheme and not to those assessed under the original scheme. While this can be regarded as a step in the right direction and provided a modest incentive to cooperate, the CMP was set too low.[66] However, from October 2008 when the policy shift occurred, it was increased to £20 per week as part of a phased increase. Most significantly, from April 2010, all payments of child support have been ignored when calculating the parent with care's entitlement to benefits.[67] It was estimated that this change – with the state and non-resident parents both contributing – would lift 80,000–90,000 children out of poverty.[68] Further, the duty to cooperate with the CSA under section 6 (and the associated reduced benefit direction) was abolished (from 2008). As Wikeley comments, 'at one level this is commendably egalitarian . . . and means that "the system will no longer discriminate against people simply because they are poor"'.[69] Not surprisingly, applications to the CSA from lone parents on benefits have risen since this change – evidence it could be said 'that carrots, not sticks, are the best way forward'.[70]

While the above change is the one most clearly linked to reducing child poverty, other reforms may also help to enhance the assessment and collection of child support: for example, the 2008 Act uses the non-resident's annual tax return as the basis for an assessment of child support. This was implemented incrementally for new applications.[71] In addition,

---

64 Maclean and Fehlberg (n 10).
65 Child Poverty Act 2010; Department for Education/Department for Work and Pensions (2011).
66 T Ridge, 'Supporting children? The impact of child support policies on children's wellbeing in the UK and Australia' (2005) 34 *JSP* 121.
67 Changes announced in Department for Work and Pensions, *Raising Expectations and Increasing Support; Reforming Welfare for the Future* (Cm 7506, TSO 2008) para 7.15.
68 Henshaw Report (n 16) 19. Research published by Gingerbread has confirmed the impact the change has had in lifting significant numbers of lone parent families out of poverty: C Bryson, A Skipp, J Allbeson, E Poole, E Ireland and V Marsh, *Kids Aren't Free: The Child Maintenance Arrangements of Single Parents on Benefit in 2012* (London: Gingerbread/Nuffield Foundation 2013), 49.
69 Wikeley (n 63) 443; quoting Peter Hain in debates on the Bill: HC Deb 4 July 2007, vol 462, col 981.
70 Child Poverty Action Group, 'CPAG response to Strengthening families, promoting parental responsibility' (CPAG 2011) para 47. See also C Bryson, n 68.
71 Initially, from December 2012, the new scheme applied only to parents with four or more children with the same father; from July 2013 this was extended to parents with two or more children by the same father and now applies to all new applications.

new enforcement measures were introduced in 2010, including taking money from bank accounts.

The shift to voluntary, 'family-based' agreements

The above reforms, particularly the fundamental separation of child support from benefit payments, are brave and welcome changes. However, it is not all good news: the removal of the duty to cooperate noted was driven by another major shift in policy in the 2008 Act towards private, 'family-based' child support agreements which re-privatises the issue of child support. Although this was one of the key principles identified by Sir David Henshaw in his report, the policy of reducing the role of the state gained momentum with the Coalition government.[72] In 2011, Works and Pensions Minister, Maria Miller stated:

> The Government is clear about the importance of families and how strong stable family relationships produce the best results for children. Too often in the past the Child Support Agency has been used as a threat that can make the difficult time of separation worse instead of encouraging people to work together and take responsibility for their child. When couples split up they generally know what is best for them and their children without the state interfering. Thousands of parents are already working together to make their own maintenance arrangements without the help of the Agency and tell us these arrangements are working well. We want more people to come to their own maintenance arrangements which are in the best interest of the child and offer value to the taxpayer.[73]

It is undeniably the case that the scheme and the Agency which ran it may have 'driven a wedge'[74] between parents in the past; that it has 'trapped parents' (particularly those under s.6); and that it may have 'entrenched conflict' and 'reduced the likelihood of 'co-parenting''.[75] Coercion is by no means the only way of securing payment. It is also possible that, if parents 'own' their agreement, they may well be more likely to abide by its terms. But is it really this simple? Are parents suddenly going to be able to talk openly about money without conflict, resentment, or fear or worse? Well, yes, for some, of course – just as some parents have always been able to resolve the issues arising from separation rationally and without recourse to formal methods. Gingerbread has commented:

> Voluntary agreements can work well. For example, families with a voluntary agreement are more likely to receive the full amount on time than those receiving maintenance through the CSA. . . . But a moment's reflection reveals the obvious: that if parents are in agreement, by definition the money is more likely to be paid. . . . It is not the

---

72 See Department for Work and Pensions, *Strengthening Families, Promoting Parental Responsibility: the Future of Child Maintenance* (Consultation, Cm 7990, 2011); Department for Work and Pensions, The Government's Response to the Consultation on *Strengthening Families, Promoting Parental Responsibility: the Future of Child Maintenance* (Cm 8130, 2011).
73 M Miller, 'Child Maintenance reforms will put children first' www.childmaintenance.org/en/news/article 17.html [accessed 20 February 2011].
74 DWP, *Strengthening Families* (n72) para 6.
75 House of Commons, General Committee *Draft Child Support Maintenance Calculation Regulations* (HC 11 September 2012) col 3.

fact that an arrangement is voluntary which makes it work; rather it is down to the circumstances of the parents who entered into the agreement.[76]

Voluntary, 'family-based' agreements have a good chance of being successful, for instance, where: the parents have lived together; they have separated recently; relations between them are amicable; the household income is higher; there is continuing engagement between the non-resident parent and the child or children; and the parent with care is also in paid work.[77] Here, the role of the Child Maintenance Options Service (and formerly C-MEC) in providing clear information to parents,[78] booklets, a helpline, a template for agreements and even a maintenance calculator is a positive one (although the booklet's inclusion of payments in kind as an *alternative* to regular payments is unhelpful and should be resisted because of its inherent unreliability).[79] But it should be remembered that information is not the same thing as independent advice and, second, that any resulting such agreements are non-enforceable. Further, 'the history of child maintenance payments in Britain and elsewhere suggests that this co-operative Nirvana will only be obtained by a minority of parents who are not living together'.[80] At the time of the Bill's passage, Wikeley also expressed his doubts about the likely success of this policy, commenting that 'any existing power imbalances between parents will simply be reinforced, to the detriment of children's interests'. He cites research by Fran Wasoff which demonstrated that women were often willing to reduce their own (and, by implication, their children's) financial claims in order to achieve what they saw as more important relationship objectives.[81]

However, matters do not rest there. As part of the drive towards 'encouraging' private agreements, the present government has amended the child support legislation so as to introduce a mandatory gateway for parents who wish to make an application to the statutory child maintenance scheme (operated by the 'Child Maintenance Service' on behalf of the DWP)[82] for a binding agreement. The Welfare Reform Act 2012 enables the taking of such steps as are considered appropriate to encourage the making and keeping of family-based agreements and, in particular, before accepting an application 'to invite the applicant to consider . . . whether it is possible to make such an agreement'.[83] Further, child maintenance arrangements can only be made if the non-resident parent agrees or 'without such an arrangement child support maintenance is unlikely to be paid'.[84] This mandatory gateway is said to be operated with a 'light touch',[85] and victims of domestic violence and parents

---

76 Gingerbread, 'Strengthening families promoting parental responsibility – government plans for child maintenance: Gingerbread response to the consultation' (London: Gingerbread 2011) para 18.
77 Wikeley, Davis and Young (n 49).
78 The child maintenance options website sits alongside the 'Sorting out Separation' website (SOS), which provides information to separating parents: www.sortingoutseparation.org.uk [accessed 26 October 2016].
79 Child Maintenance Options, 'Talking about money: a child maintenance decisions guide' (2015) 37
80 Parkinson (n 46) 822.
81 Wikeley (n 63) 446; F Wasoff, 'Mutual Consent: Separation Agreements and the Outcome of Private Ordering in Divorce' (2005) 27 *JSWFL* 237.
82 The Child Support Agency itself is being closed down, a process it is currently projected will be completed by 2018. Parents who have an assessment (under the old scheme) are being informed that this will come to an end and they should try to secure a family based arrangement, using Child Maintenance Options, or if unable to do so, apply to the Child Maintenance Service for a new assessment.
83 Welfare Reform Act 1012, s 136.
84 Ibid. s 137.
85 DWP, *Strengthening Families* (n72) 17.

under the age of 18 are exempt from the filter but, for many other lone parents, the prospects of securing a freely formed family agreement must be so weak that this will simply add delay and anxiety to already difficult times.

As alarming as the erection of a barrier to prevent access to anything more than information and advice is the government's decision to charge fees for use of the statutory scheme. In 2008, the Labour government had passed a provision which gave them the power to charge fees;[86] however, this had not been implemented. The Coalition government, despite encountering opposition to its plans in the House of Lords, supplemented those provisions.[87]

Fees were provisionally set as a £100 upfront application charge (reduced to £50 for those on benefits, with £20 taken upfront). There was then to be a further deduction from sums collected to contribute towards the ongoing costs of collecting child support at a rate of 20 per cent of the maintenance from the non-resident parent (on top of maintenance payment itself) and seven per cent from the parent with care, which would be deducted from the maintenance payment.[88] In Maria Miller's view, 'the charge will encourage more parents to reach agreement together without automatically falling back on the state to resolve the issue'.[89] In other words, charging is seen as a route to influence behaviour: so-called 'behaviour economics'. The government also justified this as both fair and offering value to the taxpayer, with the statutory system of child support remaining 'heavily subsidised'.[90] CPAG and Gingerbread are among the organisations which made their opposition to these changes very clear. In its response to the consultation which preceded the Act, Gingerbread pointed out that many parents currently use the scheme from necessity and not from choice.[91] It went further:

> We wish to place on record our fundamental disagreement with the government's intention to deliberately seek to deter parents with care raising children from using the statutory maintenance system if they need to, and to levy financial charges against them – even where they have demonstrably no alternative but to use the statutory service if their children are to be adequately financially supported by the other parents.[92]

In committee, Dr Eilidh Whiteford MP commented that

> the vast majority of parents with care are women. It is deeply unfair that collection charges will be levied on parents with care who, through no fault of their own, have a former partner who refuses to meet obligations towards the children. This seems to me to be punishing the children for the sins of the fathers.[93]

---

86 Child Maintenance and Other Payments Act 2008, s 6 following the recommendation in Henshaw's Report that charging should be introduced.
87 Welfare Reform Act 2012, ss 140–1. The House of Lords backed an amendment blocking the measures, introduced by the former Lord Chancellor, Lord Mackay, by 270 to 128: HL Deb 25 January 2012, vol 735, cols 1090–1106.
88 DWP, *Strengthening Families* (n72) paras 25–32.
89 Miller (n 73).
90 General Committee (HC 11 September 2012) (n 75) col 40.
91 Gingerbread (n 76) para 10.
92 Ibid. para 10; see also CPAG (n 69).
93 General Committee (HC 11 September 2012) (n 75) col 12.

Despite the opposition to the introduction of fees, the government remained committed to them,[94] and they were introduced in 2014. In response to the criticisms it did scale down the charges: the person with care making the application has to pay an application fee of £20 unless under the age of 18 or a victim of domestic violence or abuse.[95] Where the collection (collect and pay) service is used, the non-resident parent's fee is 20 per cent of the daily amount of child support maintenance he is liable to pay while a four per cent collection fee is deducted from the payment the parent with care receives.[96] Parents can avoid these charges by choosing the 'Direct Pay' route, whereby the paying parent pays the receiving parent directly. 70 per cent of parents using the child maintenance service in 2015–2016 opted for this.[97] The reduction in the fee and the option to avoid additional charges by paying maintenance directly do mitigate the severity of the original scheme, it does not demonstrate any real understanding of the hardships facing single parent families on low incomes who may be put off applying because of the charge,[98] may make regular payments more uncertain for those using 'Direct Pay' and does not address the issue of principle. Despite the rhetoric about these changes furthering the interests of children by enabling parents to form their own agreements, which will help to lift more children out of poverty, cost saving and operational efficiency have more than a little to do with these reforms.

Where are we now?

Some twenty-five years after the implementation of the 1991 Act is an appropriate point to take stock again of the statutory child support scheme: what was it trying to achieve? What success, if any, has there been? Does the hopeless naivety of which Cretney accused the original drafters[99] continue today in the optimism surrounding family-based agreements? Or does the withdrawal of the state have other motivations? To try to answer these questions entails revisiting the earlier discussion concerning whether the child support scheme was driven by fiscal or social policy. What seems clear is that both have been drivers, with the emphasis shifting over the years.

As an instrument of social policy, the child support legislation has been and continues to be an exercise in setting norms:[100] 'responsible' parents pay for their children even if they do not live with them. As Ann Estin has commented,

> the construction of child support enforcement as a social policy problem rests on several key assumptions. One is that a biological connection between an 'absent parent' and a child is sufficient basis for imposing a legal responsibility for the child's support.

---

94 It did postpone introduction until the new gross income scheme was fully implemented: Department for Work and Pensions, Supporting Separated Families; Securing Children's Future Public Consultation (Cm 8399, 2012) 19.
95 Approximately 30 per cent of applications are exempt from application fees, almost all because of domestic violence: DWP, *Child Maintenance Service 2012 Scheme Experimental Statistics* (2016) 6.
96 The Child Support Fees Regulations 2014.
97 DWP (n 95) 8.
98 Bryson *et al.* (n 68) 121.
99 Cretney (n 15).
100 Carbone (n 13) 3.

Another is that absent parents are capable of paying support in an amount sufficient to make a real contribution to their children's lives.[101]

Examining these two assumptions in turn requires us to ask first if there is now consensus that a biological connection (irrespective of social parenthood) creates responsibility; or putting it another way, that the 'responsibilisation' strategy has been successful at least in creating the norm. This is crucial if the shift towards much more widespread voluntary agreements is to work. According to Mavis Maclean success has, indeed, been achieved:

> the great achievement of the CSA has been the establishment of a new social norm: that all fathers should pay for all their children. No child should experience material disadvantage between its parents, whether that relationship was formal or informal. Although most men query their own assessment, very few query the principle. This was not the case prior to the CSA.[102]

In his report, Henshaw took a somewhat different view:

> improving enforcement of social norms and responsibilities was a key objective in the creation of the CSA. . . . However, 16 years later the figures [of parents receiving maintenance] have barely changed. . . . [T]here is a widespread belief . . . that it is possible and, in some cases, acceptable to avoid paying.[103]

There may well indeed be a high level of agreement among the general population that fathers ought always to pay child support.[104] But, in research conducted for C-MEC to try to understand the behaviour of parents with no formal child maintenance arrangements in place, it was found that 'although there was universal support among those interviewed . . . for the principle of paying child maintenance, many viewed their own situation as the exception to the rule'.[105] This would suggest that opposition goes beyond disputes as to quantum. Consensus in the abstract is not that much of a consensus.

Even if there is a degree of consensus about a non-resident parent's responsibility to pay child support, this may now be threatened by the emphasis being given to voluntary agreements. At the time of the 2008 reforms, Parkinson commented that 'Britain risks going backwards . . . in terms of community acceptance of the child support obligation':[106] that fear is now much greater in the light of the current government's shift in focus. A survey of 2,000 parents who had contact with the Child Maintenance Options Service between

---

101 AL Estin, 'Moving beyond the child support revolution' (2001) 26 *L Social Enquiry* 508.
102 Maclean and Fehlberg (n 10) 19, citing a paper given to a Department for Work and Pensions seminar in 2006.
103 Henshaw Report (n 16) 12.
104 For example, in 2004 81 per cent of people surveyed took this view, see V Peacey and L Rainford, 'Attitudes towards child support and knowledge of Child Support Agency research report 226', Department for Work and Pensions (London: TSO 2004).
105 S Andrews, D Armstrong, L McLernon, S Meglaw and C Skinner, 'Promotion of child maintenance: research on instigating behaviour change, research report 1' (2011) www.childmaintenance.org/en/publications/index.html [accessed 16 March 2012].
106 Parkinson (n 46) 823. See also, Baroness Hollis and Lord Skelmersdale in committee stage of the Bill: HL Deb 31 January 2008, cols GC382-383, GC427.

July 2008 and January 2010 revealed that more than two-thirds of parents with a family-based arrangement were 'happy' with it, compared to a third of those who had used the CSA.[107] Given the difficulties with the CSA perhaps this is surprising but it reinforces the view that providing parents with valuable information will assist *some* to come to a fair agreement. However, recent statistics from the DWP suggest that it is appropriate to emphasise that it will only be some parents. In 2015–2016 a phone survey of Child Maintenance Options 'customers' found that only 25 per cent had gone on to form family based arrangements (a figure which was consistent with previous years) following their contact. Further research by Gingerbread has cast doubt on the durability of such arrangements.[108] Moreover, it is, of course, dependent upon the parents being willing and able to cooperate.

And what does this mean for the drive to eradicate child poverty? Although the target of halving child poverty was missed in 2010,[109] figures for the year 2009–2010 show that child poverty was at its lowest for 25 years.[110] It would seem that the former government's strategies, which included its policy towards child support (although it also included other measures, such as spending £150 billion on working tax credits between 2004–2009)[111] had some impact even if not enough. On coming into power the Coalition government took the view that the former government's policies had 'stalled'[112] and in 2014 the Social Mobility and Child Poverty Commission declared the target of eradicating child poverty by 2020 to be unattainable.[113] The number of children in absolute poverty has risen by half a million since 2010.[114] 26 per cent are still regarded as living in poverty.[115] Shortly after regaining power with a majority, the Conservative government reaffirmed its commitment to reducing child poverty but went on to repeal both the binding targets in the Child Poverty Act (which was renamed the Life Chances Act 2010) and the established measures of child poverty. In place of what Iain Duncan Smith, the then Secretary of State for Work and Pensions, condemned as the 'deeply flawed' relative measure of poverty is a new, controversial, measure of child poverty based on numbers in workless households and child educational attainments at 16.[116]

With the change in approach to child support, re-privatising the responsibility, together with the very significant changes being made to benefits, the fear is that despite the

---

107 A Allen and A Goldstein 'Survey of child maintenance option outcomes 2009/10: research report 4' (2012) www.childmaintenance.org/en/publications/index.html [accessed 16 March 2012].
108 Bryson *et al.* (n 68). DWP, Effective Family-based Child Maintenance Arrangements (2016) 3.
109 Save the Children, 'No child left behind: a child poverty strategy 2011–2014' (2010).
110 CPAG (n 70). However, as the measure is one of relative poverty some people were lifted out of poverty by the fall in general living standards.
111 Department for Education/Department for Work and Pensions, *Child Poverty: Tackling the Causes of Disadvantage and Transforming Families' Lives* (Cm 8061, 2011) 1.
112 Ibid. This included the policy of using child support to help reduce child poverty: in 2011 Iain Duncan Smith stated that child support by itself did not have a statistically significant impact on child poverty. Letter to Chair of Work and Pensions Select Committee (January 2011) available at www.publications.parliament.uk/pa/cm201011/cmselect/cmworpen/writev/cmec/sos2.pdf [accessed 26 October 2016].
113 Social Mobility and Child Poverty Commission, *State of the Nation* (2014) available at www.gov.uk/government/organisations/social-mobility-and-child-poverty-commission [accessed 05 February 2017].
114 Welfare Reform and Work Act 2016.
115 CPAG (n 70) www.cpag.org.uk/child-poverty-facts-and-figures [acessed 27 October 2017].
116 DWP, *Press Release* (n 39). As noted above, the *majority* of families in poverty by the current measure are those where a family member is in work.

government's declared commitment, child poverty could rise substantially.[117] It is an 'era of austerity' but it would seem that some vulnerable and needy families will have to bear the brunt of the renewed emphasis upon the child support scheme being 'value for money for the taxpayer' – considerations of fiscal policy.

We saw earlier that commentators do not agree on how valuable a tool child support is in reducing child poverty and this leads us to the second of the assumptions Estin identifies above: can non-resident parents pay sufficient amounts to make a difference to their children's lives? The answer is, of course, that the degree to which this is possible depends on the type of family involved. Those on higher incomes can mitigate the economically harmful effects upon children of parental separation, while for others on a low income or on benefits themselves, paying child support is very difficult and will not be sufficient by itself. Enabling parents with care to keep any child support obtained as well as their benefits has lifted children out of poverty. Moreover, evidence from organisations such as Gingerbread suggests that even small amounts of regular child support make a difference and even payments made at the lower, flat rate help.[118] So while child support may not reduce child poverty figures overall, it can and does at least alleviate the poverty of the poorest lone parent families who receive it regularly.[119]

All of this would lead to the conclusion, therefore, that we should not be taking any steps which make it *more* difficult for lone parents to secure regular support from the other parent by an over-reliance on private agreements, the introduction of a filter, or a regime of charging which is designed to act as a disincentive to seek state help and reduces the sum parents with care then receive if they rely upon the Child Maintenance Service to collect payments. It is true that some parents are circumnavigating these hurdles: latest figures reveal that just under half of those who were surveyed after contacting Child Maintenance Options went on to use the statutory scheme via the Child Maintenance Service, that approximately one-third avoid any charges (because of domestic violence) and that two-thirds avoid collection charges by using Direct Pay[120]. However, there will always be a significant number of determinedly resistant parents in relation to whom parents with care, anxious to secure child support, will require help that ought to be freely available as part of the state's responsibility towards children. The dismal reality is that, at a time when many parents living together need two wages to support a family, over-dependence upon the private responsibility of the non-resident parent and the parent with care to resolve child support issues will continue to leave too many children in poverty and leave them disadvantaged.

---

117 See UK Children's Commissioners, *Report of the UK Children's Commissioners UN Committee on the Rights of the Child: Examination of the Fifth Periodic Report of the United Kingdom of Great Britain and Northern Ireland* (2015), paras 8.12-8.18; R Dickens, 'Child poverty in Britain: past lessons and future prospects' (2011) 218 (1) *Natl Inst Econ Rev*, R7-R19. Browne, J and A. Hood, *Living Standards, Poverty and Inequality in the UK 2015–2016 to 2020–2021* (London: Institute of Fiscal Studies 2016) 2.
118 Bryson *et al.* (n 68).
119 See C Skinner and G Main, 'The contribution of child maintenance payments to the income packages of lone mothers' (2013) 21 Journal of Poverty and Social Justice 47 and M Hakovirta, 'Child maintenance and child poverty: a comparative analysis' (2011) 19 *Journal of Poverty and Social Justice* 249.
120 DWP (n 108) 3. The Department for Work and Pensions is conducting a 30 month evaluation of the reforms: see DWP, 'Child Maintenance Reforms Evaluation' Strategy (2014) www.gov.uk/government/uploads/system/uploads/attachments_data/file/387584/child-maintenance-reforms-evaluatiom-strategy.pdf [accessed 26 October 2016].

Bibliography

Aldridge H et al., *Monitoring Poverty and Social Exclusion* (Joseph Rowntree, York 2011).
Allen A and Goldstein A, 'Survey of child maintenance options outcomes 2009/10: research report 4' (2012) www.childmaintenance.org/en/publications/index.html [accessed 16 March 2012].
Andrews S et al., 'Promotion of child maintenance: research on instigating behaviour change: research report 1' (2011), http://webarchive.nationalarchives.gov.uk/20120716161734/http://www.childmaintenance.org/en/pdf/research/Main-Report-Vol-I.pdf [accessed 9 February 2017].
Bartfield J, 'Child support and the postdivorce economic well-being of mothers, fathers, and children' (2000) 37/2 *Demography* 203–13.
Belfield C et al., *Living Standards, Poverty and Inequality in the UK: 2015* (Institute for Fiscal Studies/Joseph Rowntree Foundation, London 2015).
Bradshaw J, 'Child support and child poverty' (2006) 14/3 *Benefits* 199–208.
Bradshaw J and Millar J, *Lone Parent Families in the UK* (Department of Social Security, London 1990).
Browne J and Hood A, *Living Standards, Poverty and Inequality in the UK: 2015–16 to 2020–21* (Institute of Fiscal Studies, London 2016).
Bryson C et al., *Kids Aren't Free: The Child Maintenance Arrangements of Single Parents on Benefit in 2012* (Gingerbread/Nuffield Foundation, London 2013).
Carbone J, 'Child support comes of age: an introduction to the laws of child support' in JT Oldham and MS Melli (eds), *Child Support: The Next Frontier* (University of Michigan Press, Ann Arbor, MI 2000) 3–15.
Centre for Longitudinal Studies, *User's Guide to the Second Millenium Cohort Study* (Institute of Education, University of London, London 2007).
Child Maintenance and Enforcement Commission, 'Maria Miller targets CSA debt mountain', 2011, www.childmaintenance.org/en/news/article30.html [accessed 16 March 2012].
Child Maintenance Options, 'Talking about money: a child maintenance decisions guide' (2012) www.cmoptions.org/en/pdfs/refresh/talking-about-money-aug-2015.pdf [accessed 9 February 2017].
Child Poverty Action Group, *Putting the Treasury First: The Truth about Child Support* (CPAG, London, 1994).
Child Poverty Action Group, *CPAG Response to Strengthening Families, Promoting Parental Responsibility* (CPAG, London 2011).
Child Poverty Action Group, 'Child poverty facts and figures' (2016). www.cpag.org.uk/povertyfacts.htm [accessed 27 October 2016].
Child Support Agency, *Quarterly Summary of Statistics, February 1997* (TSO, London 1997).
Collier R, 'The campaign against the Child Support Act: "errant fathers" and family men' (1994, July) 24 *Family Law* 384–87.
Collier R, 'Engaging Fathers? Responsibility, Law and the "Problem of Fatherhood"' in Bridgeman J, Lind C and Keating H (eds), *Responsibility, Law and the Family* (Ashgate, Aldershot, UK 2008) 169–90.
Cretney S, *Principles of Family Law*, 7th edn (Sweet & Maxwell, London 2002).
Department for Education and Skills, *Social Mobility: Narrowing Social Class Educational Attainment Gaps* (TSO, London 2006).
Department for Education/Department for Work and Pensions, *Child Poverty: Tackling the Causes of Disadvantage and Transforming Families' Lives* (Cm 8061, London 2011).
Department of Social Security, *Children Come First* (White Paper, Cm 1264, London 1990).
Department for Work and Pensions/Child Support Agency, *Summary of Statistics* (TSO, London 2006).
Department for Work and Pensions, *A New System of Child Maintenance* (White Paper) (TSO, London 2006).
Department for Work and Pensions, *Raising Expectations and Increasing Support; Reforming Welfare for the Future* (Cm 7506, TSO, London 2008).

Department for Work and Pensions, *The Government's Response to the Consultation on Strengthening Families, Promoting Parental Responsibility: The Future of Child Maintenance* (Cm 8130, London 2011).

Department for Work and Pensions, *Strengthening Families, Promoting Parental Responsibility: The Future of Child Maintenance* (Consultation, Cm 7990, London 2011).

Department for Work and Pensions, 'Child Maintenance Service 2012 scheme experimental statistics' (2016) www.gov.uk/government/uploads/system/uploads/attachmentdata/file/564283/child-maintenance-service-2012-scheme-aug.pdf [accessed 26 October 2016].

Department for Work and Pensions, *Supporting Separated Families; Securing Children's Future* Public Consultation (Cm 8399, London 2012).

Department for Work and Pensions, 'Child maintenance reforms evaluation strategy' (2014) www.gov.uk/government/uploads/system/uploads/attachmentdata/file/387584/child-maintenance-reforms-evaluation-strategy.pdf [accessed 26 October 2016].

Department for Work and Pensions, 'Effective family-based child maintenance arrangements' (2016) www.gov.uk/government/uploads/system/uploads/attachmentdata/file/542849/effective-family-based-child-maintenance-mrch-2016.pdf [accessed 26 October 2016].

Dickens R, 'Child poverty in Britain: past lessons and future prospects' (2011) 218 *Natl Inst Econ Rev*, R7–R19.

Duckworth L, 'Single parents now head a quarter of all British families' *The Independent* (27 September 2002).

Duncan Smith I, 'Letter to Chair of Work and Pensions Select Committee' (January 2011) www.publications.parliament.uk/pa/cm201011/cmselect/cmworpen/writev/cmec/sos2.pdf accessed [26 October 2016].

End Child Poverty, 'Why end child poverty' www.endchildpoverty.org.uk/why-end-child-poverty/the-effects [accessed 24 October 2013].

Estin AL, 'Moving beyond the child support revolution' (2001) 26/2 *Social Enquiry* 505–28.

Fabian Commission on Life Chances and Child Poverty, *Narrowing the Gap* (Fabian Society, London 2006).

Garland D, *The Culture of Control* (OUP, Oxford 2001).

Garrison M, 'The goals and limits of child support policy' in JT Oldham and MS Melli (eds), *Child Support: The Next Frontier* (University of Michigan Press, Ann Arbor, MI 2000) 16–45.

Gingerbread, *Strengthening Families Promoting Parental Responsibility – Government Plans for Child Maintenance: Gingerbread Response to the Consultation* (Gingerbread, London 2011).

Grice A, 'CSA faces major reform after being branded "not fit"' *The Independent* (9 February 2006).

Hakovirta M, 'Child maintenance and child poverty: a comparative analysis' (2011) 19 *Journal of Poverty and Social Justice* 249–262.

Henshaw D, Report to the Secretary of State for Work and Pensions, *Recovering Child Support: Routes to Responsibility* (Cm 6894, London 2006).

House of Commons, General Committee *Draft Child Support Maintenance Calculation Regulations* (HC, London 11 September 2012) col 3.

James A, 'Responsibility, children and childhood' in J Bridgeman, H Keating and C Lind (eds), *Responsibility, Law and the Family* (Ashgate, Aldershot, UK 2008) 145–66.

Keating H, 'Children come first?' (1995) 1 *Contemp Issues in Law* 29–44.

Legler P, 'The impact of welfare reforms on the child support legislation' in JT Oldham and MS Melli (eds), *Child Support: The Next Frontier* (University of Michigan Press, Ann Arbor, MI 2000) 46–68.

Maclean M and Fehlberg B, 'Child support policy in Australia and the United Kingdom: changing priorities but a similar tough deal for children?' (2009) 23/1 *IJLPF* 1–24.

Meyer D and Hu M, 'A note on the antipoverty effectiveness of child support among mother-only families' (1999) 34/1 *J Hum Resources* 225–34.

Miller M, 'Child maintenance reforms will put children first' www.childmaintenance.org/en/news/article17.html [accessed 20 February 2011].

Parkinson P, 'Re-engineering the Child Support Scheme: an Australian perspective on the British government's proposals' (2007) 70/5 *Modern L Rev* 812–36.

Peacey V and Rainford L, *Attitudes Towards Child Support and Knowledge of Child Support Agency, Department for Work and Pensions Research Report* no. 226 (TSO, London 2004).

Ridge T, 'Supporting children? The impact of child support policies on children's wellbeing in the UK and Australia' (2005) 34/1 *Journal of Social Policy* 121–42.

Save the Children, *No Child Left Behind: A Child Poverty Strategy 2011–2014* (London 2010).

Sheldon S, 'From "absent objects of blame" to "fathers who want to take responsibility": reforming birth registration law 13' (2009) 31/4 *Journal of Social Welfare and Family Law* 373–89.

Skinner S and Main G, 'The contribution of child maintenance payments to the income packages of lone mothers' (2013) 21/1 *Journal of Poverty and Social Justice* 47–60.

Social Mobility and Child Poverty Commission, *State of the Nation* (2014) available at www.gov.uk/government/organisations/social-mobility-and-child-poverty-commission [accessed 9 February 2017].

Spencer N, *Childhood Poverty and Adult Health* (End Child Poverty, London 2008).

Spencer N, *Health Consequences of Poverty for Children* (End Child Poverty, London 2008).

Thatcher M, *The Downing Street Years* (Harper Collins, London 1995).

United Kingdom Children's Commissioners, *Report of the UK Children's Commissioners UN Committee on the Rights of the Child: Examination of the Fifth Periodic Report of the United Kingdom of Great Britain and Northern Ireland* (London 2015).

United Kingdom Office for National Statistics, *Inequalities in Life Expectancy at 65 in UK* (London 2007).

Wasoff F, 'Mutual consent: separation agreements and the outcome of private ordering in divorce' (2005) 27/3–4 *Journal of Social Welfare and Family Law* 237–50.

Wikeley N, 'Child support reform – throwing the baby out with the bathwater' (2007) 19/4 *Child Family Law Quarterly* 434–57.

Wikeley N, Davis G and Young R, *Child Support in Action* (Hart Publishing, Oxford 1998).

11 The Universal Credit

A 'great rationaliser' for the 21st century

Ann Mumford

Introduction

The Universal Credit aims to make things simpler for workers receiving a low income, or no income at all. This chapter aims to make our understanding of the Universal Credit a little more complex. It starts with the proposal that broad efforts towards reform in government structure and benefit provision represent more than a political party's hopes to make an impact upon government (even if only for the sake of impact) while the opportunity persists. Rather, they also reflect significant changes in society that may have been building over time, and in this sense may present an historical benchmark, or an opportunity to reflect on how much has changed since the last, important effort at reform.

For these reasons, this chapter undertakes to construct an isomorphic, institutionalist analysis of the Universal Credit, which is a replacement for Jobseeker's Allowance, Housing Benefit, working Tax Credit, Child Tax Credit, Employment and Support Allowance, and Income Support.[1] When the Universal Credit was first introduced, its proposal purported to attack New Labour tax credit initiatives which largely had been well received in the literature;[2] and, additionally, which had contributed to reductions in levels of child poverty. The motivations for reforming the tax credits involved simplicity and work incentives, but not apparently regretful assertion that funds were not available to continue an otherwise worthwhile initiative. Thus one starting point for this chapter was to query why these justifications were used, and to investigate a suspicion that the transfer from 'wallet to purse' that the tax credits in part aimed to achieve could be ascribed with credit for causing confusion. This chapter adopts an isomorphic, institutional approach to the Universal Credit, because such analyses enable 1) consideration of the interaction between governments and taxpayers in policy formation, and 2) wide ranging considerations of social change in the family. With these foci, the chapter considers the source of some of the 'confusion' that the Universal Credit aims to tackle.

Isomorphic, institutional analysis: setting the stage

This chapter will integrate discussions surrounding the Universal Credit in the United Kingdom (UK) into existing, socio-legal literature engaging with New Labour's 'working

---

1 www.gov.uk/universal-credit [accessed 22 September 2015] *per* The Welfare Reform Act 2012.
2 See, *inter alia*, R Blundell, '2001 Lectures – British Academy' in *2001 Lectures – British Academy* (Oxford: Oxford University Press 2001); J Bradshaw, 'Child poverty and child outcomes' (2002) 16 *Children & Society* 131; and B Lund, '"Ask not what your community can do for you": obligations, New Labour and welfare reform' (1999) 19 *Critical Social Policy* 447.

families tax credit' (as then was; later, Child Tax Credit).[3] The methodological approach will be grounded specifically in literature describing trends towards isomorphism in governmental institutions. To understand this approach, it is necessary to begin with a groundbreaking article, written by DiMaggio and Powell in 1983, arguing that business, and government processes and agencies, are being driven by homogenisation.[4] Corporate and public bodies respond to change by mimicking what similar organisations do, they explained, largely to achieve some sort of stasis in the midst of disruption.[5] Legislation according rights to groups of persons can cause exactly the sort of disruption that may lead to the pursuit of bureaucratisation, or homogeneity.

The value of institutional analysis has been noted particularly for what might be described as 'normal times'. Although few historical periods are without crises of some sort, the 'New Labour' period from 1997–2007, before the economic crisis of 2008, might serve as a 'normal time' for these purposes. This, also, is not to suggest that this period, having been designated 'normal', did not contain social inequality; rather, it is to emphasise the difficulties of the period after 2008. It is only by comparison, or on a sliding scale, that the pre-2008 period might be described as 'normal' – a term with particular resonance in institutionalist scholarship. For example,

> [t]he institutionalist approach . . . has a good toolbox to explain, for 'normal times', social policy continuity and what has been termed 'progressive change', that is, the kind of change showing no brutal departure from a developmental path but with a specific direction nonetheless.[6]

Institutionalism, generally, has a long history in legal analysis, roughly dividing into two schools: old and new. The 'old' institutionalism focused upon formal means of achieving what could be described as good outcomes; in a sense, it was pragmatic.[7] The 'new' institutionalism is interested in the impact that institutions have upon society, and the way that they interact. It acknowledges that law does not proceed in a strictly 'top-down' fashion. It is because of the acknowledgement of this complexity that several insights are possible when mining the isomorphic literature for approaches to some of the changes in tax and benefit law, generally; and, specifically, with respect to the Universal Credit. Simply, institutional analysis allows a deeper analysis of the language, and symbolism, underpinning legislative initiatives.

---

3 Tax Credits Act 2002 c.21, repealed by Welfare Reform Act 2012 c. 5 Sch. 14(1) para. 1.
4 PJ DiMaggio and WW Powell, 'The iron cage revisited: institutional isomorphism and collective rationality in organizational fields' (1983) 48 *American Sociological Review* 147–60.
5 Ibid.
6 B Vis, K van Kersbergen and T Hylands, 'To what extent did the financial crisis intensify the pressure to reform the welfare state?' (2011) 45 *Social Policy & Administration* 338, 339.
7 AL Stinchcombe, 'On the Virtues of the Old Institutionalism' (1997) 23 *Annual Review of Sociology* 1, 8, arguing that '[t]he old institutionalist theory of Selznick and others is that reason and good sense are values, and formality a means to reason and good sense. Selznick's theory would predict Bentham's success . . . In part the new institutionalism would predict that Bentham should have lost out, particularly among lawyers who are dependent on predicting what the other lawyers who run the court will decide. The profession of law depends on isomorphism, that the arguments they make will be the same as the arguments that the court will accept'. Stinchcombe is referring to Bentham's work with rules of evidence, in that Bentham was opposed to heavily exclusive rules of evidence, and advocated investing trust in a court's discretion. Stinchcombe, citing W Twining, *Rethinking Evidence: Explanatory Essays* (Evanston, IL: Northwestern University Press 1990).

The introduction of the Universal Credit has meaning beyond its professed objectives of simplification and economic efficiency. A clue may be found in its reception. As this chapter will discuss, the Universal Credit has been widely criticised by authors who suggest that the reforms are unlikely to achieve their objectives. This is not simply a matter of disagreement, in that, it is not merely the case that the Conservative party believe that the reforms will assist people living in poverty, and critics of the Conservative party insist that it will not. Rather, the Universal Credit may represent a reaction against placing a market value on traditionally unpaid care work, and the disruption in gender power relations that threatened, or promised, to accompany this.

An institutionalist approach is perhaps less novel if one recalls that, in some ways, institutionalism is quite similar to the approach of Schumpeter,[8] whose evolutionary analysis of economics has been much discussed in recent years.[9] Schumpeter is famed for suggesting that wealth is destroyed by capitalism, in a process he described as 'creative destruction'.[10] Schumpeter drew attention to the importance of the governing class in this process, and as such would have been enormously interested in the differences between the political parties supporting, and opposing, the Universal Credit.[11] He would have appreciated that the introduction of the Universal Credit is not simply a reflection of the economic times, but, in some sense, connected to power.[12]

Whether one is engaging with DiMaggio and Powell, or with Schumpeter, sociological analyses of law, generally, tend to focus upon the administration of law, and its impact, and thus provide an ideal context for analyses of tax and benefit legislation targeted at influencing behaviour. Indeed, it would appear to be ideally suited for the specificities and bureaucracies of tax and benefit legislation, the impacts of which often are felt as much in their administration, as in the bare structure of their underpinning legislation. Part of the appeal of institutional analysis is the enthusiasm with which it embraces bureaucracy.[13]

Returning to the 1983 article of DiMaggio and Powell, in this piece the authors emphasised the significance of what might be dismissed as mundane, structural changes,

---

8 Joseph A Schumpeter (1883–1950), Austrian-American economist. His approach to the 'tax state' and 'fiscal sociology' has always been enormously influential, but largely among tax scholars and economic sociologists. Since the economic crisis in 2008, however, he is much discussed on BBC Radio 4 (for just one example, see 'Schumpeter Rising', 14 January 2009, www.bbc.co.uk/programmes/b00glndm) as both one who might have predicted the banking collapse and one whose ideas might provide a way forward.
9 An electronic search of Hansard performed on 2 April 2012 returned 19 references to Schumpeter in Parliament and in written evidence.
10 JA Schumpeter, *Capitalism, Socialism and Democracy* (London: Routledge 1994) Ch VII. He emphasises (at 82) that this is Marx's idea.
11 Ibid. 13: 'Schumpeter perhaps fits uncomfortably with Selznick as a comember of an old institutional school. But one of the positions he holds in common with the old institutionalists is that the form of competition among organizations is historically variable, depending a good deal on the values of the governing class and their challenges.'
12 Ibid. 12. 'Schumpeter thought that many economic institutions that facilitated capitalism as we know it depended on values other than capitalism. Imperialism and mercantilism were driven by the value of power as much as by profit'.
13 This is part of the 'new institutionalism', which '. . . has been characterised by renewed interest in the concept of ideas . . . The explanation of institutional change has often been regarded as the Achilles heel of historical institutionalism, and it has been argued that the concept of ideas has been introduced to enable comprehension of both the path of institutional change as well as the origins of change itself'. L Holm Pedersen, 'The political impact of environmental economic ideas' (2005) 28 *Scandinavian Political Studies* 25, 27.

and insisted that these should be studied for a variety of pragmatic clues to deeper changes. In perhaps their most famous paragraph, they wrote:

> ... the causes of bureaucratization and rationalization have changed. The bureaucratization of the corporation and the state have been achieved. ... Today, however, structural changes in organizations seem less and less driven by competition or by the need for efficiency ... Instead, bureaucratization and other forms of organizational change occur as the result of processes that make organizations more similar without necessarily making them more efficient. Bureaucratization and other forms of homogenization emerge, we argue, out of the structuration (Giddens, 1979) of organizational fields. This process, in turn, is effected largely by the state and the professions, which have become the great rationalizers of the second half of the twentieth century.[14]

Similarity among organisations need not merely be driven by, for example, a desire for efficiency, but also may include the hope or pursuit of legitimacy. The challenge is that a drive for efficiency may undermine efforts towards legitimacy. In some ways, DiMaggio and Powell are using homogeneity in ways similar to the twenty-first century emphasis on efficiency (and they more or less mean the same thing). Homogeneity is pursued because there is comfort, or safety, in similarity, and the absence of disruption appears to be more efficient. The difficulty with drives towards homogeneity/efficiency is that such processes that may start well, but in the end also may produce ultimately inefficient results.

Large bureaucracies, like government, are subject to pressures from a number of sources, including the weight of market forces. Governments are pressured to be more efficient, to be more homogeneous, and to save money. Thus, DiMaggio and Powell ask, '[u]nder what circumstances are institutional norms more important than alternative processes, such as market forces, in shaping this distribution?' They conclude that institutional norms (drives towards homogeneity) tend to win over market forces, in particular, during 'periods of nationalism'.[15] The rise of nationalism may be linked to forces in the economy; or, in some studies, has been connected to the influence of elite members of society.[16]

Applying institutional analysis: unlocking feminist potential

The institutional analysis deployed in this chapter is undertaken with an eye upon the feminist potential of such analyses. This literature is enthusiastic about the potential, but predicated upon some cautions. First, the search for similarities in bureaucracies can be misleading.[17] Second, the demand for accountability, so perfectly illustrated by the conditionality of the Universal Credit, should be considered not just from the perspective of the information

---

14 DiMaggio and Powell (n 5).
15 Ibid.72.
16 JM Whitmeyer, 'Elites and popular nationalism' (2002) 53 *The British Journal of Sociology* 321.
17 Thus, Bogoch, when analysing the gender factor in interactions between lawyers and clients, observed that '... some hold that there is no isomorphism between particular linguistic structures and social functions and that the same feature may serve different functions, even in the same culture'. B Bogoch, 'Gendered lawyering: difference and dominance in lawyer-client interaction' (1997) 31 *Law & Society Review* 677, 679–80, citing S Harris' Questions as a mode of control in magistrate's court' 49 *International Journal of Sociology of Language* 5–27.

that is produced, but also against the background of the bureaucratic pressures that gave rise to the call for accountability.[18]

The institutionalist analysis which follows – which in a sense would ask whether the Universal Credit is evocative of what DiMaggio and Powell would have described as a 'great rationalizer'[19] of otherwise irrational bureaucracy; i.e. the drive to isomorphism – is divided into two parts. The first part considers the feminist potential of isomorphic analysis, as applied to the Universal Credit. The second part considers the Universal Credit as part of a wider, legislative project of equality based initiatives; in other words, as part of a bureaucracy. The chapter concludes with the suggestion that the confusion which the Universal Credit was introduced to address is perhaps ascribable to changes in the role of women in the economy, as differentiated from paperwork, or bureaucratic language. Thus, this chapter relies upon a theory developed to analyse bureaucracy, to suggest that the Universal Credit, despite its publicity, is not about bureaucracy. Rather, the Universal Credit addresses the confusion that resulted from Labour's war on child poverty.

To make this case, it is necessary first to explain the feminist potential of institutional analysis. Mackay *et al.* suggest that feminist, institutional analysis is potentially very useful, but only in a limited sense. It can help to identify why something has happened, but it is relatively unhelpful in providing solutions, or useful next steps.[20] This is an objective of this chapter, to consider reasons why the Universal Credit was introduced, and from within the specified context of bureaucracy. It is a salient enough project, and one which invokes Cornell's lament that '. . . we cannot understand the backlash against even the most meagre civil rights of women and the restoration of inequality through the traditional explanations of the distribution of political power'.[21] Yet in attempting to answer this question, Cornell turned to systems theory. She was motivated by '. . . seeing the gender hierarchy restored, in which anything associated with the feminine is disparaged, devalued, feared, and ultimately, repudiated'.[22] She explained that a systems theory analysis would provide insight into this, as '[t]o fully explain this process of restoration of inequality, we need a systems explanation of how the gender hierarchy is perpetuated and intersects with the law so as to effectively undermine the legitimacy of women's demands for justice'.[23] Thus, her analysis explained why any step forward for gender equality within the legal structure inevitably seemed to face resistance and undermining.

This chapter, while not relying on systems analysis, will ask some similar questions. For example, is the Universal Credit an inevitable, politically motivated dismantling by the

---

18 MT Hannan and J Freeman, 'Structural inertia and organizational change' (1984) 49 *American Sociological Review* 149, 153.
19 The title of their 1983 article (n 5).
20 '. . . we argue that a synthesis of SI [sociological institutionalism] and feminist gender analysis can systematically identify and track the norms as well as the symbolic and cultural factors that play an important role in gendering institutions and their practices. As such, the incorporation of elements of SI into a feminist institutionalism can remedy some of the difficulties associated with certain other institutionalisms, such as an overemphasis on a narrow conception of the "rational" actor and on formal institutions and practices. Nonetheless, though promising, we argue that a feminist institutionalism based upon SI on its own would be insufficient to tackle the core questions of gender, strategic action, power, and change'. F Mackay, S Monro and G Waylen, 'The feminist potential of sociological institutionalism' (2009) 5 *Politics and Gender* 253, 254.
21 DL Cornell, 'The philosophy of the limit, systems theory and feminist legal reform' (1991) 26 *New England Law Review* 783, 784.
22 Ibid.
23 Ibid.

Coalition government of Labour's successful tax credits initiative? Or, is the Universal Credit a reaction against structural changes; and, if so, in what way (mimetic, normative, or coercive)? A White Paper explaining the government's proposals for the Universal Credit was published in November 2011.[24] The paper starts by suggesting that it has been accepted by 'successive governments' that 'fundamental reform' of the welfare and benefits system is needed.[25] Previous governments did not try to embark upon a process of reform, however, because they believed it to be too 'difficult' a task. The report evocatively suggests that '[i]nstead of grasping the nettle, [past governments] watched as economic growth bypassed the worst off and welfare dependency took root in communities up and down the country, breeding hopelessness and intergenerational poverty.'[26] Thus, very early on, the White Paper has detailed some important assumptions underlying the Universal Credit: first, that benefits have stopped assisting some who live in poverty, and have started to become the cause of poverty; second, that the process by which this has occurred is fraught with complexity, and difficult to unravel; and, finally, that there is a culture of dependency in some communities, which has prevented parents from teaching their children how to find work in the marketplace.[27] On this point, Bennett, in written evidence to the Parliamentary select committee, highlighted the language used in the White Paper. She explained that 'some language used in the White Paper (e.g. 'welfare dependency') labels claimants and seems to contradict its focus on financial disincentives to work'.[28] Lister echoed these criticisms, and warned that '[t]he use of such terms is stigmatising and contributes to the "othering" of people living on benefits'.[29]

The Universal Credit will operate such that only one carer will receive the payment. The Women's Budget Group (WBG) have warned that, given that it is likely that this payment may be claimed for men, then this could have a disruptive effect on the management of the financial resources of families living in poverty.[30] Additionally, the WBG caution that, with families living in poverty, research has proven that finances are much more likely to be managed by women.[31] The combination of these factors may have a very deleterious impact on women and children living in poverty.

---

24 A White Paper, Universal Credit: Welfare that Works (Cm 7957) (11 Nov 2012).
25 Ibid.1.
26 Ibid.
27 In this chapter, 'marketplace' is a term that will be used to refer to the portion of the economy which pays workers for their efforts. It is a term that is used to avoid the suggestion that, for example, parenting does not involve work. There will be general agreement that parenting does involve effort, of course, but the tasks of parenting may be delegated to others for payment. When the delegation does not involve other family members, the etymology of the White Paper is that this will involve 'work', especially as payment will be involved. 'Marketplace' is thus a term that emphasises the importance of both payment and recognition. For a general discussion of the importance of word choice in analyses of unpaid labour, see generally, E Appelbaum, and T Bailey, 'Shared work/valued care: new norms for organizing market work and unpaid care work' in H Mosley, J O'Reilly and K Schömann (eds), *Labour Markets, Gender and Institutions: Essays in Honour of Günther Schmid* (Cheltenham, UK: Edward Elgar 2002) 136–65, 146.
28 'Written Evidence' House of Commons Session 2010–11 Select Committees Work and Pensions Committee, Submitted by F Bennett. www.publications.parliament.uk/pa/cm201011/cmselect/cmworpen/writev/whitepap/contents.htm
29 'Written Evidence' House of Commons Session 2010–11 Select Committees Work and Pensions Committee, Submitted by R Lister.
30 Ibid., submitted by The Women's Budget Group.
31 Ibid.

Given this, why was the Universal Credit introduced? If the question is one of budget cuts, then why has the system of delivering the benefits been targeted? The Institute for Fiscal Studies (IFS) have explained that 'perceived problems' with the current system include, *inter alia*, the impact upon recipients of withdrawal from benefits, and the difference in benefits that are received in work, and out.[32] To simplify the system, the Universal Credit takes the place of the following benefits: income-based jobseeker's allowance;[33] income-related employment and support allowance;[34] income support;[35] housing benefit;[36] council tax benefit;[37] and, child tax credit and the working tax credit.[38] The reorganisation has been criticised, however, as focused on gender. Described as 'the key plank of the "welfare reforms"' of the Coalition government,[39] the Women's Resource and Development Agency in Northern Ireland suggests that the impact of the Universal Credit is to 'unashamedly prioritise' the 'primary, usually male, earner at the expense of the second, usually female, earner'.[40] The WBG agree, and have cautioned that they '. . . are seriously concerned about financial proposals which concentrate financial resources and power into the hands of one person, especially where this may exacerbate existing gender inequalities'.[41]

The Universal Credit as part of a wider, legislative bureaucracy

The Universal Credit in many ways may be understood as a reaction against what preceded it. Early research into the child tax credit concluded that it was likely to increase labour market participation, although the costs of child care might require further attention.[42] The child tax credit was described as part of an approach which involved 'welfare ends through market means'.[43] Blundell, in the 2001 Keynes Lecture in Economics, optimistically suggested that the tax credits, when viewed as part of Labour's wider package of tax initiatives, 'could work', and, in fact, were potentially a '. . . relatively low cost way of enhancing earnings and self-sufficiency'. [44]

---

32 Universal Credit: a preliminary analysis, M Brewer, J Browne, Institute for Fiscal Studies (IFS), Briefing Note, 2011 - Ifs.org.uk Review. www.ifs.org.uk/docs/uc_case.pdf. (PowerPoint Presentation), slide 5.
33 Welform Reform Act 2012, s 33(1)(a), replacing the Jobseeker's Act 1995.
34 Ibid. s 33(1)(b), replacing Part 1 of the Welfare Reform Act 2007.
35 Ibid. s 33(1)(c), replacing s 124 of the Social Security Contributions and Benefits Act 1992.
36 Ibid. s 33(1)(d), replacing s 130 of the SSCBA Act 1992.
37 Ibid. s 33(1)(e), replacing s 131.
38 Ibid. s 33(1)(f), replacing the Tax Credits Act 2002.
39 H Dean, 'The ethical deficit of the United Kingdom's proposed Universal Credit: pimping the precariat?' (2012) 83 *The Political Quarterly* 353.
40 B Hinds, 'The Northern Ireland economy: women on the edge? A comprehensive analysis of the impacts of the financial crisis', Women's Resource and Development Agency (June 2011) 8 www.wrda.net/Documents/The%20NI%20Economy%20-%20Women%20on%20the%20Edge%20Report.pdf [accessed 22 September 2015].
41 Women's Budget Group, 'Universal Credit and gender equality' (June 2011) www.wbg.org.uk/RRB_Reports_13_4155103794.pdf [accessed 22 September 2015].
42 R Blundell, A Duncan, J McCrae, and C Meghir, 'The labour market impact of the Working Families' Tax Credit' (2000) 21 *Fiscal Studies* 75.
43 P Taylor-Gooby, T Larsen, and J Kananen, 'Market means and welfare ends: the UK welfare state experiment' (2004) 33 *Journal of Social Policy* 573.
44 R Blundell, '2001 Lectures – British Academy' in *2001 Lectures – British Academy* (Oxford: Oxford University Press 2001), 477, 519.

As with the Coalition, the (then, new) Labour government also commenced its term in office with welfare reform initiatives – what eventually was enacted as the Welfare Reform and Pensions Act 1999.[45] In his analysis of that bill, Lund suggested it was typical of the 'rights/obligations' structure of New Labour philosophy.[46] He explained that rights became closely linked with duties, so that expectations of the state could not be perceived as unconditional.[47] He emphasised, though, that '. . . the promotion of social inclusion by the elevation of obligation remains an important element of New Labour's thinking on the "third way"'.[48] New Labour attempted to emphasise the 'processes' that led to social exclusion and 'benefit dependency',[49] rather than simply mandating solutions and budgetary efficiencies.[50] Nonetheless, budgetary efficiencies clearly were a priority.

'Welfare to work' was placed at the centre of New Labour's policies, possibly based on influences from Clinton-era initiatives in the US.[51] By 2008, the UK government modified its approach slightly by 'renewing' the tax credits initiative through focusing on the needs of families as they moved into and out of work – a renewal based on a certain amount of optimism that paid work had successfully been introduced into some families.[52]

In this sense, the means testing aspect of the Universal Credit is not new. Indeed, Sainsbury reminds us that '[c]onditionality has been a feature of the benefit system since its inception: requiring claimants to fulfil some kind of obligation (mostly to do with preparing or looking for work) is rarely challenged and has become an almost core tenet of welfare policy in the UK'.[53] Celebrated as the UK's 'first' tax credit,[54] the predecessor to the Child Tax Credit, the Working Families Tax Credit (WFTC) was in many ways designed to be all things to all people. Newspapers critical of the Prime Minister described the tax relief as a form of nanny relief tax, with some middle class overtones.[55] In truth, however, the WFTC, later the Child Tax Credit – in many ways the target of the Universal Credit – was linked to New Labour's Child Poverty platform to reduce child poverty.

---

45 *per* The Welfare Reform and Pensions Act 1999 (Commencement Order 1999) Order 1999, 1999 No. 3309 (c.88).
46 B Lund, '"Ask not what your community can do for you": obligations, New Labour and welfare reform' (1999) 19 *Critical Social Policy* 447.
47 Ibid. 451.
48 Ibid. 452.
49 A term apparently first noticed in use among government ministers in 1987. R Walker and M Wiseman, 'Sharing ideas on welfare' in R Walker and M Wiseman (eds), *The Welfare We Want? The British Challenge for American Reform* (Bristol, UK: The Policy Press 2003) 14.
50 Ibid. 17.
51 R Walker, 'Does work work?' (1998) 27 *Journal of Social Policy* 533.
52 N Smith, 'Tackling child poverty dynamics: filling in gaps in the strategy' (2008) 7 *Social Policy and Society* 507, 507–8.
53 Ibid. 105. Similarly, in 1975, when reviewing the early proposals for the introduction of a tax credit system, Adler observed that '[o]ne important point which no one seems to have put forward, however, is that the finer control over the economy which is made possible by the rapid adjustment of credit levels and tax rates is achieved at the price of making the incomes of poor people dependent on types of measures to regulate the economy which are not used at present'. ME Adler, IFS conference on proposals for a tax-credit system, Institute for Fiscal Studies, London, 1973 (1975) 4 *Journal of Social Policy* 97, 97.
54 E McLaughlin, J Trewsdale, and N McCay, 'The rise and fall of the UK's first tax credit: The Working Families Tax Credit 1998–2000' (2001) 35 *Social Policy and Administration* 163.
55 A Mumford, 'Marketing working mothers: contextualizing earned income tax credits within feminist cultural theory' (2001) 23 *Journal of Social Welfare and Family Law* 411.

The 'all things to all people' aspect of the WFTC was criticised by Newman, who suggested that New Labour operated in an 'imaginary post feminist world', in which there was a 'supposed new consensus' on women, work and the economy.[56] Yet, she and others acknowledge that there is some consensus; for example, that families headed by lone mothers with dependent children are most 'vulnerable' to poverty.[57] In this sense, upon their introduction, the tax credits were recognised as 'major reforms'.[58] The intention was not to remedy existing defects in the system, but to facilitate 'modernisation'.[59]

The credits also were conspicuously linked to a campaign to 'end child poverty'.[60] By 2002, Bradshaw described the prospects for improving rates of child poverty as 'pretty good', and linked the introduction of these tax credits to the positive outlook (as well as, at that point in time, what was perceived to be a relatively healthy economy).[61] Bradshaw's observation should be considered in light of two factors. First, this was during a period when, globally, statistics pertaining to child poverty were steadily worsening.[62] Second, these credits were introduced against the backdrop of the stark reality that, in 1997, the UK had the highest rate of child poverty in Europe, achieved after a period in which (since 1979) rates of child poverty had tripled.[63] New Labour made these statistics a target of their time in office. Indeed, one of the final pieces of legislation published by the outgoing Labour government was the Child Poverty Act 2010.[64]

So, how should this history be approached? Institutionalist mimicry is not driven simply by a desire to avoid difficulty, in that, if every organisation acts in the same way, then one is less likely to be challenged for aberrant practices. Nor is mimicry the explicit product of the state's design – quite the opposite.[65] Rather, organisations and individuals who respond well to external forces (such as equal pay legislation) tend to be capable of forming new 'sets of social arrangements', as opposed to trying to impose the new rights, or a new order, upon the old arrangements.[66]

The introduction of a drive against child poverty, in significant part through increasing women's market participation, may have presented just such a disruptive force for the

---

56 J Newman, *Modernising Governance: New Labour, Policy, and Society* (Thousand Oaks, CA: SAGE 2001) 155.
57 N Smith, 'Tackling child poverty dynamics: filling in gaps in the strategy' (2008) 7 *Social Policy and Society* 507, 513.
58 R Walker and M Wiseman, 'Making welfare work: UK activation policies under New Labour' (2003) 56 *International Social Security Review* 3.
59 Ibid. 4.
60 Ibid. 8–9.
61 J Bradshaw, 'Child poverty and child outcomes' (2002) 16 *Children & Society* 131, 137.
62 See H Levy, C Lietz, and H Sutherland, 'Swapping policies: alternative tax-benefit strategies to support children in Austria, Spain and the UK' (2007) 36 *Journal of Social Policy* 625 discussing UNICEF statistics in 2005.
63 V-H Phung, 'Ethnicity and child poverty under New Labour: a research review' (2008) 7 *Social Policy and Society* 551.
64 R Dickens, 'Child poverty in Britain: past lessons and future prospects' (2011) 218 *National Institute Economic Review* R7.
65 As Edelman argued, '[l]aws that regulate the employment relation tend to set forth broad and often ambiguous principles that give organizations wide latitude to construct the meaning of compliance in a way that responds to both environmental demands and managerial interests'. LB Edelman, 'Legal ambiguity and symbolic structures: organizational mediation of civil rights law' (1992) 97 *American Journal of Sociology* 1531.
66 'Institutional theory in the organizational literature has argued that institutional entrepreneurs create new sets of social arrangements in organizational fields with the aid of powerful organizational interests, both inside and outside of the state'. N Fligstein, 'Markets as politics: a political-cultural approach to market institutions' (1996) 61(4) *American Sociological Review* 656.

government. One of the driving theses of isomorphism is that organisations become similar through institutional forces. New Labour and the Coalition faced the 'pressure' of child poverty statistics equally,[67] but the Coalition resisted focusing on gender economic inequality. Indeed, the Coalition government appeared determined to undermine existing New Labour initiatives that, either directly or indirectly, responded to gendered poverty.[68]

This could be described as a coercive reaction, by the Coalition government, against an increase in women's market participation, perhaps against a backdrop of a declining availability of jobs overall. The insistence upon a 'Big Society' filling the gaps left by their dismantling, however, is key.[69] Even as government support is removed for some services, the insistence that charities should step in as substitutes is an admission that support, itself, is needed.[70] The focus on economic disadvantage was introduced not simply by tax credits, but also by the Equality Act 2010. The inclusion by the Equality Act 2010 of socio-economic disadvantage as a factor to which governments must pay attention when exercising their duties was heralded as an important change in the law.[71] Lord Lester described the obligation as 'admirable' but 'unenforceable'[72] because of the absence of a requirement to invest further resources into combating socio-economic disadvantage. Yet, the basic requirement that a government might have to account for its decisions was not insignificant, and may lead to rights of challenge through judicial review.[73]

These are classic arguments (i.e. the private/public divide), and, indeed, the problematisation by a new government of arguably successful initiatives by a previous government is not new. Neither is the rhetoric behind the consolidation of a range of pre-existing benefits into a single 'Universal Credit', paid to one member of a couple, justified on the basis of simplifying a 'confusing' system, which George Osborne and Iain Duncan Smith are endeavouring to 'rescue'. As the Universal Credit dismantles a benefit system introduced by New Labour, which could have been claimed as one of their more successful initiatives, it re-writes history in this sense, and presents the tax credit system as another, inherited problem that the (then) Coalition had to fix. From the perspective solely of political advantage, however, the Universal Credit potentially may produce two, perhaps unexpected disadvantages. First, the presentation of a single, universal credit, paid to one member of a

---

67 Grimshaw and Rubery describe '... the liberal collectivist approach of New Labour with the reinforced neo-liberalism of the coalition government'. D Grimshaw, and J Rubery, 'The end of the UK's liberal collectivist social model? The implications of the coalition government's policy during the austerity crisis' (2012) 36 *Cambridge Journal of Economics* 105.
68 For example, in its 2011 *Plan for Growth*, the government announced that it would be 'scrapping plans for regulations that would have cost businesses over £350 million a year, including stripping back proposed regulation on dual discrimination and third party harassment from the Equalities Act 2010'. HM Treasury, Department for Business, and Innovation and Skills, *The Plan for Growth* (The Stationery Office 2011), 7.
69 Morris observed that, '[i]t might seem paradoxical to consider the need for legal devices to support the Big Society, which is, after all, expected to be a movement of the people, in which they find local solutions to local problems without falling back on state support'. D Morris, 'Charities and the Big Society: a doomed coalition?' (2012) 32 *Legal Studies* 134.
70 Ibid. 153. The reliance on charities to fund the 'Big Society' has been highlighted as misguided, and indeed '[t]he assumed natural alliance of symbiotic aims' between governments and charities is 'sadly lacking'.
71 See, most significantly, S Fredman, 'Human rights transformed: positive duties answers positive rights' Oxford Legal Studies Research Paper no. 38/2006 (2006) 1 http://papers.ssrn.com/sol3/papers.cfm?abstract_id=923936 [accessed 22 September 2015].
72 MT Dacin, 'Isomorphism in context: the power and prescription of institutional norms' (1997) 40 *The Academy of Management Journal* 46.
73 As noted by Fredman (n 72).

couple, has been received as presenting a clear, economic disincentive for marriage (an institution which the Conservative Party in particular would wish to be perceived as supporting).[74] Second, paying the credit to a single family member is likely to undermine financial independence for women, which could contribute to the perceived 'women's problem' for the Conservative Party's popularity.[75]

In this context, the question of the difference between tax and benefits is increasingly complicated. Early responses to the WFTC (as noted, the predecessor to the Child Tax Credit) commented upon the importance of labelling what might otherwise be described as a benefit a tax credit, and thus, in effect, symbolically giving similar recognition to both marketplace workers (who pay taxes) and parents who do not work outside of the home. The term 'working families' also clearly was imbued with meaning, conveying either 'the government recognises that it takes work to care for a family', or, 'this credit will help families living in poverty to find work', depending upon the inclinations of the observer. This question also is linked however to relatively recent challenges in the literature between benefits (or welfare) and tax preferences.

Analysis of the Universal Credit provides an illustration of this. The credit is designed to encourage recipients to find marketplace work, so is it of benefit to the economy, or to society? Additionally, there is the difficult question, obfuscated by this reform, of encouraging recipients to find jobs, when employment rates are low. As Sainsbury starkly reminds us: '. . . the benefit system cannot create jobs, and no reform of benefits could ever do so'.[76] He reminds us of this however, while suggesting that there was 'no doubt' that the welfare changes introduced by the Coalition government '. . . contains ideas for a massive simplification of the benefit system that are innovative and bold'.[77] He cautions, however, that some aspects of the proposed reform have 'been interpreted as "more stick than carrot" and poorly timed, in the prevailing economic and employment circumstances, and that the advantages of a radical simplification of the benefit system may consequently be lost to view'.[78]

Also potentially 'lost to view' are the varieties of different families who will receive the Universal Credit. The 'move from purse to wallet' can be analysed as part of an isomorphic journey, as follows: child care is 'gendered' in that it is largely performed by women. This has led both to the exclusion of women from the marketplace, but also to the receipt by women of money from the state to assist parents with children. The funnelling of money to women, to the 'purse', was disruptive, and led to the confusion decried by the Coalition in their drive for reform. Restructuring benefits so that money flows to the wallet both

---

74 See, e.g. P Butler, 'Cuts blog', *The Guardian* (30 March 2012) www.guardian.co.uk/society/patrick-butler-cuts-blog/2012/mar/30/working-tax-credit-cuts-marriage-lose-lose-situation [accessed 22 September 2015].
75 See, e.g. J Ashley, 'Women will need more than a spread in *Grazia* Magazine to vote Tory', *The Guardian* (18 March 2012), www.guardian.co.uk/commentisfree/2012/mar/18/women-grazia-vote-tory-budget?newsfeed=true [accessed 22 September 2015].
76 Ibid. 106. Similarly, Dean suggested that '[t]he Universal Credit may go some way to relieving the poverty of low-paid workers, but it will do nothing to compensate for the injustices or adverse effects of the precarious labour market.' D Hartley, 'The potentially counterproductive effects of in-work benefits for low-paid workers', a paper prepared for 10th Anniversary ESPAnet Conference, 6–8 September 2012, University of Edinburgh, UK 358 www.cas.ed.ac.uk/__data/assets/word. . ./Dean_-_Stream_5.doc [accessed 22 September 2015].
77 R Sainsbury, '21st century welfare - getting closer to radical benefit reform?' (2010) 17 *Public Policy Research* 102.
78 Ibid. 107.

178 Ann Mumford

maintains stasis, however reduced, in terms of the state providing financial assistance to children and their families, but also lessens the disruptive potential of funnelling too much money into the 'purse'.

The interaction between the Universal Credit, and the financial crisis, is significant. In his March 2012 Budget Speech, George Osborne expressed regret for his decision to reduce the availability of child benefit.[79] The Universal Credit, however, and its promise of simplification, was not mentioned once. Perhaps the combination of too many reductions on the 'purse' was appreciated as a potential, political difficulty. Of course, the proliferation of reductions in women's wealth, and the insistence that they should bear the brunt of 'difficult' financial decisions, is not unusual. A gender budget analysis of the European Social Fund (ESF) by the agency for gender equality in Germany is instructive in this regard. The ESF is the European Union's main financial instrument for supporting employment in the Member States, as well as promoting economic and social cohesion. The ESF spending amounts to around 10 per cent of the EU's total budget. Gender budgeting analysis demonstrated that the programmes for overcoming the financial crisis, while aiming for 'equality' (perhaps mindful of gender budgeting obligations), persisted in underfunding programmes with high representations of women.[80]

So, the Universal Credit in this sense is part of a pattern that is not new. What is different, however, is tensions between women's growing financial power, against a backdrop of a gendered marketplace. This produced a dichotomy, this chapter argues, that the Coalition felt could only be resolved with a 'universal', even de-gendered, tax reform.

Conclusion

Institutional analysis, involving a search for mimetic, normative or coercive isomorphism, commonly has involved studies of gender rights legislation. Thus, for example, in the instance of equal pay initiatives, studies have sought to determine how organisations have reacted to what they would perceive as disruptive legislation. The sorts of reactions that are of interest in institutionalist studies include awareness training courses, and the production of paperwork. Inevitably, similarity between organisational responses, even where the responses are counter-productive,[81] and especially if the responses seem to be relatively well intentioned,

---

79 'Mr Deputy Speaker, in the Spending Review, we took the difficult decision to remove child benefit from families with a higher rate taxpayer . . . All sections of society must make a contribution to dealing with the deficit – without this measure we wouldn't get the job done'. Budget 2012 statement by the Chancellor of the Exchequer, the Rt Hon George Osborne MP (21 March 2012) http://hm-treasury.gov.uk/budget2012_statement.htm [accessed 22 September 2015].

80 Specifically, '[t]he biggest share of the budget is allocated to measures in which women and men are "equally" represented (from 41 to 60 per cent). *Measures with a high representation of women (more than 60 per cent) had significantly smaller budgets*, whereas the measures with female participation rates of less than 40- and 20 per cent had significantly higher budgets'. R Frey and B Savioli, 'Gender budgeting in the European Social Fund', Agentur für Gleichstellung im ESF (March 2011) www.esf-gleichstellung.de/fileadmin/data/Downloads/english_site/gb-report-2009_agency_gender_equality_esf.pdf [accessed 22 September 2015] (emphasis added).

81 An institutional analysis of marriage is illustrative in this respect: 'We use DiMaggio and Powell's approach to explaining isomorphism to outline institutional pressures that can help us understand the persistent decision to marry. Isomorphism describes the tendency toward similarity and status quo in institutions over time. DiMaggio and Powell focused on firms and industry organizations, and they explained why, when people seek and pursue innovation in organizations, they ultimately return to established organizational arrangements.' S Laurer and C Yodanis, 'The deinstitutionalization of marriage revisited: a new institutional approach to marriage' (2010) 2(1) *Journal of Family Theory & Review* 58, 65.

attract attention. In some ways, institutionalist analysis could be described as the search for mimicry.

This chapter has suggested that institutionalist analysis should turn to questions of tax, gender, and, specifically, the Universal Credit. These topics are ideal for a search for rights within a bureaucratisation process, also serving to highlight the impact of unintended consequences from legislative initiatives. The Universal Credit does not take notice, for example, of the pre-existing impact of the economic downturn upon women's employment opportunities. A reduction in women's employment levels has had an impact far beyond those individual women who lost their jobs. The Universal Credit, thus, enters the bureaucratic mix at a sensitive time, with a greater need than before to consider the gender impact of such reforms. Assurances that the Universal Credit will prompt recipients to enter the workforce also need to be examined carefully.

Ultimately, this chapter has suggested that the future of the Universal Credit must be considered against the backdrop of its history. Child poverty levels were reduced under New Labour, and levels of women's marketplace participation were improved. The question that persists now is whether these successes will be preserved and, if so, how the Universal Credit will assist.

Bibliography

Adler ME, 'IFS Conference on proposals for a tax-credit system', Institute for Fiscal Studies, London 1973 (1975) 4 *Journal of Social Policy*, 97.

Appelbaum E and Bailey T, 'Shared work/valued care: new norms for organizing market work and unpaid care work', in H Mosley, J O'Reilly, and K Schömann (eds), *Labour Markets, Gender and Institutions: Essays in Honour of Günther Schmid* (Cheltenham, UK: Edward Elgar 2002), 136.

Ashley J, 'Women will need more than a spread in *Grazia* Magazine to vote Tory', *The Guardian* (18 March 2012), at www.guardian.co.uk/commentisfree/2012/mar/18/women-grazia-vote-tory-budget?newsfeed=true [accessed 30 January 2017].

Biggart NW, *Readings in Economic Sociology* (Oxford: Blackwell 2008).

Blundell R, '2001 Lectures – British Academy' in *2001 Lectures – British Academy* (Oxford: Oxford University Press 2001).

Blundell R, Duncan A, McCrae J and Meghir C, 'The labour market impact of the working families' tax credit' (2000) 21(1) *Fiscal Studies*, 75.

Bogoch B, 'Gendered lawyering: difference and dominance in lawyer-client interaction' (1997) 31(4) *Law & Society Review*, 677.

Bradshaw J, 'Child poverty and child outcomes' (2002) 16(2) *Children & Society*, 131.

Brewer M, Browne J, and Jin W 'Universal Credit: a preliminary analysis', Institute for Fiscal Studies (IFS), Briefing Note, 2011 – IFS.org.uk Review. www.ifs.org.uk/docs/uc_case.pdf [accessed 30 January 2017].

Brien S, 'Examination of witnesses, Work and Pensions Committee – Minutes of Evidence', Government White Paper on Universal Credit (London: 26 January 2011).

Butler P, 'Cuts blog', *The Guardian* (30 March 2012), www.guardian.co.uk/society/patrick-butler-cuts-blog/2012/mar/30/working-tax-credit-cuts-marriage-lose-lose-situtation [accessed 30 January 2017].

Campbell CM, and Wiles P, 'The study of law in society in Britain' (1975) 10(4) *Law & Society Review*, 551.

Cleaver F and Nyatsambo R, 'Gender and integrated water resource management', in RQ Grafton and K Hussey (eds), *Water Resources Planning and Management* (Cambridge: Cambridge University Press 2011), 311.

Conley H and Page M, 'The gender equality duty in local government: the prospects for integration' (2010) 39(3) *Industrial Law Journal*, 321.

Cornell DL, 'The philosophy of the limit, systems theory and feminist legal reform' (1991) 26(3) *New England Law Review*, 783.

Dacin MT, 'Isomorphism in context: The power and prescription of institutional norms' (1997) 40(1) *The Academy of Management Journal*, 46.

Dean H, 'The ethical deficit of the United Kingdom's proposed Universal Credit: pimping the precariat?' (2012) 83(2) *The Political Quarterly*, 353.

Dean H, 'The potentially counterproductive effects of in-work benefits for low-paid workers', paper prepared for 10th Anniversary ESPAnet Conference, 6–8 September 2012, University of Edinburgh, UK.

Department for Work and Pensions, *Universal Credit: Welfare that Works*, Government White Paper (Cm 7957) (London: 11 November 2012).

Dickens R, 'Child poverty in Britain: past lessons and future prospects' (2011) 218(1) *National Institute Economic Review*, R7.

DiMaggio PJ and Powell WW, 'The iron cage revisited: institutional isomorphism and collective rationality in organizational fields' (1983) 48(2) *American Sociological Review*, 147.

Edelman LB, 'Legal ambiguity and symbolic structures: Organizational mediation of civil rights law' (1992) 97(6) *American Journal of Sociology*, 1531.

Fligstein N, 'Markets as politics: a political-cultural approach to market institutions' (1996) 61(4) *American Sociological Review*, 656.

Fredman S, 'Human rights transformed: positive duties and positive rights', Oxford Legal Studies Research Paper no. 38/2006 (2006), at http://papers.ssrn.com/sol3/papers.cfm?abstract_id=923936 [accessed 30 January 2017].

Frey R and Savioli B, 'Gender budgeting in the European Social Fund', Agentur für Gleichstellung im ESF (March 2011), at www.esf-gleichstellung.de/fileadmin/data/Downloads/english_site/gb-report-2009_agency_gender_equality_esf.pdf [accessed 30 January 2017].

Gilbert N and Gilbert B, *The Enabling State: Modern Welfare Capitalism in America* (Oxford: Oxford University Press 1989).

Grimshaw D and Rubery J, 'The end of the UK's liberal collectivist social model? The implications of the coalition government's policy during the austerity crisis' (2012) 36(1) *Cambridge Journal of Economics*, 105.

Hannan MT and Freeman J, 'Structural inertia and organizational change' (1984) 49(2) *American Sociological Review*, 149.

Harris S, 'Questions as a mode of control in Magistrate's Court', 1984 (49) *International Journal of Sociology of Language*, 5.

Himmelweit S, 'The welfare reform bill will erode women's financial independence', *The Guardian* (23 January 2012), at www.guardian.co.uk/commentisfree/2012/jan/23/welfare-reform-bill-women-independence [accessed 30 January 2017].

Hinds B, 'The Northern Ireland economy: women on the edge? A comprehensive analysis of the impacts of the financial crisis', Women's Resource and Development Agency (June 2011), at www.wrda.net/Documents/The%20NI%20Economy%20-%20Women%20on%20the%20Edge%20Report.pdf [accessed 30 January 2017].

HM Treasury, Department for Business, Innovation & Skills, *The Plan for Growth* (London: The Stationery Office 2011).

Holm Pedersen L, 'The political impact of environmental economic ideas' (2005) 28(1) *Scandinavian Political Studies*, 25.

Laurer S and Yodanis C, 'The deinstitutionalization of marriage revisited: a new institutional approach to marriage' (2010) 2(1) *Journal of Family Theory & Review*, 58.

Levy H, Lietz C and Sutherland H, 'Swapping policies: alternative tax-benefit strategies to support children in Austria, Spain and the UK' (2007) 36(4) *Journal of Social Policy*, 625.

Lie J, 'Sociology of markets' (1997) 23 *Annual Review of Sociology*, 341–60, 341.

Lund B, '"Ask not what your community can do for you": obligations, New Labour and welfare reform' (1999) 19(4) *Critical Social Policy*, 447.

Mackay F, Monro S and Waylen G, 'The feminist potential of sociological institutionalism' (2009) 5(2) *Politics and Gender*, 253.

McLaughlin E, Trewsdale J and McCay N, 'The rise and fall of the UK's first tax credit: the Working Families Tax Credit 1998–2000' (2001) 35(2) *Social Policy and Administration*, 163.

Morris D, 'Charities and the Big Society: a doomed coalition?' (2012) 32(1) *Legal Studies*, 132.

Mumford A, 'Marketing working mothers: contextualizing earned income tax credits within feminist cultural theory' (2001) 23(4) *Journal of Social Welfare and Family Law*, 411.

Newman J, *Modernising Governance: New Labour, Policy, and Society* (London: SAGE 2001).

Painter C, 'The UK coalition government: constructing public service reform narratives' [2012] *Public Policy and Administration*, 1.

Phung V-H, 'Ethnicity and child poverty under New Labour: a research review' (2008) 7(4) *Social Policy and Society*, 551.

Prasad M, 'Tax "expenditures" and welfare states: a critique' (2011) 23(2) *Journal of Policy History*, 251, at p. 252.

Sainsbury R, '21st century welfare – getting closer to radical benefit reform?' (2010) 17(2) *Public Policy Research*, 102.

Schumpeter JA, *Capitalism, Socialism and Democracy* (London: George Allen and Unwin 1994).

Smith N, 'Tackling child poverty dynamics: Filling in gaps in the strategy' (2008) 7(4) *Social Policy and Society*, 507.

Speaight A and Hamilton P, 'Restoring the rule of law to financial services compensation', www.hm-treasury.gov.uk/d/consult_finregresponses_0a.pdf [accessed 30 January 2017].

Stainback K and Kwon S, 'Female leaders, organizational power, and sex segregation' (2011) 639(1) *The Annals of the American Academy of Political and Social Science*, 217.

Stinchcombe AL, 'On the virtues of the old institutionalism' (1997) 23(1) *Annual Review of Sociology*, 1.

Taylor-Gooby P, Larsen T and Kananen J, 'Market means and welfare ends: the UK welfare state experiment' (2004) 33(4) *Journal of Social Policy*, 573.

Twining W, *Rethinking Evidence: Explanatory Essays* (Evanston, IL: Northwestern University Press 1990).

UK Women's Budget Group, *A Gender Impact Assessment of the Coalition Government Budget* (June 2010), http://wbg.org.uk/RRB_Reports_12_956432831.pdf [accessed 30 January 2017].

Vis B, van Kersbergen K and Hylands T, 'To what extent did the financial crisis intensify the pressure to reform the welfare state?' (2011) 45(4) *Social Policy & Administration*, 338.

Walker R, 'Does work work?' (1998) 27(4) *Journal of Social Policy*, 533.

Walker R and Wiseman M, 'Making welfare work: UK activation policies under New Labour' (2003) 56(1) *International Social Security Review*, 3.

Walker R and Wiseman M (eds), *The Welfare We Want? The British Challenge for American Reform* (Bristol, UK: The Policy Press 2003).

Whitmeyer JM, 'Elites and popular nationalism' (2002) 53(3) *The British Journal of Sociology*, 321.

Women's Budget Group, 'Universal Credit and gender equality' (June 2011), at www.wbg.org.uk/RRB_Reports_13_4155103794.pdf.

Index

absent parents 149–51, 154–5, 160
accountability 170–71
affection 69, 129
ageing 3, 58, 68–70; *see also* older couples
agreements 98, 131, 151, 155, 157–61; prenuptial 103, 130–1; private 5, 148, 155, 163; voluntary 157, 161
allocation 10, 21, 60, 90
allocative rules 112
American Law Institute 3, 90–2
analysis: institutionalist 167, 171, 179; multivariate 27, 36–7
ancillary relief 114, 121
arrears 12–15, 154
assets 10, 58, 89–90, 93–6, 120, 125, 129; division of assets acquired during marriage 96–7; premarital 89–90, 97
attainment, educational 42–3, 153, 162
Auchmuty, R 108
austerity 74–87; effects 74–5; measures 3, 6, 74, 85–6
Australia 65, 92, 150
autonomy 4, 17, 59, 69

Belgium 82–3
benefit income 12, 15
benefit system 149, 152, 172, 174, 176–7
benefits 6–7, 18, 110, 151, 154–6, 162, 172–3, 177; state 102, 110, 142, 151
bereavement 3, 60
big money cases 95
breadwinners 15, 60, 94–5; male 40–2, 48, 50, 54
Brexit decision 84–5
burden of coping 25, 28, 30, 35, 37
bureaucracy 6, 169–71
bureaucratization 169–70

Canada 4, 92, 95, 101, 107
capital 92, 94, 136, 154

capitalism 168
cards, credit 7, 9, 11–13, 15, 17
care work 74, 81, 83, 123; unpaid 84, 168
careers 54, 93, 95, 126
caregiving 4, 51, 56, 137
carers 53, 82–4, 171; primary 82–3
change: catalysts for 68; and resistance 64–6
charities 86, 176
child benefit 13, 30, 178
child care 18, 91, 98, 154, 173, 177
child maintenance 5, 148, 155, 157, 159
Child Maintenance and Enforcement Commission, *see* C-MEC
Child Maintenance Options Service 158, 161
child maintenance premium (CMP) 156
child poverty 6, 153–4, 171, 174–5; and child support 148–63
Child Poverty Act 162, 175
Child Poverty Action Group 152
child support 5, 148, 150–1, 153–7, 159, 161–3; and child poverty 148–63; legislation 148, 151, 153, 155–6, 158, 160; paying 150, 153, 162
Child Support Acts 5; 1991 Act 150–1; background 148–50
Child Support Agency, *see* CSA
child tax credit 167–8, 173–4, 177
childcare 26, 53, 89, 91, 94–5; valuation 89–95
children 9–15, 17–19, 46–9, 52–4, 81–4, 91–4, 104–6, 148–63; adult 67, 143; dependent 41, 47, 174; poverty, *see* child poverty; raising 106, 126, 148, 152
churning 13–14
citizenship 55, 81–5; rights 81–4
citizenship rights, social 74, 81–2
civil partnerships 2, 4, 102, 107, 112–14, 139, 143
civil unions 102, 104, 108, 112
class, social 22, 30, 33, 37, 58, 61, 74
clean break 120, 149

close personal relationship 1–4, 6, 7–9, 15–16, 19, 21, 37, 40, 87, 144
C-MEC (Child Maintenance and Enforcement Commission) 150, 155, 158, 161
CMP (child maintenance premium) 156
cohabitants 3, 5, 89, 91–3, 95–9, 134–46; commitment 139–42; female 99, 135; inheritance tax liability 136, 145; non-parenting 141, 146; property claims by 136–7˙
cohabitation 91, 93, 98–9, 102, 134, 138–41, 143, 145–6; unmarried 89, 94
commitment 74, 76, 80, 108, 135–6, 145–6, 148, 162; cohabitants 139–42; expression of 140–1
common money 48–50
community 79, 90, 129, 171
compensation 79, 90, 95, 121, 124
competition 81, 170
conflict 58–9, 64, 66, 68–9, 157; ongoing 66
confusion 141, 167, 171, 177
consensus 5, 148, 152, 160–1, 174
consent 103
constructive trusts 135
consumption 59, 69, 90–1, 96, 98, 127
contract 93, 99, 108, 113, 130–1, 134
contract law 89, 98
contractual thinking 3, 89–99
contributions, indirect 91–2, 94–6, 98
control, financial 11, 24, 60, 69
co-ownership 92, 98–9
co-parenting 157
coping 22, 25, 28, 30–1, 37, 69; burden of 25, 28, 30, 35, 37
core values 77–8, 80, 87
corrective justice 98
costs 21, 54, 56, 93–4, 137–8, 142–3, 149, 152
council houses 14–15
council tax benefit 6, 172
counter-service 89, 93, 98–9
couple identities 62, 69
couple relationships 3, 7–8, 17, 89, 91, 93, 95, 97–9
couples: dual-income 40, 42, 44, 46, 55; gay 104, 109; heterosexual 9, 41; intact 64, 107; lesbian 101, 105, 108; married 2, 22, 25, 36, 40, 54, 104, 110; younger 42, 45, 67, 70
credit 2, 7–19, 40, 167, 173, 175, 177; cards 7, 9, 11–13, 15, 17; and debt 7–8, 10, 40
credit card debts 12–13

CSA (Child Support Agency) 15, 150–2, 154–7, 161
culture 16, 58, 128, 172

deadbeat dads 151
debt, and credit 7–8, 10, 40
debt advice 10–11
debts 7–19, 25, 40, 58, 78, 99; problematic personal 2, 7, 9, 11, 19
decisions, irrational 125–6
dental care 27, 31
dependency 1–2, 7, 17, 142, 172
depression 14, 17
deprivation 22, 24, 26–7, 31, 33, 35–7, 62, 85; differences between spouses 26–30; impact 33, 35, 37; material 2, 23, 26, 30, 36–7; non-monetary 23; physical 24; relative 23–4, 36; scores 27, 37
differential treatment 144–6
different-sex couples: married 107; unmarried 107
different-sex marriages 112–13
different-sex partners 102, 114
disability 51–2, 70
disadvantage, economic 92–3, 175
discretion, redistributive 119, 128
discretionary powers 89, 120
discrimination 78–9, 82, 110, 123, 144; sex 79
disposable income 11, 97
distress, psychological, *see* psychological distress
distribution: fair and reasonable 134, 142–3, 146; income 21, 23, 25, 29–30, 54; intra-household 22
distribution of property 4, 108, 118–19, 123, 131; on divorce 120–2; gender, fairness and equality 122–4; and justice at the end of relationships 124–5
division of assets acquired during marriage 96–7
division of labour 92–3, 104, 122; gendered 3, 84, 112
divorce 4, 65, 90–1, 101–2, 111–12, 114, 118–25, 131; distribution of property 120–2; law 111–13; reallocation of property 118–31
domestic cohabitation, *see* cohabitation
domestic labour 4, 74, 91, 93, 105, 109
downsizing 62, 69
dual-income couples: economic inequalities in 44–6; increase in 42–4; Spain 39–56
duties 18, 85–6, 102–3, 107, 112–14, 150–1, 156–7, 174; of third parties 102–3, 113

Index

earnings 16, 44, 52, 60, 91–2, 94, 126–7
ECHR (European Convention on Human Rights) 82, 144
economic disadvantage 92–3, 175
economic inequalities: between men and women depending on type of household 46–8; in dual-income couples 44–6
economic irrationality 131
economic relations 103–4, 108
economic rules 109, 111
economic value 4, 130
economics 1, 59, 170, 174
ECtHR (European Court of Human Rights) 145–6
education: level of 33, 42; university 42, 46
educational attainment 42–3, 153, 162
educational level 39, 42, 44, 46, 48, 54
EFSF (European Financial Stability Facility) 77
egalitarian relationships 41, 55
employment 9, 15–16, 18, 39, 44, 47, 54–5, 78–81; status 31, 33, 36
equality 1, 3–4, 53–4, 74–5, 77–81, 83–7, 108, 121–3; duty 85–6; economic 46; formal 5, 101, 104, 110, 112, 118; gender 49, 74, 78–81, 84, 118, 171, 178; principle 80–1, 85, 109
eradication of poverty 155–6
ESF (European Social Fund) 179
EU Survey of Income and Living Conditions, *see* EU-SILC
European citizenship rights 3, 74, 81
European Convention on Human Rights (ECHR) 82, 144
European Financial Stability Facility (EFSF) 77
European social citizenship 74, 80
European Social Fund, *see* ESF
European social solidarity 81, 84
European Union 3, 26, 39, 41, 75–6, 79–81, 84, 87; gender equality 78–80
EU-SILC (EU Survey of Income and Living Conditions) 23, 28, 41
exclusion, social 58, 173
exit options 17–18
expenditure 8, 11–13, 15–16, 22, 28, 150; responsibilities 25, 36

fair and reasonable distribution 134, 142–3, 146
fairness 70, 121–3, 128–9
familialisation 18, 49

families: change 15–16; formation 11–12; investing in 12–13; lesbian 105; lone parent 149–50, 152–3; single parent 150–1, 160; types 154–5
family home 97, 103, 118
family life 13, 50, 52, 82–3, 97, 109, 118, 121
family members, individual 2, 22
family-based agreements 148, 157–8
fatalism 25, 28–31, 34–7; levels of 33–5, 37; measure 26, 31, 35–7; scores 28–30, 33, 35, 37
fathers 52–3, 93–4, 112, 152–3, 159, 161
Fawcett Society 86
feckless fathers 151
female poverty 86–7
financial arrangements 6, 25, 36–7, 61, 64, 68–9
financial control 11, 24, 60, 69; gendered division of 24
financial interdependence 3, 120, 140, 145–6
financial strain 2, 21–5, 29, 33, 35–7
fiscal policies 1, 3, 42, 50, 150, 162

gay couples 104, 109
gender: differences 22, 24; and distribution of property 122–4; equality 49, 74, 78–81, 84, 118, 170, 177; inequalities 4, 40–1, 49–50, 54, 80, 172; relations 6, 39, 41–2, 50, 52, 54, 56, 68–9; Spain 39–56
gender justice 81, 122
gender roles, traditional 54–5, 78
gendered division of financial control 24
gendered division of labour 3, 84, 112
gendered power relations 123
GHQ (General Health Questionnaire) 26, 28–31, 33, 36; measure 29, 31–3, 36
gifts 89–90, 97, 99, 129
government policy 42, 50, 52, 55–6, 156

health 23–4, 61, 66–70; problems 63–4, 67; psychological 21–6, 30–1, 33, 37
homogeneity 106, 167, 169
household income 10, 16, 22, 29–34, 36–7, 152, 158
household money 49; *see also* common money; management 10, 65
housewives 40–2, 48, 54, 91–2
housework 104
Human Rights Act 144–5

identities 7, 62, 68, 70, 80, 102; couple 62, 69
identity politics and justice 110–12

Index

IFS, *see* Institute for Fiscal Studies
inclusion 41, 74, 76, 80, 175
income: benefit 12, 15; disposable 11, 97; distribution 21, 23, 25, 29–30, 54; household 10, 16, 22, 29–34, 36–7, 152, 158; independent 30, 32–4, 37; low 17, 22, 160, 162, 167
independent income 30, 32–4, 37
indirect contributions 91–2, 94–6, 98
individualisation 8
inequalities: gender 4, 40–1, 49–50, 54, 80, 173; social 22, 55, 167
inequality: experience of 23; restoration of 171; societal 21–2
inheritance tax 107, 136, 143–5
Institute for Fiscal Studies (IFS) 173
institutional analysis 6, 167–71, 178
institutionalist analysis 167, 171, 179
institutions 80, 102, 113, 168, 177–8
intact couples 64, 107
intentions 14, 99, 113, 135, 175
interdependence, financial 3, 120, 140, 145–6
interdependency 1–2, 7, 11, 16
intestacy 134–46; event of 135–6; Law Commission reform proposals 137–9; law of 134–5, 137, 145; rules 5, 134–6, 138–9, 143–4, 146
intestate succession, *see* intestacy
intra-household distribution 22
intra-household inequality 2, 21–37, 50, 58
invaluable value 125–6, 128–30
investments 17, 25, 66, 97–8
Ireland 2, 23, 25, 27, 36, 77, 89, 145
irrational decisions 125–6
irrationality, economic 131
isomorphism 168, 171, 176, 178
Italy 76–7

justice: corrective 98; and distribution of property 124–5; gender 81, 122; and identity politics 110–12; social 76

labour 3, 84, 89, 95, 112–13, 122, 125, 172–3; division of, *see* division of labour; domestic 4, 74, 91, 93, 105, 109
Law Commission for England and Wales 5, 92–5, 134–5, 138–40, 142, 144, 146; intestacy reform proposals 137–9
legal recognition 109, 134, 138, 145
legal rights 83–4, 141
legislative changes 5–6, 18
legitimacy 80, 170–71

lesbian families 105
liability 144, 154–5
life 8–9, 11, 14, 16, 18, 58–9, 65–6, 68–70; family 13, 50, 52, 82–3, 97, 109, 118, 121
life interest, spouse's 136, 138, 142
lifetime transfers 144
LIIS (Living in Ireland Survey) 23, 25–6, 28, 36
lived experience of inequality 21, 23
Living in Ireland Survey, *see* LIIS
loans 7, 12, 99
lone mothers 14, 17, 174
lone parent families 149–50, 152–3
lone parents 18, 149, 156, 159, 163

maintenance 5, 8, 55, 62, 103, 137, 143, 148–50; arrangements 155, 157
male breadwinners 40–2, 48, 50, 54
male partners 42, 45, 55
management 7, 15–17, 25, 27, 50, 58, 171; money 10, 58–9, 61, 63, 65, 68–9; of scarce resources 22–4
manual workers 63–4
market prices 93, 98, 123
marketplace 171, 176
marriage 89–91, 93–9, 101–14, 120–2, 124–7, 139–41, 145–6, 177–8; model 5, 146; and money 62; same-sex 2, 102, 108, 112, 114; unbundling marriage law 102–3
married couples 2, 22, 25, 36, 40, 54, 104, 110
married women 44, 54, 61, 92
material deprivation 2, 23, 30, 36–7; differences between spouses 26–30
material property 124, 127
matrimonial property 114
migrants 3, 84
minimum duration requirement 141, 146
money 16–17, 39–43, 47–9, 53–5, 58–70, 121–2, 156–7, 177–8; advice 7, 10–11; big money cases 95; management 10, 58–9, 61, 63, 65, 68–9; and marriage 62; ownership and meaning 48–50; ownership of 40, 42, 61
mortgages 15, 66, 91, 95
mothers, lone 14, 17, 175
multivariate analysis 27, 36–7

nationality 81–2, 84
negotiations 50, 104–5
New Labour 167–8, 174–5, 179
non-contributory pensions 51–2
non-discrimination 18, 75, 77–8, 80–1, 84

non-parenting 139, 141
non-parenting cohabitants 141, 146
norms 6, 45, 48–9, 160–1; institutional 169
Northern Ireland 83, 85, 172

obligations 4, 102–3, 108, 110, 113, 121, 174, 176
occupational social security 79
old age 50, 60, 67, 69–70
older couples 42–5; money practices 3, 58–70
ordinary least squares (OLS) 30
organisations 82, 155, 159, 162, 168, 170, 175–6, 178
ownership, of money 40, 42, 61

paperwork 171, 178
parental leave 53
parental separation 148, 162
parenthood 140, 149
parenting 8, 17, 106, 109, 141, 146, 152
parents: absent 149–51, 154–5, 160; lone 18, 149, 156, 159, 163
partners: elder 41; male 42, 45, 55; surviving 135
partnership 3, 8–9, 12, 14, 16, 59–60, 112, 121; *see also* civil partnerships
payments 137, 144, 153, 155–6, 158, 160, 163, 172
pensions 1–3, 41–2, 50–2, 60, 63–4, 70, 155–7, 162; contributory 51–2; non-contributory 51–2
physical well-being 23–4, 127
positive effects, significant 31, 35–6
poverty: children, *see* child poverty; eradication 155–6; female 86–7; gendered 176; relative 152
power 22, 24, 58, 60, 62, 64, 67–70, 137; discretionary 89, 120; imbalances 66–70, 158; relations 50, 123
powerlessness 28, 33, 35–7
precariat 16, 18, 40
premarital assets 89–90, 97
prenuptial agreements 103, 130–1
prices, market 93, 98, 123
primary carers 82–3
private agreements 5, 148, 155, 163
private sphere 75, 81, 87, 118–19
professional/managerial backgrounds 64, 66–7
profitability 131
promotion 5, 55, 76, 79, 145, 174
property: adjustment 123–4, 131; common 49; distribution of, *see* distribution of property; material 124, 127; matrimonial 114; rights 124, 128; unmarried cohabitants 134–46
protection 5, 79, 135, 139, 143, 145; social 82
psychological distress 2, 22–5, 28–33, 36; fatalism measure 29, 31; higher levels 2, 36; lower levels 25, 31
psychological health 21–6, 30–1, 33, 37
psychological stress 23–4, 28
psychological well-being 2, 21, 23–5, 27
public opinion, surveys 137–8, 141–2
public policies 2–3, 5–6, 39, 41, 50, 52–3; effects on families 50–4
public spending 1, 3, 74, 86–7

reciprocity 89, 98–9
recognition 80, 83, 107–8, 110, 114, 119, 121, 139–40; legal 109, 134, 138, 145; third-party 113
redistributive discretion 119, 128
redistributive valuation 129
regression results 31, 35
relations, economic 103–4, 108
relationship breakdown 1, 3, 8, 17, 64, 89–90, 92, 109
relationships: close personal 1–9, 11, 13, 15, 17, 19, 21, 37; couple 3, 7–8, 17, 89, 91, 93, 95, 97–9; egalitarian 41, 55; long 69–70
relative deprivation 23–4, 36
relief: ancillary 114, 121; tax 173
remarriage 90
re-partnering 60, 69
reprivatisation 5–6, 148
resistance 58, 171; and change 64–6; strategies for 67–8
resources 21–2, 24–5, 59–60, 67, 69–70, 84, 121, 125; individual 58
responsibility 5–6, 16–18, 22, 27–8, 52–3, 91, 149–51, 160–2
retirement 3, 51–2, 59–63, 69; transitions to 62–4
rhetoric 3, 113, 151, 160, 176
rights 5–6, 75, 82–5, 101–2, 134–5, 145–6, 174, 176; European citizenship 3, 74, 81; legal 83–4, 141; property 124, 128
rules: allocative 112; economic 109, 111
same-sex couples 2, 4, 41, 101–14, 135; difficulties for research 106–10; distinctive traits 104–6
same-sex marriage 2, 102, 108, 112, 114
samples 28–30, 36, 41, 64, 68, 106
savings 10, 15–16, 25, 28, 58, 93–4, 97

Index

scarce resources, management 22–4
Schecter, E 108
separation 111, 134, 149, 154, 157; parental 148, 162
sex 47–9; discrimination 79
sexual orientation 4, 107, 110
sharing 7, 25, 28, 37, 54, 103–4, 109, 111
SILC (Statistics on Income and Living Conditions) 40–1
simplicity 138, 142–3, 146, 167
single parent families 150–1, 160
single-person households 46–7
social citizenship: European 74, 80; rights 74, 81–2
social class 22, 30, 33, 37, 58, 61, 74
social exclusion 58, 173
social inequalities 22, 55, 168
social justice 76
social protection 82
social science 103, 109, 113, 127
social security 7, 58, 60, 148; occupational 79
social solidarity, European 81, 84
social welfare benefits 3, 128
societal inequality 21–2
solidarity 3, 49, 74–85, 87, 90; degree of 87
South America 67–8
Spain, gender differences 39–56
spending, public 1, 3, 74, 86–7
spouses: former 135, 152; surviving 135–6, 142–4, 146
stability 9, 69, 139–41
stakeholders 93, 139, 142–3, 146
state benefits 102, 110, 142, 151
Statistics on Income and Living Conditions, *see* SILC
status quo 62–3, 69, 114, 178
step-families 67, 143
strain, financial 2, 21–5, 29, 33, 35–7
stress, psychological 23–4, 28
structural changes 60, 169–70, 172
succession, intestate 134–46
surveys, public opinion 137–8, 141–2
surviving spouses 135–6, 142–4, 146

tax: credits 167, 173, 175–7; differential treatment 145–6; inheritance 107, 136, 143–5; taxpayers 142–3, 149, 157, 159, 162, 167
third parties, duties 102–3, 113
tolerance 75, 77–8, 80
traditional gender roles 54–5, 78
transitions 9, 16, 60–2, 93
treatment, differential 144–6
triple jeopardy 85
trusts 134, 138, 142; constructive 135

unemployment 13–14, 21, 24, 29, 36, 50, 55, 86
Universal Credit 6, 18, 167–79
unmarried cohabitants, property 134–46
unmarried different-sex couples 107
unpaid care work 84, 169
unpaid work 55, 96, 121

valuation 89, 97, 127, 130–1
value 118–19, 121; adjustment at end of relationships 127–31; calculable 128–31; economic 4, 130; settling 119; transfers of 144; valuable and invaluable 125–7
variance 22, 24, 37

wages 11, 16, 50, 54, 63–4, 163
wealth: acquisition 1, 128; redistribution 55
welfare benefits 7, 81; social 3, 128
welfare dependency 171
well-being 21, 24–5, 59, 70, 130; physical 23–4, 127; psychological 2, 21, 23–5, 27
wills, making 137–8
women 1–4, 16–17, 24–8, 39–42, 44–56, 69–70, 78–87, 177–8; married 44, 54, 61, 92; working 78–9; young 45, 54
work 13–15, 82–5, 91–5, 123, 128, 155, 157–8, 172–5; unpaid 55, 96, 121
workers 82, 167; manual 63–4
working tax credits 15, 162, 167, 173
working women 78–9
work-life balance 53–4

young women 45, 54